WYCLIFFE IN THE MAKING:
The Memoirs of W. Cameron Townsend
1920–1933

Wycliffe in the Making

The Memoirs of

W. Cameron Townsend

1920-1933

Hugh Steven

Harold Shaw Publishers
Wheaton, Illinois

Library of Congress Cataloging-in-Publication Data

Steven, Hugh.
    Wycliffe in the making : the memoirs of W. Cameron Townsend, 1920–1933 / by Hugh Steven.
       p.   cm.
    ISBN 0-87788-890-6
    1. Townsend, William Cameron, 1896–   . 2. Wycliffe Bible Translators—Biography. 3. Summer Institute of Linguistics. I. Title.
    BV2372.T68S74 1995
    266'.0092—dc20
    [B]   95-33102
                                                                                      CIP

02 01 00 99 98 97 96 95

10 9 8 7 6 5 4 3 2 1

For William Cameron Townsend

*Who had the courage, the faith, and the imagination
to carry his God-given vision from the abstract
into reality*

Contents

Foreword

In 1945 the government of Peru invited Cameron Townsend to launch a linguistic program on behalf of the ethnic groups of the Amazon jungle. An interested government official quizzed him about his plans.

"How will you get your students to the isolated tribal villages, Señor Townsend?"

"By small airplanes."

"How many airplanes do you have, Señor Townsend?"

"None, but I expect that God will provide."

"Who will fly those airplanes, Señor Townsend?"

"Volunteer pilots."

"How many pilots do you have, Señor Townsend?"

"None, but I expect that God will provide."

"How will you maintain those planes, Señor Townsend?"

"With volunteer mechanics."

"How many mechanics do you have, Señor Townsend?"

"None, but I expect that God will provide."

"How will you keep your students well, Señor Townsend?"

"With volunteer doctors."

"How many doctors do you have, Señor Townsend?"

"None, but I expect God will provide."

The interview concluded and Townsend said goodbye to the official, promising that he would return. The official, as he himself related years later, said, "There goes the most *loco gringo* I have ever seen!"

Fifty years later, without a single Summer Institute of Linguistics aviation fatality in Peru, some have called Cameron Townsend "the *gringo* least *loco*" they had ever seen. However, it was not for aviation that Townsend was most noted, but for addressing the problem of how to provide written language, literacy, and the Scriptures for the hundreds of pre-literate language groups around the world.

Even those accomplishments might not have left a mark unless Townsend had joined hands with his Creator in a can-do vision. Where others saw roadblocks, Townsend saw steppingstones. Where others saw enemies, he saw friends. Where others were doubtful, he was faithful. Where others were presumptuous, his obedience was carefully timed.

In 1982, just months before his death at age eighty-five, the Peruvian government presented Townsend with the highest honor Peru can give to a foreigner: *La Orden el Sol del Perú* ("The Order of the Sun of Peru"). Peru's president, Fernando Belaunde Terry, made the presentation and summed up his remarks by saying, "The Peruvian government recognizes once more the outstanding service Mr. Townsend has made to the communities of the jungle, and the great work he has done in spreading the Good News, culture, and brotherhood for which he has worked so intensely and fruitfully, exalting spiritual values among the isolated minority language groups of Peru."

Dr. Richard Pittman
Director, International Relations
Wycliffe Bible Translators

Preface

In October 1980 I drove Cam Townsend from his daughter's home in Southern California to the Wycliffe office in Huntington Beach. It was a rare opportunity for me to have Uncle Cam (as most people called him) all to myself, and I made the most of the thirty-minute trip. I wanted to know his opinions and feelings about some of the new directions Wycliffe Bible Translators (WBT) and the Summer Institute of Linguistics (SIL) were taking. I also wanted to understand more precisely some of the circumstances that led to the development of his working principles and methods under which WBT and SIL have operated with keen sensitivity on the world stage of cross-cultural missions.

Just as our trip ended, I asked Uncle Cam how he felt about anthropologists and others who had accused SIL of destroying indigenous peoples' cultural values. After a short pause, he said:

> Sometimes when a country or person is unhappy with us, it is because their pride has in some way been wounded. This is one of the reasons why it is important to give credit whenever possible to national peoples and host countries for their assistance in our work. I have observed that many who speak out against us often change their opinions and in time become our friends when we have extended Christian love, courtesy, and hospitality to them.
>
> I know the world is changing, but our message of service to others has not. We must, with sincere love, look for ways to serve the anthropologists and those who hold an opposing view. When we first began in Mexico, I told our new workers that at all times we must remember we are guests in Mexico; that we must be genuine friends and neighbors to all people without regard to race, creed, or religion. We must serve all people, particularly ethnic minorities. We are called to serve their governments with humility, compassion, and most of all, with a spirit of true human love and friendship.
>
> This must always be our attitude, even when we might have to face an unfriendly or hostile crowd, as I did in my early days in

Guatemala. When that happened, I greeted everyone with a smile. I refused to regard anyone—even when there was a danger of being chopped up by their long knives—as my enemy. My motto then, as now, was, "By love serve one another," even when you think they might kill you.

We must never forget our God is the God of the impossible. But he expects us to still march around Jericho. We have a specialized task and we must keep on with this task. I believe we who have been called into WBT and SIL have a special responsibility. Over the years I have emphasized the importance of sticking to our methods. Many of our methods and principles are unique to SIL and have served us well. Unfortunately, not all of our people understand the importance of operating under these principles and methods. *Few people have really understood my soul.*

I never forgot that sentence, and I took that as a challenge to try to understand what he meant. In his book *Care of the Soul,* Thomas Moore said, "Soul has to do with genuineness and depth. [Soul] is tied to life in all its particulars—good food, satisfying conversation, genuine friends and experiences that stay in the memory and touch the heart. Soul is revealed in attachment, love, and community." Anyone who knew Cameron Townsend understood this description was quintessential Townsend. Uncle Cam loved good food and took seriously the scriptural injunction to be hospitable. He believed the rituals of eating and talking together were the small civilities that held friendships together. It was through genuine hospitality that he nurtured old friendships and developed new friendships with strangers. He believed it was part of a missionary's responsibility to seek ways and means of extending genuine hospitality and friendliness to all people, irrespective of rank or station in life. One humble Indian man once said of Townsend, "I know he loves me because he speaks and listens to me with the same respect and attention he gave to the president of our country." In Cam's mind, Christ's call was to care for people as well as to preach the gospel.

So how could I as his biographer discover Cameron Townsend's soul? How could I invite the reader to discover his uniqueness? Townsend revealed his soul through the choices he made and his reactions to the natural events of everyday circumstances. My desire has been to uncover these clues through researching the chronicled events of his life prior to establishing Wycliffe Bible Translators, as recorded in his personal diaries, journals, and letters beginning in 1920 through 1933.

As I read these letters, I saw that Cameron Townsend wasn't always certain what God was doing in his life, but he was completely sure that he had been called by God. Thus when he read that the Scriptures called believers to rejoice always, to give thanks in all things, to pray without ceasing, and to be careful not to quench the Spirit, a principle emerged in his mind. It's the simple principle of *trusting God no matter what.* Cameron Townsend believed that "many people quench the Spirit by being down in the mouth rather than rejoicing, by planning rather than praying, by murmuring rather than giving thanks and by worrying instead of trusting in him who is faithful."

The faith principles and mission methods that emerged from Townsend's soul in the 1920s and 1930s are timeless and have value and wisdom for today. Not to chronicle his early life would be to deprive ourselves of Wycliffe Bible Translators' formative history and the early pilgrimage of one of the world's great mission leaders. This book, then, is my tribute to the memory of a man which, I hope, will inspire readers with faith, imagination, and courage to believe that God can be trusted, *no matter what.*

Acknowledgments

After the death of William Cameron Townsend on April 23, 1982, Cal Hibbard, Townsend's personal secretary of many years, began gathering primary source material for historians and others who might want to write factual histories of Townsend's life and the development of Wycliffe Bible Translators (WBT) and the Summer Institute of Linguistics (SIL). Cal and his wife, Cornelia, began to archive Townsend's letters, papers, diaries, journals, photos, and other important documents. Cal was the one who first found the files and received permission from the Central American Mission to have them copied. He was ably assisted by Dr. Richard Pittman, former SIL Deputy Director for Asia and the South Pacific, and long-time personal friend and understudy to Cameron Townsend.

Cal, a long-time friend and encourager of my work as a writer, early on urged me to write a follow-up to my book *A Thousand Trails*. This new project moved ahead when Hyatt Moore became director of the U.S. Wycliffe organization and gave me full rein and support to continue pursuing what had been in my mind for over five years. To these colleagues I extend heartfelt gratitude. The book would not have happened without their support and encouragement.

A word of appreciation also to the Central American Mission, who generously gave their consent to photocopy over a thousand letters and documents and let them become part of the Townsend Archives. The task of selecting and photocopying the letters and documents of the Central American Mission fell to Wilson Stiteler, former assistant treasurer of Wycliffe in the U.S. This story would not have the depth and completeness it does without his valuable contribution.

The basic material for the book, nearly three thousand letters and other documents, came neatly packaged in yearly increments. For their invaluable help in systematizing this material, I wish to thank Elsie May Hartog, Florence Nickel, Winnie Gentry, Gladys Zellmer, and Harriet Nielsen.

I want also to thank Dr. Pittman and Cal Hibbard for their careful editing, editorial and historical comments, and Elaine Townsend for her corrections and encouragement.

My thanks also to Dr. Kenneth L. Pike and his wife Evelyn, who were eyewitnesses to the early development of WBT and SIL, and who gave me helpful anecdotes and insights into the early life of the Townsends. Other eyewitnesses to WBT and SIL's early history are Dr. Benjamin Elson, Otis Leal, Herman Aschmann, Dr. George Cowan, and Dr. Richard Pittman, who have remarkable understanding of Cameron Townsend's unique management style and soul. I thank them for their considerable help and insight.

Bill and Marjory Nyman, along with Bill's sister Mary Ann Mooney, and her husband Earl Mooney, also gave helpful insights, recalling their father's wise and vital counsel as the first secretary-treasurer during Wycliffe's fledgling years.

I owe special thanks and appreciation to Anna Marie Dahlquist, whose father, Ed Sywulka, was one of the first two students to attend Townsend's linguistic course in 1934 at Breezy Point near Sulphur Springs, Arkansas. I thank her for permission to use parts of her notes and other documents relating to the Chichicastenango Conference and early history of the Central American Mission.

My thanks also to David Brainerd Legters (hereafter referred to as David Legters) for the remembrances of his father, L. L. Legters, and the survey trip to Brazil in 1926.

My appreciation to Bruce Grayden, friend, colleague, and former editor of Wycliffe Australia's *Beyond Words,* for his support and encouragement and for permission to use material from his article "Languages of God." Other encouragers include Ethel Wallis, who cheered me on from the sidelines. I am also grateful to the mission's subcommittee of Trinity United Presbyterian Church in Santa Ana, California, and the intercessors there who prayed faithfully for the completion of this book. Only eternity will reveal their singular role. My appreciation also to the small but fervent Wednesday prayer group of Granville Chapel, Vancouver, Canada.

To Stephen Board, a colleague of many years and publisher at Harold Shaw Publishers, many thanks for his endorsement and enthusiasm for the book, and to Lil Copan for her fine editorial work.

Finally, to Norma, my wife and dearest friend, companion, collaborator and editor, a special word of thanks and appreciation for her objective criticism, her editorial suggestions, and her ability to untangle my sometimes ponderous prose. She continues to be an indispensable partner in our writing ministry with Wycliffe Bible Translators.

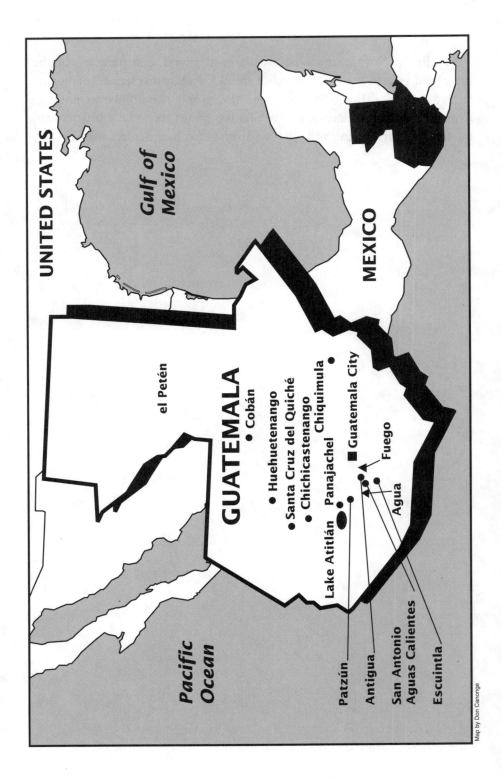

UNITED STATES

Gulf of Mexico

MEXICO

Pacific Ocean

el Petén

GUATEMALA

● Cobán

● Huehuetenango

● Santa Cruz del Quiché

● Chichicastenango

Chiquimula ●

■ Guatemala City

Lake Atitlán   Panajachel

Fuego

Agua

Patzún

Antigua

San Antonio Aguas Calientes

Escuintla

Map by Don Canonge

Introduction
The Plain Man

William Cameron Townsend was a plain man. Born in Riverside County, California, in 1896, there was little to distinguish him from the herd. No angular jaw or square shoulders that tapered to a narrow waist. No thick, wavy hair. Just a rail of a man whose thin hair was cut high above his ears. When the time came for him to wear glasses, they were plain wire-rimmed. His voice was slow and deliberate, without affectation, the plain, folksy drawl of a Southern Californian farmer. For that's what he was, a farmer, a plain man of the earth.

His father was a truck farmer who, with his two sons' help, peddled vegetables and fruit to the markets of Downey, Clearwater, and Santa Ana, California. His brother was a man comfortable with tools that ground, scraped, drilled, planed and sawed. The plain man didn't have his brother's skill, but he had a feel for the good earth. He believed if it were nourished and tilled, encouraged and loved, it could produce more than it knew it could. And this same God-given, intuitive talent to nurture, encourage, and love spread to people. That was the genius of William Cameron Townsend.

From farmer, to student, to Bible salesman, to founder of Wycliffe Bible Translators (WBT), the Summer Institute of Linguistics (SIL), and Jungle Aviation and Radio Service (JAARS), he had an ability to inspire people to become more than they believed they could become. Herman Aschmann, long-time Wycliffe member and translator of three New Testaments for the Totonac people of South Central Mexico, recalls:

> When I first met Cameron Townsend in 1938, I didn't have very good feelings about my abilities. The little I learned of linguistics that year [at "Camp Wycliffe," the linguistics school Townsend and L. L. Legters began before the Summer Institute of Linguistics was founded], was indeed little. But there was something about that summer of study that rang my bell. I wanted to know more. We students all needed someone to make us feel we could master something hard like learning unwritten languages and translating the Bible into those

languages. Cameron Townsend ("Uncle Cam," as we came to call him) was the one who had the gift and heart to do that.

Uncle Cam helped me and others to activate our faith and imagination to try hard things for God. He was always going out on a limb, which made me uncomfortable, and yet things worked out right in the end. He seemed to think anybody could do anything if God were in it. And we believed him. I think we believed him because of the way he listened to unimportant people like me. I sometimes wonder what would have become of me if my life hadn't been challenged by this man's vision.

Dr. Benjamin Elson, former executive director for Wycliffe International and the Summer Institute of Linguistics, concurred:

Uncle Cam had the ability, as do all great leaders, to bring out the best in the men and women he led, to lead them forward toward the goals they believe are important, yet without violating their own individuality.

His leadership was marked by a deep, personal concern for others. He always had a smile, an attentive ear, a word of encouragement and support. I remember him as having a forgiving, compassionate attitude toward those under his leadership.

While Cameron Townsend may have looked prosaic, there was nothing prosaic about his faith, his vision, or his intellect. Because Cameron Townsend believed the primary task of the church was evangelism, he believed both time and opportunity for ministry in Christ's name on earth was, at best, short. Therefore, he lived with a sense of urgency and made use of every opportunity to fulfill this primary task. It was for this reason that he turned down a full scholarship (awarded by the eminent linguist Edward Sapir) to study for his Ph.D. in linguistics at Yale. Yet he encouraged others, including Kenneth L. Pike and Benjamin Elson, to take the time for their advanced degrees. Said Dr. Elson:

Uncle Cam turned his own opportunity down because he was more concerned about people getting the Scriptures in their own language than he was in seeking his own advancement. His energies and priorities were given to specific projects he believed were vital to the overall worldwide program of evangelism through Bible translation. Studying for his Ph.D. in linguistics would take too much time away from the prime directive of the church.

In 1935 he wrote a letter to a personal friend in which he outlined his convictions to interact with linguistic scholars on the basis of sound scholarship, rather than ideology or dogma. That conviction remains firm policy for SIL, as does the thrust of Townsend's December 18, 1935 letter to the Hon. Josephus Daniels, U.S. ambassador to Mexico:

> I have a desire, prompted by Christian convictions, to serve my fellow man. I despise scientists who use humanity as laboratory instruments in their research, but think nothing of the welfare of the people they study, just as I detest ecclesiastical emissaries who seek only to inject their dogma while leaving the people in economic, intellectual and moral stagnation. I am determined not to engage in the propagation of sects, but rather simply to give the Bible to people with whom I come in contact. Especially do I desire to see at least portions of this Book of good will and brotherly love translated and published in all the languages of the world.

This book covers the early years of Cam's missionary service when at the age of twenty-four he and his wife of five months were beginning work as missionaries with the Central American Mission in Guatemala. These years, 1920–1933, explore the period after *A Thousand Trails*, which covered the years 1917–1919, and delve into the circumstances, events, and pressures that forged the man and the principles he lived by, as well as the beginning development of WBT, SIL, and JAARS. Yet, in response to this man and his work, Otis Leal, former candidate secretary for the Wycliffe Corporation, noted, "We do not worship or think Cameron Townsend to be infallible. We recognize his fallibility. We honor him because his goals have become our goals. His vision has become our vision. Wycliffe Bible Translators is in many respects a lengthened shadow of what he is and the vision he had."

Cameron and Elvira's wedding, June 9, 1919

Chapter One

Home Sweet Home

Leonard Livingston (L. L.) Legters parked his car in front of the Mexican immigration office in Nuevo Laredo, Texas. With him was his wife, Edna, and fellow mission adventurer, William Cameron Townsend. The date was November 11, 1933. The two men paused for a moment and prayed silently. Then, as if on cue, both men gave each other a reassuring glance, smiled slightly, opened the car door, and walked into the immigration office with their documents.

People were everywhere. There were immigration officials dressed in semi-military uniforms. There were street vendors hawking tortillas, sweet breads, tamales, candy, fruit, roasted corn, and more. There were groups of soldiers and small boys with battered shoe caddies who, for a few coins, offered to shine the soldiers' shoes.

While this colorful everyday market scene gave a festive feel to the air, the unsmiling officials eyeing Legters and Townsend dampened any geniality they may have felt. They knew all too well the surfacing political tension facing the last days of Mexico's President Plutarco Calles's regime. There had been wild rumors of revolution.

This was the arena that Townsend and Legters entered as they presented their documents to an austere immigration official. After examining the two men's papers, the official motioned for the men to wait.

After about thirty minutes, the officer returned and escorted Townsend and Legters to his chief. With polite deference, the two men stood silently in front of the chief's large desk while the official continued to study their documents.

After a tension-filled wait, the officer looked up. He regarded the two men with dark penetrating eyes and said, "You, Señor Legters, have been writing articles in a magazine called *Christlike*. In that magazine you said you wanted to bring your religion into Mexico. I'm sorry, Señor Legters, Mexico has enough religion already. We cannot let you into the country. And you, Señor Townsend, you want to come into Mexico to study Indian languages. I am afraid you too are denied permission to enter Mexico."

Here they were, stopped cold even before they started. Both Townsend and Legters had believed unequivocally that God had called them to begin a new work among the ethnic peoples of Mexico. The vision for this work had been repeatedly confirmed by a variety of circumstances, the most recent being an all-night prayer session where the men and women attending a Victorious Life Conference had gone without food for an entire day to pray for God to open the door to Mexico. Had Townsend and Legters read the signals incorrectly? Surely if God was in this new venture, he would provide a way to overcome this first hurdle. Bewildered and confused, the two men returned to the car to pray and think. Cam thought back to the many ways God had led him to this moment.

On June 9, 1919 in Guatemala City, Cameron Townsend married Elvira Malmstrom, a secretary with the Presbyterian Mission in Guatemala. Cam was twenty-three, Elvira twenty-seven. The newlyweds, full of romantic idealism, prepared to leave on a bouncy thirty-mile stagecoach ride to the city of Antigua to settle down as new missionaries with the Central American Mission and continue the work Cam had begun months before as an independent missionary among the Cakchiquel Indian churches of the surrounding area. Elvira's brother, Carl Malmstrom, recently returned from France, had surprised his sister by coming to the wedding. Eager for any opportunity to interest people in mission work, Cam and Elvira seized the moment and invited Carl to go with them to Antigua, a beautiful city surrounded by three volcanos.[1]

That this was their honeymoon evening didn't seem to enter into their minds. In fact, they had planned their honeymoon to be an extended evangelistic trip. In a report to Judge D. H. Scott, treasurer of the Central American Mission, Elvira wrote:

> The first week of our honeymoon we spent holding meetings in our new little home in Antigua. The second week we went on an eighty-five mile muleback trip from the mountains to the low jungle on the coast [accompanied by Carl]. We held twelve different evangelistic services. Three people professed faith. I have to tell you that no couple has ever spent a happier honeymoon—giving out the Bread of Life!

After August 13, when Carl left for the States and their evangelistic "honeymoon" trip was over, Cam and Elvira busied themselves with the work among the Cakchiquel believers and their congregations in and around Antigua. Discouragement had settled over these small congregations—discouragement from lack of pastoral care and spiritual nurture, and periodic persecution for their faith.

In 1919, militarism, political and economic instability, and violation of human rights were frequent occurrences in Central America. Most Indian people remained in serfdom. Education was encouraged, but lack of financial support for teachers often led the pupils back to tilling farmland.

Military service was compulsory for all males twenty to sixty years of age. Throughout the country, soldiers lined up in front of barracks, bugles sounded, roll was called, and a campaign button was pinned on each soldier. Each soldier was then given a completed ballot, reading, "I hereby give my vote for Licenciado Manuel Estrada Cabrera for the term 1917-1923."

Early correspondence shows that Cameron Townsend was fiercely affected by this injustice. Yet he never spoke out publicly against a government's elected representative. For him, obedience to rulers was part of obedience and honor to God. He believed governments were placed by Divine decree to maintain law and order, based on 1 Timothy 2:2. And because he believed God put rulers in place for the good of all people, he could honor and give authorities respect—even if their office had been won by fraudulent means. Years later, when someone asked him about working under repressive governments, Cam said, "I believe we should be like the apostle Paul. As he traveled throughout the

Roman world, he knew about the excesses and injustices, yet he never once publicly complained. On the contrary, he said we should obey those who rule over us as God's ministers. I do not want anyone who goes to a foreign country to be critical of its government."

Yet, quietly, Cam tried to lessen the plight of the disenfranchised. On one occasion, he and another missionary saw a plantation owner abusing an Indian worker. The other missionary spoke out in defense of the Indian, which simply provoked the plantation owner to beat the Indian harder. The owner then ran the missionary off his plantation with a warning never to return. When Cam observed that the missionary was unable to have any further ministry among the Indians of that plantation, he resolved not to directly interfere with local politics or with the accepted customs of the plantation owners. Yet whenever he observed such a miscarriage of justice, he would stand by silently with bowed head and pray and, if possible, comfort the abused Indian with some small act of kindness.

Cam kept copious notes in his diary and letters to family and friends explaining these situations:

> With each plantation I visit, I am made painfully aware of the plight of the indentured Indian. I have found thousands of highland-born Indian people who are now entrapped by the *colono* system. This system is virtual slavery. The Indians have been brought to live and work year-round on the coastal plantations. If the Indian borrows a small amount of money from the land owner (generally to buy liquor) and cannot pay back his debt, he is forced by the government to serve the lender for a certain length of time each year at a small wage.
>
> Unfortunately, the Indian never seems to be able to pay off his debt. If the plantation is sold, the *colono* is transferred to the new master. Further, a *colono* is transferred to the plantation without his permission. On some of these plantations, I found stocks and whipping posts. One Indian told me he was whipped until he was almost unconscious. Another told me he was strung up by his thumbs and made to sit for days in the stocks unsheltered from the sun.

The ruling of these plantations paralleled the government's own heavy rule. Cam wrote:

Political conditions are in an evolutionary process and we are living in considerable uncertainty. A rising antigovernment party advocates the union of five Central American Republics. The government still maintains a firm hand but we can hardly see how this can blow over without some serious results. We pray the poor believers may not be called upon to suffer.

During this time, Cam wrote articles for various Christian periodicals, as well as a novel. *Tolo, the Volcano's Son,* tells the fascinating tale of a people who lived with their own special dignity, yet without a voice in the economic or political affairs of their own country. The language Cameron Townsend used to tell his story was simple and direct:

Two pompous generals bedecked with swords, plumes, medals and yards of gold braid, strutted impatiently into the halls of the president's reception room.

There were also beautiful dark-eyed women exquisitely dressed in the latest high-fashion Paris styles. There were businessmen of the aristocracy and men with unpolished shoes and mismatched pants and jackets, plus a poor widow dressed in black. These, along with two or three foreign investors, had exerted their "pull" and patience for an audience with the great Estrada Cabrera about matters that were of importance to them. But true to form, the president had kept most of them waiting day after day for a week. Those who waited the longest were the ones with mismatched pants and jackets and unpolished shoes.[2]

Cam hoped the novel would awaken the American Christian community to the dehumanization of more than three million ethnic people by this rich and powerful minority.

During Cam's first days in Antigua, he accepted a position from the director of the Normal School to teach English. While he and Elvira were happy for the little extra income, however small, Cam took the position primarily as an avenue for personal witness. Yet it also gave him an opportunity to learn how the Guatemalan educational system worked. His interest in education would one day play an important role in expanding SIL's work in Mexico and South America.

Cam soon began to realize that all his time could be taken up with teaching English in private homes and at the Normal School. While this was a worthwhile endeavor, he also had a growing desire to translate the Scriptures for the Cakchiquel people but knew as long as he lived in a predominantly *ladino* (Spanish-speaking)[3] environment, he would never learn to speak the Cakchiquel Indian language well enough to do this. Therefore, on his own initiative, he and Elvira made the decision to move to San Antonio, the administrative and market center for the 200,000 Cakchiquels.

The immediate problem was housing. Since the school he and Francisco Díaz (Cam's co-worker in selling Bibles) had begun a few months earlier was an unsuitable home for his new bride, Cam began to look for at least a five-acre plot on which to build their first home and a place to carry out his idea of an agricultural school and clinic for the Cakchiquels.

To Cam's dismay, no one would sell a vacant lot to him. (The only outsiders to overcome this obstacle were two saloon keepers.) The people of San Antonio were frightened by the possibility of any outsider taking over their land because too much of their land had already been gobbled up for coffee plantations by German investors. This was Cam's first disappointment. The second was the disquieting realization that his new wife was not physically well. Within two months of his marriage, Cam wrote his parents to tell them that Elvira would have to undergo a hernia operation. Other correspondence reveals that Elvira was suffering from severe headaches and fevers. This was to be the beginning of twenty-five years of health problems for Elvira.

Besides revealing Elvira's illness, Cam's early letters signaled other problems. One was the problem of Cam's over-zealous relationship to the "work" and an insensitivity to his young wife's need for time alone with him; time to bond as a couple. Then began another difficulty that troubled Elvira for many years—and may well have been the cause of what Cam described as "her nervous temperament." Elvira's aversion to a house that was in any way messy or dirty was constantly tried by an inordinate number of visitors and semi-permanent house guests.

Elvira's upbringing called for a house that was always in order and immaculately clean. Cam's upbringing was, as Elvira would one day complain, "different." Disorder did not bother him. During the first months of their marriage, Elvira never specifically complained about the large number of guests or the disorder company caused. She knew Cam relished the company of others. Their dominating motivation, after all, was to serve people and be involved "in the work." Yet their correspondence revealed their unspoken stress:

> This past week we have been blessed with visitors. The native evangelist takes all his meals with us. Mary Bishop's nephew and servant came for dinner every day. And Mr. Wilson, the young U.S. government agricultural explorer from Pasadena [California], of whom I wrote when I first came down, was with us for a couple of weeks. On top of this, we have been busy [with our Indian work], Elvira has not been at all well, and the cook has been out of sorts for a few days.

While Cam and Elvira waited and prayed about how they might purchase land, they busied themselves with a congregation that had been established by the Central American Mission. In a letter home, Cam wrote, "We are in the midst of wonderful meetings. Every night the crowds grow. Last night we put out extra benches and there were still many who had to stand. There have been several conversions as well. We are looking forward to much greater things."

Cam had learned early the art of letter writing. These letters he wrote to his parents, whom he addressed as "The Home Folks," had a profoundly deeper meaning for him than the casual writing of a letter to a friend. Since Cam's father was deaf—the result of working in the ironworks in Colorado and Pennsylvania—letter writing was his principal way of communicating with his world. Colleagues and friends remember that if there happened to be a lull in a conversation at a dinner party, it was common practice for Cam to suddenly take out a piece of paper and pen from his briefcase and begin writing a letter to someone.

In a December 15, 1920 letter, Cam reported over two hundred people had come to their special meetings and fifteen had "confessed" the Lord for the first time. His plan was to begin a Wednesday night men's Bible class. He then said:

> We had a sad affair last Thursday. The administrator of the post office was shot by an eighteen-year-old boy he had scolded. Three hours before, I had spoken to the administrator and given him a tract. He promised to attend the meetings that night, but he never came. In all probability, he went to a Christless grave. He thought he had plenty of time.
>
> No letter from you this week. We wonder when your Christmas presents will reach us. The postmaster said that all mail from the States is slow. When it does come, it sure will be welcome.
>
> The past week has been full as always. We had a watch night service last Wednesday night from eight until midnight. The chorus sang, the native pastor gave a message, yours truly gave over an hour's talk. There were many testimonies, including Elvira's. We spent the last hour in prayer.
>
> After the service, the believers served tamales, coffee and bread. The evenings are cold, but those tamales had enough chile in them to warm a person from head to toe. In every way it was a blessed service. We slept late on Thursday, but by ten o'clock we gathered at the chapel for a picnic. Elvira was not at all well but decided to go along in order not to disappoint the believers. We went to a hill on the outskirts of town that was covered with a great cypress forest and found a delightful spot way up on the side of the hill.
>
> We sang songs, had rope jumping, and in every way had a jolly time. At noon we divided up into our individual groups and ate dinner. The place we selected overlooked the whole valley of Antigua. The most prominent structures in view were the old ruins. Stretched out and surrounding the city were beautiful coffee plantations. And then, due south, the old mountain *Agua* lifted her majestic peak. To the right towered the volcanos of *Fuego* and *Acatenango*. It was truly a beautiful sight.

During the early months of 1920, much of Cam's and Elvira's correspondence reflected the concern they both had for the completion of what was to become their cornstalk house on a piece of land they were finally able to rent. Their letters exude both a thankfulness for the Lord's provision and a confidence that—in spite of a lack of creature comforts—they were exactly where the Lord wanted them at that moment. While Elvira spoke warmly about their new "home sweet home," the lack of running water or electricity, combined with the constant battle to keep a dirt-floor house dust and dirt free, exacted a greater toll on her Swedish sensibilities than she was at first willing to admit. In a letter dated March 1, 1920, Cam wrote:

> Dear Home Folks,
> At last we are settled in our new home. Water for drinking and cooking has to be drawn from a community well a half block away. We both bathe in a cold stream as do the other villagers. At night we read by candlelight and a tiny lamp, and when Elvira cooks, it is over an open fire with green wood that results in so much smoke that she says it nearly kills her. Elvira is now in the dining room visiting with a girl who has just brought a present of several eggs, some beets and tomatoes. Her little brother and sister are admiring everything about the house.

The new house's structure shocked local people. Never before had the Cakchiquels of San Antonio seen the interior of a house built with partitions. In fact, when they saw Cam place upright poles *inside* the house, he came under considerable ridicule. "What good are such posts?" they said. "They serve no purpose. They will only get in the way." However, when the people saw how the partitions made separate rooms, they nodded their heads in approval. The cornstalk house became a curiosity that everyone wanted to see. Continuing his March 1 letter, Cam wrote:

> I am sitting at the desk where I can look out of the window over a beautiful hill. I would give you a description of the whole house but as it isn't finished yet, you will have to wait. I just heard the little seven-year-old girl say that she doesn't want to go home. She was here all afternoon; yesterday, too. It means that Elvira won't get many letters written.

One of the first letters Elvira wrote from their new home was to Judge Scott:

Thank you for your precious letter and for the $100.00. We are praising the Lord for the wonderful way he is caring for us. As you know, neither Mr. Townsend nor I came outfitted to the field as missionaries generally do. And then having to equip a home besides. But, little by little, we are getting things as we need them.

A great change has taken place on this lot since January. Then it was simply a heap of rubbish on uneven ground, pockmarked with deep holes. It looked hopeless. But now the odd little cornstalk hut looks neat and pretty with flower-bordered walks in front and to the side of the house.

Our vegetable garden is growing strong. We have a chicken corral made out of cornstalks where we have a few chickens that have been given to us. Besides the chickens, we have two sheep, also given. We are quite proud of our little place and thankful to the [Cakchiquel] sister who was kind enough to let us build on her lot when no one else in the village would sell us land. We rent the lot for a yearly sum of only $2.00 in gold. We hope some day the sister will be willing to sell this piece of land and we will be able to build a permanent home. Cornstalks only last about four years. Meanwhile, we are just as happy as can be and love our "home sweet home."

The other night two Indians broke through part of the fence, we believe to steal some of our equipment or livestock. Fortunately their noise woke us up, and when they heard our voices, they fled. "The angel of the Lord encampeth round about them that fear him, and delivereth them" [Psalm 34:7, KJV].

There is much sickness among the Indians. Since most of them are poor, they come first to us to see if we can help them. We want to buy a small supply of simple remedies when we go to Guatemala City for an upcoming missions conference. The hardest thing for me to deal with is the awful way most of them live in filth and uncleanliness. They seem to be afraid of water. I struggle to get the children to come to school with their hands and faces washed. But praise God, he shows us even through all the dirt and "live ones" [lice], they are precious souls for whom Christ died. We cannot help but embrace and love them.

Cam added his note to Elvira's letter to Judge Scott:

Supper's over and Elvira's busy teaching a bunch of young men how to sing "When the Roll is Called up Yonder." They're eager to learn and don't wait to be invited to come. If this keeps up the way it has, we'll be busy most of the time receiving callers. It doesn't leave much time for studying or writing, etc., but the Lord and his disciples had little time for leisure, for that matter, even to eat.

I can never think of the Lord as cloistered away with a bunch of books around him. Rather, he walked and talked with people, studied them, and made his message simple and clear to fit their needs. We find, too, that the more we are among the Indians, the sooner we'll learn their language.

One of Elvira's early prayer requests had to do with learning the difficult Cakchiquel language. Again to her friend and committed supporter, Judge Scott, Elvira wrote:

Do pray that we may quickly learn this "awful" language. No grammar or books of any kind to study from makes it harder. We have a little book in which we mark down the different words and phrases the Indians tell us when we visit them. However, some of the words have such difficult sounds, it is almost impossible to write them down. But surely the language of the Cakchiquels is the Lord's just as much as English, Spanish or Swedish, and we know he will give us this Indian language that we may soon be able to explain the Gospel to them in their own tongue.

However inappropriate for a trained field linguist or anthropologist to refer to the sounds of an ethnic language as "awful," it was, for Elvira, a perfectly honest and refreshing reaction. Anyone who has tried to mold one's facial muscles and train one's vocal cords to reproduce the unfamiliar sounds of a new language can easily identify with her dilemma. And without a background in comparative or descriptive linguistics, Cam and Elvira had set for themselves an outrageously impossible task.

*Cameron and Elvira in Cakchiquel dress
standing by their cornstalk house*

Chapter Two

Implicit Trust

The difficult task that Cam and Elvira had set for themselves was to analyze and speak the Cakchiquel language with enough confidence and skill to enable them to translate the Scriptures. Even with today's electronic tools—computers, tape recorders, data banks—and a host of scholarly aids, most modern-day linguists find the systematizing and analyzing of words highly demanding.

Cam had to learn how to distinguish and analyze such language challenges as stress, pitch, intonation patterns, and rhythm. He did this without the aid of sophisticated recorders that can repeat and play at a variety of speeds for careful analysis. He had to listen, and strain to listen, over and over, to the fast-paced normal Cakchiquel conversation in the marketplace, in the field, and wherever he heard the language being spoken in everyday activity.

Besides struggling with a completely unfamiliar, complex grammatical system, Cam also had to learn the differences among this language's verb forms. For him, the English forms seemed simple. For example, in English there are five forms of the verb *to eat* (not counting compound forms): *eat, eats, eating, eaten,* and *ate.* But *each verb* in Cakchiquel had the potential of 100,000 different forms! A single verb can be used to indicate time, number of subjects, number of objects, location of the subject(s), and several aspects of action.

Cam found some of the Cakchiquel sounds almost impossible to distinguish. In Cakchiquel, the sound that a letter such as *k* would make includes not only the sound that is similar to the English *k,* but another *k* that sounds like a deep cough; another comes out with a kind of pop; and the hardest of all of the Cakchiquel *k* sounds is a sort of choking sound. The last two are further differentiated by the up or down direction of the speaker's Adam's apple! Speaking and analyzing Cakchiquel became even more puzzling when Cam began to understand that this language did not conform to any recognizable Latin or European language patterns.

Dr. Eunice Pike, one of SIL's first women linguists and translators, gave an important insight into Townsend's linguistic contribution when she wrote:

> In the 1920s, [Townsend] made a structural analysis of the Cakchiquel verb system. In so doing, he became one of the first men in the world to succeed in analyzing a complicated native language system in reference to the structure of itself. Most people with a European background, who had previously attempted to analyze American Indian languages, tried to force their analyses into a Latin mold.[1]

While Eunice Pike rightly credits Cameron Townsend for being one of the first men in the world to succeed in analyzing a Mayan language in relation to its own linguistic structure, the genesis of this notion came from another man.

In August 1919, a young Cameron Townsend met a Dr. Gates, an American archaeologist in Antigua. Cam told Dr. Gates about his interest in studying the Cakchiquel language with the intention of then translating the New Testament. Dr. Gates urged Cam to simply observe and listen to the Cakchiquels using their language in everyday occurrences. Then mimic, Gates told him, practice and use every occasion to use the words he had learned. Dr. Gates introduced Cam to the writings of Dr. Edward Sapir, then considered one of America's greatest linguists. From Dr. Sapir, Cam learned "the descriptive approach" to language learning and analysis, the basics of which included resisting the temptation to superimpose the rules of English or Latin grammar onto "pre-literate" unanalyzed languages of the Americas.

During the spring and summer of 1920, while struggling with Cakchiquel verbs and furnishing a new house, Cam and Elvira also dealt with the more fundamental problems: dishonest civil servants and a violent political coup. On April 26, 1920, he wrote his parents, "It was probably due to the unsettled [political] conditions here that you failed to receive our letters for such a long a time. We know a great deal of our mail has been stolen, but praise the Lord we have found the leak and things have been straightened out."

He also expressed how disappointed he and Elvira were over the loss of provisions, books, and other items his parents had sent them.

Apart from one lengthy letter Elvira wrote to her parents in Chicago describing the "unsettled conditions," little is known about what Cam and Elvira thought during those turbulent days. This was partly because Elvira's letters are lost to history, and because Cam and Elvira did not want their families to be overly concerned.

At a deeper level, during those turbulent times, Cam's focus was characteristically selective and often highly optimistic. Younger directors and colleagues sometimes criticized Cam for what they thought was a reluctance to confront the reality of a situation. But, for Cam, any country's turbulent political climate meant simply a renewed opportunity to trust God for the impossible. A poem Cam included in a letter to his parents reflects this implicit trust:

> Trust Him when dark doubts assail you;
> Trust Him when your strength is small.
> Trust Him when, to simply trust Him
> Seems the hardest thing of all.

Yet, while Guatemala's political realities swirled around Cam and Elvira, their letters revealed a calm counterpoint to the April 1920 revolution. In May, Elvira wrote her brother and sister-in-law to congratulate them on acquiring their own home: "I am sure it must be great fun and I wish you the happiest and coziest little nest there ever was. I mean in Chicago, for down here in San Antonio ours is the happiest little house there EVER was." Elvira then spoke about the increasing amount of time they spent meeting medical demands and their feelings of inadequacy in meeting these needs:

> I have been treating sick babies and children with hookworm. I love to treat the sick, but wish I knew more about medicine. There is no doctor here and the medical needs are great, particularly among the poor Indian people. They simply have no money to spend on medicines or doctors. When we go to the States, we both plan to take a medical missionary course. I especially am interested in this.

A month after the revolution, Cam's letter to his sister and brother-in-law spoke about taking on another school teacher for thirteen dollars per month. The letter also told about Cixto Guaján, a young Indian evangelist who was to be paid nine dollars per month, and about Antonio Bac, an energetic forty-year-old Quiché man he had helped come to faith in Jesus Christ a year earlier.[2] He wrote, "Since Antonio Bac has a large family and has proven to be an outstanding evangelist among his own people, his salary is to be twelve dollars per month."

With every passing day, Cam was gaining greater knowledge and insight into what he called "Indian work." (This would later become "Work with national or ethnic peoples.") His enthusiasm for this new emphasis spilled over into his personal correspondence. To his family and friends he expressed his affection and gratitude for their monetary support. His letters also revealed his intuitive emphasis that national believers be trained to become independent of expatriate missionaries. Contrary to some in his own mission, Cam had no misgivings about training Indian believers to evangelize their own people in the vernacular language:

> We are giving our national workers at least four days of intensive training every month. What these men lack in formal Bible training they make up for in their spiritual vitality. They accomplish much as they go about from town to town all over the highlands and among the plantation Indians of the coast. Would to God that we had a dozen such fellows like Antonio Bac to evangelize these towns.
>
> The Lord is giving us a wonderful vision of a gospel work among the Indians. We look to him to prepare us to be used in a much

needed, though humble, way. We see a great need and a great opportunity. We also see nothing in ourselves to meet this need but we do see in him all that is needed. And we see in his Word that the most humble and useless instrument surrendered into his hands can be filled with his power and used greatly for his honor and glory.

May we always be found in the attitude of full surrender and absolute faith. Give us your prayers as liberally as you have been giving us of your means.

This letter also contained a short update on Elvira's continuing health problem:

Elvira's health doesn't seem to improve. The doctor prescribed a year of going easy but it seems impossible down here. We haven't been able to hire a cook, so Elvira has been doing all the housework in addition to her many other mission duties. You can readily understand that standing on her feet is hard on her hernia which is getting worse. She keeps up a brave front and turns out more work than I do. But we realize something must be done. Mr. Smith was led of the Lord to send forty dollars. This could pay for a passage home. It seems this may be a guidance. He will make it clear.

On the heels of his May 3 letter to his family, Cam wrote a fuller account of his feelings about the work in the *Central American Mission Bulletin*. The article showed seeds taking root of what would one day become Wycliffe Bible Translators:

Here we have a congregation of eighty believers. There is a strong representation of young people, as well as men, women, and children. We have a competent young teacher in the day school, and therefore I do not have to dedicate much time to the school, though if I could, it would be time well spent. Some of the brethren who don't know how to read are putting the finishing touches to a room for the school teacher so he can live here and thus start a night school to teach them to read. He has been living in Antigua and goes back and forth on foot.

The one interest now is to learn to read God's Word. If it were not for this, they would contentedly go through life without knowing a single letter. What they have heard of God's Message gives them a burning desire to read it for themselves. The desire is so strong that after carrying heavy burdens all day, they light a piece of fat pine for a torch, take out their Spanish Bibles, and after asking the Lord to open their understanding, begin to spell out the letters.

Over two dozen in the various congregations have learned to read with no other teacher than a brother who can read already and with no other textbook than the [Spanish] Bible. God grant that some day we may be able to put large parts of the Bible into their own tongue! For even when they learn to read Spanish, they do not understand a large part of it.

The bulletin ended with a short paragraph about that all-important box of clothing, books, and miscellaneous items that Cam thought had been stolen during the revolution. It appeared the Indian carriers had left the box at the home of a believer when they had come under cannon fire by the revolutionaries.

On May 10, a government commission visited San Antonio and the newly established school that was being held in a former chief's house. In Cam's words, the visitors "marveled at what the children were learning—as well as seeing them come to school neat and clean." Mixed with Cam and Elvira's joy and pride over the affirmation by the governmental commission was the pain of seeing some of the believers persecuted for their faith:

Just yesterday some Indians from San Andrés Itzapa asked if we would take in two of their little girls, one eight and the other ten. [Cam and Elvira had already taken in one orphan girl, Tomasa, who had been living with them for eight months.] The parents of these girls are the only believers in their town and have suffered much for their faith. Their home was burned and their possessions smashed by an angry mob. The parents said they cannot stand to see their children growing up in total ignorance.

One of the Indian sisters has taken them into her home. We are paying all the expenses. After a few weeks when we have been able to get away for a short rest, we will take them into our home. There are other orphan girls, presently staying with relatives, who would like to come to us. If the Lord gives us strength, we want to take them in as well. We realize this is no small task, and ask you to pray with us in this matter that we may be guided by the Lord.

We don't know what is going on in Antigua. Yesterday we heard the sound of gun and cannon fire in the distance. We learned one was killed and several wounded. With all the shooting we heard this morning, we are afraid there is more bloodshed.

Throughout his life, Cameron Townsend demonstrated a practical confidence in God's promise to fulfill the purposes of his Word. Cam wanted his ideas and efforts to serve those most in need of spiritual help and social reform. On June 21, 1920, during a brief vacation and second "honeymoon" at the Friends Mission Center in the colonial town of Chiquimula, a hundred and thirteen miles from Guatemala City, Cam poured out his heart for the spiritual and practical needs of Guatemala:

Dear Home Folks,
We are still enjoying a delightful rest here with the Friends missionaries. They are a consecrated group of people. Their plant includes a commodious mission home, a boy's school with buildings to accommodate forty boys, and a girl's school, which is now housed (temporarily) in palm buildings, for fifty girls.

The receipts of the mission for one year are $17,000.00. Most of this comes from channels other than the Friends Board. How the Lord has honored their faith! Cannot as much be done for the Indians? Let us pray. Our Lord has promised that if we abide in him and his Word abides in us, we may ask what we will and it shall be done unto us. *Let us abide, pray, trust.*

Cam took a keen interest in how other people executed their mission responsibility. He was particularly interested in physical buildings and their practical functions. When he and Elvira returned from their vacation at the Friends Mission Center on July 27, he wrote Judge Scott:

We thought you would be interested in knowing more about the work [of the Friends Mission]. Although we differ in many points of doctrine, they are dear children of God and are doing a wonderful

work. Their plant is one of the best organized and most complete
that I know of in missionary work in Guatemala, as well as all of
Central America. There are many things we can learn from them,
especially about unity of purpose that is most evident among their
missionaries.

By mid-year, "Indian work" appeared more and more frequently in
Cam's correspondence. His July 27 letter revealed a special meeting with
the Central American Mission leaders and a concerned time of prayer
over this issue. There was also a call to prayer for the large number of
people who were coming down with malaria, particularly those who
lived and worked around Lake Patzún and Panajachel. The same letter
also revealed Cam's creative thinking and constant desire to link people
in the United States as partners with him in his vision, and marked
Cam's first bold step that would eventually lead him out of the Central
American Mission:

> The Lord has put it in our hearts to do more for the poor and op-
> pressed people of this land. We feel, as do many missionaries here
> in Guatemala, that the ethnic minorities have largely been neglected.
> Many have urged us to consider this as our primary mission effort
> and we are now giving most of our time to this work. Also, we feel
> the conditions we face here on the field should be brought before
> the people in the homeland. The result is the enclosed paper [a
> ten-page booklet on the plight of Guatemala's Indians]. We have
> talked this over with other missionaries and they suggested publishing
> a semiannual leaflet dealing with the situation. We know this will
> mean extra work, but if it meets with our board's approval, we would
> be glad to undertake this extra work for the glory of God.

A week later, on August 4, after a short evangelistic trip to the Patzún
Lake area, Cam wrote to Judge Scott, affirming once again his deep
interest in Indian work:

> We had special meetings in Patzún for four days, mainly Bible studies
> each morning and afternoon with Indians. In the evening we had
> gospel services in the central chapel in Spanish. The attendance was

splendid. As a result of this last trip, the Lord has filled our hearts with love for the Indians as never before. How we wish we could do more for them. If we had a dozen lives, we would give them all to telling these people about the love of God in Jesus Christ.

Elvira and Cameron with a group of Cakchiquel children from the local church in San Antonio

Chapter Three

A Companion in Lice Cracking

From mid-July to mid-September 1920, Cam and Elvira left their corn-stalk house in San Antonio and moved to the cooler highlands of Patzún. Their daily activity centered on learning and analyzing more of the Cakchiquel language. Besides gathering word lists, Cam translated the first stanza of the song, "Stepping in the Light." The purpose of this first translation attempt was to gain Cakchiquel readers for the New Testament. By teaching the people the simple words of this gospel song, Cam showed them how easily (some learned to read in a single sitting) they could learn to read, and that learning could be fun.

Cam and Elvira also produced a small grammar guide and dictionary. Both of these were to be printed into a booklet in order to "serve not just us alone, but be useful for other missionaries who will come to work among the Cakchiquels." Once again, here was a precursor to what would become standard SIL policy—making scientific, linguistic, and literacy research materials available to government agencies, universities, and others who might care to use such materials.

While encouraged by their language progress, Elvira was under no illusions that she and Cam had anywhere near the skills and understanding needed to do a full-fledged translation. She wrote:

Our pastor [Trinidad Bac, Antonio's brother] is the only one of the Indians who knows Spanish. Since he has never studied Spanish grammar, it is difficult to get him to tell us the different verb forms. If you ask him the meaning of a word in Cakchiquel, he generally gives you a whole history in the language, and you know no more after you are through than when you first asked the question.

But, praise God, we know he is giving us wisdom and understanding in learning this difficult language. Unfortunately the Indian people are ashamed of their language. They often insist on trying to speak in Spanish, even though the sounds they make are quite unintelligible.

The imprint of oppressive Spanish colonial rule had left a nation of people with deep-seated feelings of inferiority and self-deprecation. By giving the Cakchiquels the New Testament, Cam and Elvira would be giving them more than God's written Word. Such an important book as the New Testament written in their own language would serve to affirm their worth as human beings.

On September 3, 1920, Judge Scott wrote Cam and Elvira to tell them that Mr. and Mrs. William Robinson (Robbie was Cam's friend and companion on his first trip to Guatemala in 1917) had been accepted by the Central American Mission. Judge Scott added that in the last eighteen months, God had given the mission several choice young couples for service in Guatemala.

Cam's September 27 letter responded to Judge Scott's news: "We are still praying that the [work] force may be doubled in the coming year." Cam's response was that of a true admirer of Hudson Taylor. Cam frequently reminded himself and others that after Taylor and his coworkers had prayed for more workers for China, God answered with a hundred new missionaries. If God could do that in 1887, Cam reasoned God could do it in 1920. After addressing several other matters of routine business, Cam ended the letter with two items he considered providential blessing:

We believe it was of the Lord that we spent the last two months away from home because malarial fever has been raging terribly. A conservative estimate places the cases up to the present at three thousand, and it is still prevalent. We went out to visit the believers on Saturday and were horrified to see how discolored their faces were and how the fever had touched almost every home. In one place, four people were in one bed. Here at the school, where nineteen were enrolled, the attendance dropped to two. The public school attendance dropped by the same ratio.

You will be glad to know Elvira's health improved greatly during our stay at Patzún. The back-to-nature life, together with the cooler temperature, is improving her riding skill. The other day, on a steep descent, Elvira's mule lost control of her hind legs and sat down in the mud. I thought Elvira would surely fall, but she kept her seat perfectly well and the mule recovered.

When some of Cam's letters to the "home folks" come under scrutiny, they often become notable for what wasn't said. The missing commentary in his correspondence concerned the extended involvement he and Elvira had in supplying medical care during the winter malaria epidemic of 1920–21. With the exception of a handful of believers and the old woman who allowed the Townsends to rent a small lot on which to build their cornstalk house, the town of San Antonio was closed to them. Most of the people were suspicious and feared they were outsiders who wanted to exploit their land. Then came the malaria epidemic. When Cam and Elvira realized the medical professionals were bypassing those who could not buy medicine, Cam wrote to friends in the States. A woman from Troy, New York, sent money for Cam to buy quinine, a doctor in Antigua told Elvira and Cam how to treat the sick, and both began to apply their new skills. It was Elvira, however, who caught the attention of the people of San Antonio. Some years later Cam wrote in his journal:

Day after day during the height of the epidemic, Mrs. Townsend rode her mule to treat the sick, often visiting sixty homes a day. When people saw her love and tender care for the many helpless sufferers, and observed that the people who took our medicines didn't die (others around us were dying like flies), they forgot we were foreigners and became friends. Even bitter enemies became friendly when their loved ones were healed through our medicines. One day I received a wonderful thrill when a man who hadn't been too friendly called me "neighbor."

Later I discovered what the Cakchiquels mean when they use that term. It means "my companion in lice cracking." Someone goes through your scalp to find these little critters and gets them out without pulling your hair. And if you let the person do the same for you, he (or she) is your neighbor. One of the immediate results of that acceptance was the willingness of the village elders to let us buy property on which to erect a permanent station.

That incident taught me the important principle of servanthood, of using service to people to open doors of opportunity. The most vivid example of servanthood and offering a practical service before trying to present the gospel came through our Cakchiquel evangelist, Antonio Bac.

Bac was a tireless energetic evangelist, very much like the Apostle Paul. And like the Apostle, Bac was always looking for an opportunity to present the gospel of Christ. But this wasn't easy. It was particularly difficult for him to speak to strangers and to minister in places where he wasn't known. But our motto was to preach the gospel where Christ hadn't been named.

One day I sent Bac to a village that I knew to be resistant to outsiders. When he returned, he said, "I didn't accomplish a thing. The people wouldn't listen to me. When I called at the gate of a farm house, the people would ask who I was and what I wanted. I would say, 'I am an evangelist. I want to tell you how you can get to heaven.' They would say, 'Oh you lazy Indian, can't you see we are busy? We have things to do. We are farmers. You must be crazy going around talking about how to get to heaven. Get out of here.'

"That's the way it was. I couldn't talk to anyone. But I have an idea. In the army I learned to cut hair. If you, *don* Guillermo,[1] could get me a pair of clippers, a razor and some shears and a comb, I'll go back to that town and evangelize as many people as I can."

When I bought the tools and gave them to Bac, he held them in his hand and lifted his eyes toward heaven and said, "A man of God, thoroughly furnished unto every good work."

When Bac returned to the town and called at the gate of a farm and the people asked who was there, Bac would say "A barber. Does anyone need a haircut?" And since the area was remote and most of the people hadn't seen a barber in months, he would be invited in. Bac would give them a low price, cut their hair and win their friendship. Once he won their friendship, he would sit down after the haircut and talk about his Best Friend. They would listen because he had won their friendship through giving them an inexpensive haircut, but also because he had built a caring relationship.

Cam never forgot that lesson and urged his colleagues to look for practical ways to make friends, to serve people, to care. In 1959, many years later, Cam was at a special conference in Glen Eyrie, Colorado, and said:

> The Apostle Paul said, "We preach not ourselves, but Christ Jesus the Lord, and"—don't forget that *and*—"ourselves your servants."
>
> This must always be the motto of the Summer Institute of Linguistics: Your servants for Jesus' sake. Jesus didn't come saying, "I am the Son of God." He came doing good, calling himself the Son of Man. It was his servant attitude that awakened them to the reality that he was the Son of God. We must remember we serve as linguists, as Bible translators, as those engaged in scientific research, and we are also servants for Jesus' sake. After all, Jesus made himself of no reputation and took upon himself the form of a servant, and so must we.

During the decades of the fifties, sixties and part of the seventies, SIL's strategy for reaching the mostly isolated and remote ethnic people in Latin America, Papua New Guinea, and elsewhere was to establish operational centers—places of service. It was Townsend's desire to help governments in such matters as bilingual instruction, health education, and literacy. Each center, depending on the specific needs of a given country, varied in size and scope of operation. The center in Peru, for example, offered training in a variety of practical skills and professional helps: a bilingual school for training indigenous school teachers (sponsored jointly by SIL and Peru's Department of Education), paramedical training, animal husbandry, auto mechanics, and printing arts. Some of these centers have gradually been turned over to host governments for their own use.

The genesis for these early centers began with Cameron Townsend's desire to serve the Cakchiquel people of San Antonio more effectively.

The property he spoke about in his journal entry became the prototype for dozens of operation centers worldwide. The circumstances surrounding how the property was acquired to expand his school and his dream illustrate Cam's basic Promethean free spirit. Under the heading of, "An Amusing Example of Swivel-Chair Statesmanship," he wrote in his journal about how the Lord multiplied his money:

> Late in 1920, friends in California contributed six hundred dollars to help me buy an old corner saloon in San Antonio. My intention was to convert this into a chapel. But then, because of a sudden rise in the rate of exchange, I discovered I had enough money to buy the land across the street. Here I wanted to build a schoolhouse and raise a vegetable garden for the school. The reason I am telling this story is to show how God overruled the shortsighted policies of swivel-chair statesmanship in the homeland.
>
> The friends who contributed the six hundred dollars consulted a Christian leader in California who was conversant with conditions in Central America. They asked his opinion about my intention to buy out the saloon and move the school from its cramped quarters to a place where the children would not only have more than two classrooms, but also a yard in which to play.
>
> This man advised they hold their money until he could write to two of our senior missionaries and have them visit San Antonio in order for them to evaluate my plan. I realized I was young and inexperienced, and welcomed the advice of the senior missionaries. There was only one difficulty. The missionaries would have to travel three or four days on horseback each way to reach San Antonio. I wondered how the Christian leader in the homeland would have felt if he had been asked to take a seven-day horseback ride over rough mountain trails at his own expense in order to advise the expenditure of six hundred dollars. To say the least, I think he would have thought the suggestion ridiculous.
>
> However, after a delay of two months, one missionary did come. Although he was sympathetic to the project, his report to the mission leader in the States was not clearly defined and did not satisfy him.
>
> Finally, the friends from California wrote again asking my own reasons for wanting to extend the work. After my reply, they took the matter into their own hands and sent the money. The months of

delay could have been fatal. There was every possibility the saloon owner might have changed his mind about selling. The interesting thing about this event was that the rate of exchange had steadily increased and when I finally purchased the property, the six hundred dollars went twice as far as it would have at the time it was contributed.

Thus by the summer of 1920, the San Antonio Aguas Calientes Station included the cornstalk house, a school, a chapel and simple quarters for a Cakchiquel evangelist and one for the school teacher.

By October 1, Cam and Elvira were back in Patzún. Cam believed it was the Lord's will for them to be there since he could be totally immersed in the language. And they were joined by others. Cam's October 1920 report in the *Central American Mission Bulletin* announced that his brother Paul and his wife, Laura, were preparing themselves for their own adventure of faith in Guatemala. Cam ended his October report with news of a disturbing cultural practice. "We are told that in the town of Patzún a dog sells for ten pesos, a cat for five, and for four pesos you can buy a woman. That is, the father will sell his daughter to any man who asks for her and pays the father the going rate."

The 1920s saw the beginnings of great social changes in Guatemala. The automobile was making its first appearance into the mainstream of the national culture, as was the commercial cinema. Schools, rather than churches, were becoming the centers of social life. Poverty, of course, was still the single most pervasive characteristic of rural life, which meant the role of women in that environment was the slowest of all to change. This was one of the compelling reasons behind Cam's desire to have a school. He was particularly concerned for the young daughters of believers. Often these young women faced a double jeopardy—their gender and their faith. In such a repressive society, there was little educational opportunity for women to use their ingenuity beyond the traditional roles as bearers of children and domestic servants to their husbands. Cam continually looked for ways to improve the role of such women and encouraged both men and women to develop their talents. In his October letter to Judge Scott, he reveals his rising confidence that "a new day is dawning for the indigenous peoples":

We are seeing a time of special blessing in the work among the Indians. Every place we have gone it seems the Word has had a new power to convict sinners and build up believers. The workers and ourselves are filled with a love for people as never before. During the last two and a half months, there were between fifty-five and sixty confessions of faith among the Indians of our district. We are shouting hallelujah, pressing on and expecting to see greater things than these (John 1:50).

On our way home from Patzún, we visited a group of *ladino* believers. I was led to talk to them on prayer. After the message, one of the believers jumped up and asked how many would spend the night with him in prayer. Nearly half of them agreed.

We told them of the great blessings God has sent among the Cakchiquels and said we were certain these blessings were the answers to the special prayers of the brethren in the States. We are sure many in the homeland must be praying in a newer more definite way for us here. How happy we are to see the results [of your prayers].

We here are praying more than ever and trust that you will do the same. Pray especially for Trinidad Bac, our pastor in Patzún, Comalapa and neighboring districts. He is developing into a powerful preacher. He is eloquent in his use of the Cakchiquel language. We call him our Indian Paul.

One of Cam and Elvira's first visitors to the newly named San Antonio Indian Mission Station was Rev. Edward M. Haymaker of the Presbyterian Mission. On November 10, 1920, he wrote Cam and Elvira a letter of appreciation for their hospitality. The following is an edited copy of that letter:

I am writing to tell you how much I enjoyed my recent visit with you. Your little home is an example of an extremely simple life-style without the surrender of either dignity or comfort. It should serve as a model to all of what can be done with a maximum of willingness and a minimum of funds.

I enjoyed the exchange of mission ideas, our devotions together, the inspection of the school, Sunday school and church work. I was

impressed with how the Indian believers expressed their faith and
gratitude to God.

For more than a third of a century I have prayed and pleaded
with our mission board for someone to work [directly] with the Indians. But they fail to understand that he who wins the Indian for
Christ, wins Guatemala.

Rev. Haymaker's encouraging letter continued with passionate pleas for
Indian recognition. He then launched into discussion of what had clearly
troubled him for many years: how his mission board handled its finances and administered programs from the homeland.

That field programs are created *from* the field, *by* the field member,
thus eliminating unnecessary bureaucracy, was Mr. Townsend's desire
from the beginning of WBT and SIL. And one unique feature of these
organizations has been that each field entity elects its own director and
executive committee from among its own field membership. This innovative mission policy came about in part from Townsend's reading
about the bureaucracy nightmare Rev. Haymaker had to go through
with his mission:

> One thing that is much in your favor is your freedom in the matter
> of funds. In our mission we are restricted by complicated rules made
> necessary by a bureaucratic system operated by officers of a non-
> resident board, who, no matter how well-intentioned, can never con-
> trol with the highest efficiency the administration of field funds. The
> system makes it necessary for us to be perpetually adjusting classified
> appropriations based on estimates a year and a half old to the rapid
> flux and change we all are so familiar with in this country. We can
> make no financial move without prolonged correspondence with the
> home base. I am convinced your work is divinely guided.

By the end of 1920, the company of lay preachers, evangelists, and
school teachers operating out of the San Antonio Mission Station had
grown to over twenty. All of them looked to Cam for direction, support, encouragement, and vision. Wisely, Cam realized this was beyond his own energies and called for outside stimulus and spiritual
refreshment. He organized what he called the first Cakchiquel Bible

Conference. The only question was who would be the conference speaker. It should be someone who was empathetic toward ethnic peoples and sensitive to cross-cultural issues. Since Cam had just heard Mr. Howard B. Dinwiddie (director of an organization called the Victorious Life Testimony) and Dr. Robert McQuilkin of Columbia Bible College[2] as conference speakers at the Union Missionary Conference in Guatemala City, he thought one of these men would be the logical choice. He chose Mr. Dinwiddie.

Responding to Cam, Dinwiddie wrote, "I will be happy to come and do what I can, but if you want a 'Victorious Life' message for a conference of Indians, the man you want is Leonard Livingston Legters, L. L. for short. He is a former missionary to the Comanche Indians in Oklahoma. I am sure he would be delighted to come to Guatemala. He most certainly is your man."

*The first Cakchiquel Bible Conference with conference speaker,
L. L. Legters,* top center; *and conference hosts, Elvira and
Cameron*

Chapter Four

The Chichicastenango Twelve

When Howard Dinwiddie recommended L. L. Legters to be the speaker for the Cakchiquel Bible Conference, Cam asked Dinwiddie to cable Legters on his behalf. Like Dinwiddie and Robert McQuilkin, Legters traveled the country holding extensive Victorious Life conferences.

These conferences had sprung from a home Bible study held in the home of *Sunday School Times'* editor Charles Trumbull in New Wilmington, Pennsylvania. Beginning in 1910, Trumbull's study emphasized four basic disciplines of the Christian life: Bible study, prayer, spiritual growth, and mission.

Tracing the history of the conferences, Anna Marie Dahlquist in her book, *Trailblazers for Translators*,[1] noted the direct influence of the Victorious Life conferences on the grassroots shaping of many organizations, including Wycliffe Bible Translators. She writes:

> In 1911, a young Robert McQuilkin (who would later become the founder and first president of Columbia Bible College that sent out hundreds of missionaries and scores of translators) heard Trumbull speak at New Wilmington. After prayer with Trumbull, McQuilkin entered into a life of surrender and trust in Christ.

A year later, McQuilkin and his new bride moved to Philadelphia to work with the *Sunday School Times*. They began a home Bible study, which in turn led to the organization of the Victorious Life Conference (separate from the one held in New Wilmington).

The first meetings were held in Oxford, Pennsylvania July 19–23, 1913, the exact dates of the annual Keswick Convention held in England. Later, this 'American Keswick' moved to Princeton, then to Long Island, and finally to its present location at Keswick Grove, New Jersey.

The Victorious Life Conference grew out of McQuilkin's prayer group and conference. One of the main conference speakers was Howard Dinwiddie. In 1919, former missionary and Dutch Reformed pastor, L. L. Legters, in search of victory over his triple besetting sins—tobacco, hot temper, and worry—attended the Keswick Conference in Long Island.

Through McQuilkin's ministry, Legters learned the secret of surrender and trust. So enthusiastic was Legters over his new-found "victory" over his problems, that he and Howard Dinwiddie, whom he had met at the conference, formed a team and held conferences throughout the United States.

Thus when Dinwiddie cabled Legters to come to Guatemala for yet another conference, Legters said yes. That Legters was to play a unique and strategic role in the early development of Wycliffe is firmly fixed in the historical record. Yet one has to both admire and wonder about Legters' decision to go. Near Christmastime he left a wife sick with cancer to attend this meeting and did not return home until the end of March 1921.

While he apparently never fully shed his hot temper when he was angry, he did live a life of remarkable self-denial and faith. Following ideals molded by men like his namesake, Dr. David Livingstone, Legters read everything ever written on the great missionary-explorer. He was influenced and fascinated by the exploits of the French writer-explorer, Paul du Chaillu, a discoverer of the African pygmies, and the scientific writings of Alexander von Humboldt in *South America Sea Currents*. Another hero was the young, promising English star cricketer, Charles (C. T.) Studd, who gave up worldly success to become a man of God in Africa.

Legters's son, David, who was born on the Comanche reservation in 1908 where his father and mother worked as missionaries, told the story of how God provided for his father after he accepted the invitation to speak at the conference in Guatemala:

> My father had resigned his church post at what seemed to be the worst possible time. My mother (the first of two helpmates) lay dying of cancer. Medicines alone cost two hundred dollars a month. When the invitation came for him to speak at the conference in Guatemala, he felt God would have him go. After borrowing enough money from friends for a one-way train and boat ticket, he left just enough money behind to take care of his sick wife during the time he would be away, and started out.
>
> On the train to New Orleans where he would catch a boat for Guatemala, my father sat down beside a burly man who was puffing away on a cigar. "I hope you don't mind the smoke," said the man. "I just can't seem to quit." My father, who had once smoked cigars himself, said he understood because he had once been a smoker. During the conversation, my father told the man how he had come to have the strength to give up smoking and how he could also find the same strength in Christ.
>
> The man, who turned out to a lumber broker, invited my father to have dinner with him. Over dinner, where they continued to talk about the deeper meaning to life, the man took out a piece of paper and pencil and began to scribble. Finally he said. "I've just been trying to figure out how much money I would save if I quit smoking for the rest of my life. Suppose I live to be seventy, twenty years from now, I figure that would amount to about five hundred dollars."
>
> The man then reached into his pocket, took out his checkbook and wrote a check for that amount. "Here," he said, "use this for your work, and good luck."[2]

After graduating from the Dutch Reformed Hope College and New Brunswick Seminary, Legters was sent by the Dutch Reformed Mission Board to work in Oklahoma among the Comanche and Apache Indians. It was there he met his future wife, who was also interested in Indian work.

While working in Oklahoma, Legters developed a vision for the Indians of Latin America. His dream was to train North American Indians
and have them go as missionaries to Central and South America.

From Oklahoma, Legters, his wife and baby son, David, were transferred to California to begin work among the Indian groups there. A
disagreement over Indian policy arose, however, and Legters and his
family left the Dutch Reformed Church, and in 1912 took a Southern
Presbyterian pastorate in South Carolina.

The disagreement Legters had with the Dutch Reformed Church was
over the use of the vernacular languages of the groups with which he
was working. The prevailing opinion, held by the Dutch Reformed
Church at the time, was that Indians should learn English and forget
their native tongue. When Legters arrived in Guatemala and saw how
deeply concerned Cameron Townsend and Paul Burgess were about using the vernacular languages for Indian evangelism and church growth,
Legters knew God had brought him to Guatemala for this.

The end of 1920 was notable in Cam's life for more than the arrival
of L. L. Legters as the principal speaker for the first Cakchiquel Bible
Conference. Earlier in December 1920, Cam had been involved in another conference of political and historic significance. A group of visiting
diplomats from five Central American countries convened in Antigua
to discuss the possible union of all Central American countries into one.
In reality, this diplomatic congress had another agenda. In her book,
Burgess of Guatemala, Anna Marie Dahlquist writes:

> Guatemala was desperately weary of President Manuel Estrada
> Cabrera who had ruled like a mad monarch for twenty-two years.
> Peasants were tired of poverty and bondage. Educated citizens were
> tired of his inflated ego that indulged in renaming ancient towns to
> honor his relatives. Catholics were weary of his worship of Greek
> culture. They felt the magnificent temples to Minerva he erected in
> every provincial capital were usurping honor that belonged solely to
> the Virgin Mary.
>
> And so Cabrera's foes banded together under the name of "Union
> ists," ostensibly to promote the federation of the five tiny Central Ameri
> can republics, but in reality seeking to depose the hated dictator.[3]

Since Cam was learning more and more about the importance of political tact, little mention of these political overtones was made in his November 15, 1920, letter to Judge Scott. The significance of the December convention for Cam was not so much the coming together of powerful diplomatic forces, but the realization that quasi-official ceremonies could pay enormous goodwill dividends for, as Townsend's secretary Cal Hibbard said, "the liberation of minority groups." Leaving the conference's overtones behind, Cam's letter to Judge Scott described his vision for the coming year and beyond:

> You may have read in some of the American magazines about a congress that has just been held in Antigua, the ancient capital of Central America. The purpose of the congress was to try to negotiate the union of the five Central American countries into one. Delegations came from each country. In every way it was an epochal event. Toward the end of the sessions, the delegates were honored with a special mass held in one of the large cathedrals.
>
> At the suggestion of one delegate, we decided to hold a gospel service. We sent out written invitations explaining the service would be held in an old chapel in Antigua, and that Indian believers would have a special part in the program.
>
> The response was greater than we expected. Almost all the delegates attended. Even though it was on a Friday afternoon, the big chapel was filled. The large group of Indian believers sang two special hymns. Next came a quartet, composed of two Indian young men, an Indian girl and Elvira. One of the delegates had come in a mood to ridicule, but when the children from our school sang a special hymn in Spanish, and another in English, he changed instantly into a respectful listener. I gave a short, pointed message, and made it clear that anyone, Indian, *ladino* or foreigner, could find love and forgiveness through the power of the gospel of Christ.
>
> As we closed the meeting, one of the delegates asked for the floor. He said with great sincerity, and with words that seemed to fail him, "In all my life, I have never seen anything to equal what I have seen today in any other religion. I marvel at what the gospel has done for these Indian people, a race which our forefathers conquered, and

considered nothing more than beasts for their service. What I have seen here today has been a banquet for my soul."

The brother of the president of Honduras sprang to his feet and said similar things, as did the Secretary of the Congress. At the end, one of the delegates promised to try and interest the government in draining the swamps that make these towns so unhealthy at this time of year. In every way it was a wonderful meeting.

Still full of enthusiasm, Cam ended his four-page hand-written letter to Judge Scott with what became his formula for spiritual action:

> Never has the time been as ripe as it is now. We believe the Lord intends to do great things. We would appreciate you joining us in prayer. Every day we see more clearly that prayer is our greatest need, just believing prayer, prayer born in love, nourished by a vision and made effectual by faith. Hebrews 4:9-11 has strengthened our spirits these days. It seems as though we just discovered it. How important it is to rest from one's own works and let the indwelling Christ work in us all things to the honor and glory of God. Only then can Isaiah 40:31 be fulfilled.

It was at that time, January 23–25, 1921, that Wycliffe Bible Translators and the Summer Institute of Linguistics were conceived. The gestation period for SIL would last almost thirteen years (and longer for WBT), yet the framework for SIL and WBT was first cast by twelve missionaries who met together for what was called the General Indian Conference. They dubbed themselves the "Chichicastenango Twelve," after the ancient Quiché Indian town in the highlands of Guatemala where they met for that historic mission conference. This cast of characters who made up the twelve were men and women with passionate concern for those who had been neglected by established mission agencies, namely ethnic minorities in Guatemala and the rest of the Americas. This was the time, those at the conference understood, for mature reasoning and planning.

It was also during this time that many, like Townsend, came under the influence of John R. Mott and the Student Volunteer Movement. In what was the equivalent of today's InterVarsity Christian Fellowship's Urbana Missions Convention, a special missions conference was called in 1886 at Mount Hermon, Massachusetts, by D. L. Moody. Of the 250 college students attending that conference, 100 signed the pledge card that said, "God helping me, I purpose to be a foreign missionary." One of those 100 was John R. Mott. He later became a renowned missions statesman, traveling throughout the U.S., speaking in universities and seminaries. His powerful persona and enthusiasm awakened a missionary zeal in many and phenomenally affected the growth of the Student Volunteer Movement, which was born at the Mount Hermon conference. The Movement's motto was: "The Evangelization of the World in this Generation."

With this motto in mind, the Chichicastenango Twelve believed the time to act had arrived. No matter how small their number or how gigantic the task ahead of them, they were men and women of faith. Cameron Townsend asked the penetrating question, "If we are to reach the Indians for Christ in this generation, are the present means for evangelization adequate?" And the consensus of the twelve was that their mission agencies had assigned no personnel, devised no plan, and allocated no budget for Indian evangelism. In fact, many in the leadership of the established mission agencies were opposed to the notion of a Bible translation program for indigenous people. R. D. Smith of the Central American Mission voiced his opposition, saying, "Let the Indians learn Spanish, read the Spanish Bible and take part in Spanish church services."[4]

The Chichicastenango Twelve were not the first who felt mission agencies were not doing enough for indigenous peoples. In 1892, the British and Foreign Bible Society appointed Rev. F. de P. Castells to work in Central America. Castells immediately began urging the missionaries to translate the Scriptures for the Mayans and other ethnic groups. He was, however, unsupported in his vision by the resident missionaries.

The annual report of the British and Foreign Bible Society in 1902 said of Castells and his dream: "His efforts were at first severely criticized. The languages of these tribes were not thought worthy of Bible translation. They were of the opinion that any version produced would prove utterly useless. The Indians were considered too ignorant, and the Society and its agents were called visionaries."

There were also other voices calling for translation into the vernacular languages. The Presbyterian missionary, Edward Haymaker—the man who had visited Cam and Elvira in their cornstalk house—commissioned a translation of the Gospel of Mark into Quiché. And there were others: the Moravians working with the Miskitos in Nicaragua, the Baptists in Belize, Paul Burgess and his wife Dora among the Quichés, and Cameron and Elvira Townsend among the Cakchiquels. But for the most part, these were scattered, isolated groups who worked without any mission organization's backing. Clearly a new organization was needed to address the needs of the thirty distinct ethnic groups in Guatemala.

Thus the historic conference began. Legters, who normally would have left after his own conference concluded, was captivated by the pioneering nature of the Chichicastenango Conference participants and decided to stay on. The other participants included Cam and Elvira, Howard Dinwiddie, and Cam's best friend, William Elbert (Robbie) Robinson. Also attending were Rev. Paul Burgess and his wife Dora, Elvira's longtime friends and mentors. They had also become Cam's good friends, and Paul had preached at Cam and Elvira's wedding. Assigned by the Presbyterian Church (USA) to work among Spanish and German speaking people in the Quiché area of Guatemala, the Burgesses were shocked one day to learn that a group of five Quiché witch doctors had brutally murdered five young men of their German congregation and had thrown the bodies into a volcano crater to appease the spirits of the mountains. This incident caused Paul and Dora to become concerned for the spiritual needs of the Quiché people.

Like Cam, Paul Burgess had been influenced by John R. Mott. After attending the sixth international Student Volunteer Convention, in which three thousand students attended from seven hundred international schools, Paul wrote:

> The watchword, "The Evangelization of the World in this Generation," suggests the enormity of our task, and drives us to seek Divine aid. It kills apathy in us and leads us to self-sacrifice, and above all, it gives us a vision, for vision we must have if we would do great things. No one could attend this conference and hear that great audience when they sang, "Faith of Our Fathers," without realizing that this faith is living still. And everyone, too, gained a desire for a deeper and more victorious life for themselves, and for having a part in this important movement.[5]

Playing host to the twelve were Ben Treichler and his wife, Louise. And the remaining three of the conference were Herbert Toms and his wife, Mary, who worked with upper-class Spanish-speaking people in Huehuetenango, and Ella Williams, a young school teacher who worked under the Presbyterian board.

On January 23, 1921, Robbie Robinson opened the conference with prayer. He asked God specifically for wisdom and guidance on how to best evangelize the Indians of Guatemala. Paul Burgess was then appointed chairman and Louise Treichler conference secretary.

Cam injected his own particular imprimatur into the conference by quoting Psalm 119:126 and saying, "It's time for Jehovah to work for the evangelization of all the Indian peoples of Latin America in this generation. This conference should consider first the local problem, and then the Latin American problem."

There followed a lengthy discussion as to whether Indian languages were capable of expressing *all* religious thought. Paul Burgess, with his eye to scholarship, argued that indeed the vernacular languages, when properly translated, were capable of expressing the full meaning of Scripture. Howard Dinwiddie wondered aloud if any people had ever been adequately evangelized, except in their own tongue. All agreed they knew of no one who had.

Since the threat of revolution, bloody repression, and cruel exploitation were political realities in Guatemala—particularly as it related to Indian peoples—Paul Burgess urged caution against entering into the political arena. To do so would jeopardize their ability to work among the people, and thus impede the translation process.

The first day of the conference concluded with Legters acknowledging that a certain number of Indian peoples *had* been reached with the gospel through the current missions methods and the use of Spanish. He, however, moved that it was the sense of *this* body that the Indians of Guatemala should have the gospel of the Lord Jesus Christ in a written form in their own language.

Day two of the conference centered on practical methods for reaching Indian peoples in their own languages. Legters moved that Townsend and Burgess constitute themselves a translation committee. He suggested they translate the Gospel of Mark separately and afterward come together to compare their translations. The motion was carried unanimously. Cam also felt that ethnic nationals should be involved in the translation process, as well as favoring a motion put forward that the nationals themselves be trained to do the work of evangelism.

On January 24, 1921, the twelve debated the necessity of establishing this new agency, and, if established, what to name it. Paul Burgess felt there should be a completely new mission agency devoted exclusively to Indian work and suggested that it be called "The Latin American Indian Mission." For such an agency to work, Cam suggested, it must have a generous policy that gives the Indian first place.

Howard Dinwiddie said he considered it a "pity" to form a new agency and urged that the problems of Indian work be carried out through existing mission channels. He said he believed strongly in collective experience.

Paul Burgess reminded the group that Indian work was not limited to their own immediate sphere. Rather, he said, the work of evangelism and Bible translation for ethnic minority groups was related to a much larger sphere. The sphere being, of course, other ethnic groups in Latin America. Legters was particularly interested in South America, as was Dinwiddie. And both Cam and Legters had spoken about the needs in Mexico. "In order to do an effective work," Legters said, "each one of us must have a vision of working and praying for the larger field." He also spoke about the needs in Ecuador and Bolivia and told about a work among Paraguay's Indians that had been replaced by a Spanish-based work.

On January 25, the last day of the conference, the meeting began as it had every day, with a lengthy session of prayer. The group unanimously agreed to call this new agency, "The Latin American Indian Mission" (LAIM). Next they concerned themselves with hammering out their goals, operating principles, membership requirements, choosing officers, writing up a statement of purpose, and forming a doctrinal statement.

The election of officers for this newly formed mission agency shows something of the group's regard for Cam's emerging leadership ability. At Cam's suggestion, all voting was by secret ballot. The nomination for chairman was between Paul Burgess and Cam Townsend. The first ballot produced a tie. On the second ballot, Burgess had a majority.

Robbie Robinson nominated Howard Dinwiddie as general director, and he was unanimously elected.

Cam moved that Legters be asked to serve on the home council. This also was unanimously carried. The final minutes, as recorded by Louise Treichler, read as follows: "The meeting adjourned at twelve o'clock midnight after prayer. HALLELUJAH! IT IS TIME FOR JEHOVAH TO WORK."

Cameron and Elvira with a young Cakchiquel woman

Chapter Five

Testings

News of the Chichicastenango Conference and its implications for Indian work spread quickly among the various missionaries and their agencies. Louise Treichler reported to the Christian journal *Serving-and-Waiting*, "We are grateful to God that someone has finally come and investigated the work we have at heart. For a long time we have felt, and recommended to our board, that Indian work be separated from the *ladino* work, and that Mr. Townsend be placed in charge of all Indian work under the Central American Mission in Guatemala." Louise concluded her report with a most telling statement: "Do you know the only missionaries who have ever gone from Guatemala have been Indians?"[1]

Paul Burgess immediately informed his Presbyterian board that Townsend, Robinson, and he had been named a committee of three to work on a vernacular translation of the New Testament. Cam was already working at translating the Gospel of Mark into Cakchiquel.

It is clear in the minutes that the central goal of the Latin American Indian Mission was Bible translation. According to Anna Marie Dahlquist, it was also clear the Chichicastenango Twelve fully expected to recruit new missionaries who would go out under LAIM rather than under the older established agencies.

During the discussions of how these new missionaries were to be supported, Cam suggested that new members of the established missions should be associate members of LAIM and that LAIM be responsible for the financial support of its active members.

If indeed this new mission agency was to become viable, the Chichicastenango Twelve needed new recruits plus financial and prayer support. Before they could inform the public of their needs, however, they needed updated facts and figures about the various ethnic groups of Mexico, Central America, and South America.

Legters was particularly eager to study the "distribution, numbers, characteristics, and strategic centers of the various ethnic minorities." In order for him to do this effectively, he would have to make a physical survey of each area.

Four days after the conference ended, Legters began a three-month survey trip of seven indigenous minority groups. In the years to come, and until his death in 1940, Legters would return as often as possible to preach and make similar survey trips. Among these trips was a pivotal trip in 1926 to Brazil with his seventeen-year-old son, David. Legters returned from that trip brimming with enthusiasm for the ethnic minorities of Amazonia. His passion for these isolated people groups to have the New Testament in their own tongues contributed significantly to the enlarging of Cam's vision for what would become a vision of Bible translation for all of the world's ethnic groups who didn't have the Scriptures in their own language.

One of the events the conferees were eager to report was the special "Victorious Life" meetings held by Dinwiddie and Legters for the national workers. Many of the Quiché and Cakchiquel leaders who attended the meetings made spiritual commitments. Of this "awakening" Paul Burgess said, "One of the most remarkable aspects of the new awakening has been a wave of evangelistic zeal that has lifted the Indians who were already believers out of the routine of ordinary church life and has made their churches centers from which scores of evangelists are going out to evangelize their fellow countrymen."

While it was true the conference meetings gave everyone a spiritual high, Dinwiddie warned the twelve to expect testings. "They will surely come to both individuals and your mission agencies alike. They always do after such meetings."

Meanwhile, Cam lost no time in reporting his view of the "Chichicastenango Twelve" conference. His January 31, 1921, letter to Judge Scott was filled with details of the formation of the Latin American Indian Mission, its officers, and the objectives of the new agency. He emphasized the unanimity of purpose the twelve had for giving the gospel to the Indians in their own language. He told about the special meetings for the national workers and added that along with the expatriate speakers, Trinidad Bac from Patzún also spoke and was used by the Lord in a powerful way. "All of us caught a new vision of our Lord and the work to which he has called us."

Cam reported that he, Paul Burgess, and Herbert Toms had formulated the policies of cooperation with the existing mission agencies and said that all felt strongly they should remain faithful to their first allegiances. In no way did he envision this new agency being in opposition to or in competition with any established agency:

> As far as I am concerned, the organization will merely mean the opening up of a new field for support of our work in the homeland and the broadening of our vision to take in the whole Indian problem and the coordination of ideas and plans of work.
>
> It is our prayer that our own Central American Mission may under God take first rank in pushing the Indian work here in Central America. The work among the Cakchiquels is better taken care of than any other group. [As for our own work] our immediate need is for a school teacher and a trained nurse.

Cam's core values of how the work of world mission was to be carried out were fixed amazingly early in his career. One of these was the juxtaposition of the expatriate missionary and the national worker. His early correspondence reveals that he placed high value on the expatriate missionary functioning as a facilitator and guide, rather than an authoritative dispenser of religious information. Further, he championed the notion that nationals be trained to carry the responsibility for teaching and evangelism. This had been one of the principal issues under discussion during the conference at Chichicastenango.

With his request for a school teacher, Cam explained in an earlier letter, he was most anxious that it be someone who could train nationals to become teachers:

We believe a trained teacher from the homeland is needed to attend to the direction of the school and to train nationals. We also would want such a teacher to be concerned for the spiritual welfare of both teachers and pupils.

We are also asking the Lord to send a trained nurse to take over the medical and visitation work that now demands so much of our time in San Antonio. Many are still dying from malaria. [Elvira wrote that for months they had heard the wailing of people mourning over their dead.]

Saturday we buried a baby whose mother was shaking from head to foot with malarial chills during the funeral. Almost every day there are from one to three people who die in each of the two towns. A nurse could do a wonderful work, not only in dispensing medicines, but also in training mothers how to take care of their children. And to also train a number of Christian Indian women to do home visitation and evangelization. However, it should be noted that conditions here are so terrible that no one but a fully consecrated servant [of God's], who is ready to sacrifice all things, would be able to take up this work.

Cam concluded the letter with a description of Miguel Apop who, in a freak accident, had fallen off a hundred-foot cliff and had survived the fall, but only for a week: "As he lay dying, there was not a moment of bitterness. Rather, he said he believed God had spared his life in order that he might give a testimony to the people in Patzún. During the last moments of Miguel's life when those around him tried to stir him back to life, he motioned them all aside impatiently and said, 'Let me alone. I am going home to Christ.'"

By all accounts Cam should have been greatly encouraged and free from inward anxiety. By mid-February the malaria epidemic had subsided. A major prayer request for a nurse was partially answered when he received a letter from Charles Abbot of Vineland, New Jersey, who, with his sister, pledged to undertake the financial support of a missionary nurse for his station. Cam still wasn't certain just who this nurse would be, but he and others were praying that "God in his own time would send just the right person."

Other monies were coming in (modest amounts) for the school building project and for malaria medicine. And Cam and Elvira were looking forward to Cam's younger brother Paul and his wife, Laura, coming to be part of the team at the San Antonio Station. Further encouraging signs were the believers in the town of Comalapa who were enlarging their chapel, because the "whole town is interested in the gospel and they are sure many will soon accept the message."

However, these blessings were only one side of the coin. The other side was that Dinwiddie's warning had inevitably come true. Testings. Within weeks after the conference, the Chichicastenango Twelve began to experience criticism, misunderstanding, disillusionment, and illness. One of the criticisms arose over a letterhead Cam had created. As part of her February letter to Judge Scott, Elvira wrote:

> You will note that we have cut off the top part of our letterhead [the part saying, "To Preach the Gospel to the Poor. The San Antonio Indian Mission Station of the. . .]. We have left the words "Central American Mission." Mr. R. D. Smith did not approve of the letterhead and we are sorry that he altogether misinterpreted our motives. We therefore have taken off the top part so as to under no circumstances give similar ideas to anyone else.

R. D. (Ralph) Smith and a senior missionary, Abe Edward Bishop, were highly rigid board members of the Central American Mission. Both were committed to the theology of C. I. Scofield, the founder of the Central American Mission, and both were unsparing in their criticism of all whom they felt had breached their brand of orthodoxy.

Cam had high regard for Bishop, considering him something of a father figure and mentor in mission strategy. It was Bishop, after all, who had been instrumental in organizing several Cakchiquel Indian congregations long before Cam came to Guatemala. Bishop was well-known for his many years of faithful work as a bold pioneer and church planter. When Cam came to the field and displayed his innovation, dedication, and interest in Indian work, Bishop appointed him to work with the Cakchiquel congregations in and around Antigua. Now, after he learned what had transpired at Chichicastenango, Bishop was outraged by what he felt was betrayal.

Immediately Bishop drew up a list of seven criticisms and gave them to Townsend. The complete list is lost to history, but among Paul Burgess's correspondence, some of Bishop's complaints against the new mission agency and its proposed policy were found: "What place is there for a new mission which would compete with established work and distribute funds through unauthorized channels, go against the time-honored policy of assimilating Indians into Spanish-speaking churches, and encourage association with individuals who were not pre-millennialists?"[2]

Like Paul Burgess, Townsend was also receiving his share of criticism. Unlike Burgess, however, Townsend's detractors were less conciliatory. In a journal in which he reflected on that moment in time, Cam wrote:

> Prior to the establishment of our work in San Antonio, Indian work had been almost exclusively a by-product of Spanish work. At that time no missionary could speak any Indian language. Mr. Bishop employed three Indian believers to evangelize among their own people. There were two *ladino* workers who could speak the language [Cakchiquel]. One of them gave all his time to the Indian work. Even though some specialized Indian work was being done, the foreign missionaries gave only their secondary attention to the Indians, and they dealt with them through interpreters.
>
> As we lived among them and came to see that the Indians differed from the *ladinos* [Spanish-speaking people] in customs, psychology, culture, dress, and beliefs, as well as language, we came to understand that specialized methods were needed to adequately reach these people. We observed that although sixty percent of the population of Guatemala was Indian, yet one hundred percent of the missionaries in the Republic worked among the *ladinos*. We therefore relinquished, as much as possible, all responsibilities to the *ladino* portion of the population in order to give our time unreservedly to the Indians. This action caused severe criticism.

Cam's general correspondence of February and March provides only hints of his feelings about the criticism he received from Abe Bishop, R. D. Smith and others. On February 14, he wrote:

> As we look back on the events in Chichicastenango, we believe our Lord guided each step. We are yet glorying in the way he gave the Toms a new vision for Indian work, and in the fine stand the Burgesses took. [Paul] is so wonderfully prepared by God to head up the organization here on the field. I am especially pleased with the unselfish plans for cooperation with other missions. Even among missions, such unselfish motives are rare. And only as we live up to them faithfully will other missions come to believe in us.

Cam had written earlier about how much he had enjoyed the ministry and personal friendship of Legters, even though both men had completely opposite personality and operational styles. Their commonality was always their pioneer vision, courage, and heart for those ethnic peoples without the Scriptures in their own languages. Then Cam acknowledged he was going through some "pretty rough times," but said these were sent to teach him to lean hard on the Lord.

Cam also acknowledged that Legters and the visit of Howard Dinwiddie had been instrumental in bringing him out of his "wilderness journey." Clearly he was puzzled by the unfavorable response to the new mission agency by men whom he held in high esteem. "It fills our hearts with sadness to see how the Lord is hindered in Guatemala by his very servants. We pray for a revival of holiness and self-denial in all of his missionaries and in the native Church. We believe this must happen before souls can be saved by the thousands as they should. May it come soon!"

Cameron Townsend's understanding of how a person could know he or she was in the will of God was almost simplistic. He believed all Christians could discern God's will through prayer, God's Word, and the guidance of the Holy Spirit. The confirmation of being in God's will was whether or not the person was well thought of by his peers and if he was successful in executing his duties.

He became famous for saying, "Thank God that's the first 'no' out of the way." He accepted these "negatives" because he interpreted experiences in the light of Scripture. Therefore, in his thinking, a negative response was treated as evidence that God was still actively involved and wanted him to continue on until all the negatives were exhausted. It was for this reason he could look back on the events of Chichicastenango and say, with full confidence, "We believe that our Lord guided in every step."

Cam also felt this was true with regard to his marriage to Elvira. She was a woman of high principle, devoted to the Indian work. She was an accomplished secretary who kept neat and accurate records of all receipts, spoke excellent Spanish, and understood the Latin American culture well enough to write an important booklet on Latin American courtesy. It was she who preserved most of the letters, diaries, and journals from which this chronicle was taken.

With the marriage there were, however, two ongoing problems. One was Elvira's health. Her heart was weak, and there were other undiagnosed difficulties. Cam accepted this and was most solicitous of her health problems. The other problem was what people called in those days her "nervous disposition." Unlike today, however, there were few, if any, antidepressants, and even she, like Cam, did not fully understand why she wasn't the woman she was when they were first married two years before. Elvira's March 7 correspondence to a Mrs. Young reveals for the first time her feelings about the pressure she had been under, and her intention to return to Chicago:

> You will be surprised to know that I am leaving for the States with Mr. Legters. I expect to arrive in Chicago [by way of New Orleans] on the 31st of this month, or the 1st of April. Mr. Townsend will remain in Guatemala until some time this summer when he expects to come home to get me.
>
> I am simply tired out and need a short rest. Two years ago the doctor told me I needed a rest. We believe it is the Lord's will for me to go [home] now. It is hard to leave the work just now, for I do love the Indians dearly. But meanwhile [God] can use me at home to tell the people there about the long-neglected people of this land. I ask you to pray for me that God may send me home to be a blessing.

On March 7 Cam wrote a lengthy letter to his good friend Judge Scott. This letter, among all of his correspondence, is singularly distinct for the depth of his honest feelings and frustrations with Elvira's dramatic mood swings. The letter is all the more extraordinary when one realizes that this was a time when many in the evangelical community considered nervous breakdowns or overt emotional difficulties—particularly for missionaries—to be somehow sub-spiritual. It would take others later to assure many Christians that having emotions was simply part of what it means to be human. In an earlier February letter he had written, "Day by day we are coming to know God better and better. We trust in him as Provider, Healer, Leader, Giver of Peace, Shepherd, our Righteousness, and the Ever-present One. He has had to bring us through some pretty hard lessons to teach us to lean on him."

This was an important truth for Cam. And just as the apostle Paul told the Corinthians in 2 Corinthians 7:5-6 that he would have felt emotionally unsupported if it hadn't been for the physical presence and comfort of his good friend, Titus, so Judge Scott became Cam's "Titus" in his time of great bewilderment and need.

A view of the mountains near Chimaltenango, where Cameron visited on evangelistic campaigns

The Dark Night of the Soul

Politeness and diplomatic decorum were as much a part of Cameron Townsend's operational style as walking and breathing. It was almost unheard of for him to give a colleague a direct order. This diplomatic talent, a talent he had perfected into a fine art, was leadership by gentle suggestion diligently pursued. If, for example, he wanted the director of a particular SIL to host a special dinner for a government official, he might say matter-of-factly, "Wouldn't it be nice to have a dinner for so-and-so to thank him for his friendship?" If the director was attuned to Cam's style, the special dinner was soon announced, the director making sure Townsend knew of the dinner in order for him to put it on his calendar. In response, Cam would smile broadly and say, "What a grand idea!" and then compliment the director for the director's astute thoughtfulness.

One could interpret Cam's style as a psychological desire to avoid unpleasant realities. However, he willingly tackled hard and difficult policy issues, especially as they related to WBT and SIL. And he repeatedly demonstrated great courage and moral leadership in the face of political adversity. In March 1981, when SIL member Chet Bitterman was martyred by the M-19 terrorists in Bogotá, Colombia, Cameron Townsend, then in his eighty-fourth year, flew immediately to Bogotá.

By doing so he lent his presence and spiritual strength with which to comfort the widow and members of the SIL Colombia branch. He was also careful to assure the Colombian government he held them in high esteem.

When he faced personal difficulty, however, Townsend usually accepted it as an opportunity to draw upon God's grace. He was fond of saying, "God's grace is sufficient for all of life's difficulties."

His life of faith, however, was not as fully developed in 1921 as it would one day become. His March 7 letter to Judge Scott is notable for its candor, its human cry for help, and for his need to have another human being understand his pain and grave concern for Elvira's health:

Some time ago you wrote to us about our plans to return to the U.S. for a rest. We had hoped that such a trip would not be necessary for several years. But a week ago we decided it would be wise for Mrs. Townsend to go as soon as possible. She had written you that we would go to Lake Atitlán where she could have a complete rest for two months. However, her condition has become worse and we believe it is necessary for her to get completely out of the work for several months.

We now have sufficient funds on hand to make a trip to the States. We believe God definitely directed you to send us money at this time because, dear Judge, her condition simply can't drag on any longer.

I want to write to you very frankly because I feel you should know and because we believe you have a deeper interest and sympathy in us and in our work than most anyone in the homeland, aside from our home folks.

At the time we were engaged, Elvira was in poor health. The earthquake[1], the influenza, and all of the duties she had to do left her nerves in bad shape. We were engaged in February. In April or March, she planned to go to the States for a good rest before getting married, but no funds came through for such a trip.

Doctor Hedges came in June, and after examining her, forbade her to marry until she had at least six months rest at home. However, everything had been arranged for our marriage and the doctor reconsidered and gave his permission, providing she was very careful about the amount of work she did.

wife issues

But she wasn't careful. When I went ahead with the work, she refused to lag behind. For over a year now we have been terribly hampered in the work by her condition. In her extreme nervousness, she loses control of herself and says and does things painful to me and hurtful to our work. These demonstrations have become more and more frequent until now they are almost daily and often in public.

We have looked constantly to the Lord for relief and at times there are wonderful periods of blessed communion. Then it's joy beyond expression. We know he is teaching us some special lessons. However, the prevailing conditions are such that we cannot continue to work here, nor can we plan for new missionaries to come while things are the way they are.

Therefore, Elvira's return to the States should be now. We believe it is fortuitous that she can sail on March 24 for New Orleans at the same time as Mr. Legters. If there are sufficient funds, I plan to go to the States and pick her up in about July or August.

During these months alone, I hope to do a lot of language work. And if funds come in, to build the school and chapel. I would like this to be out of the way when we return. I tell you all this in confidence so that you may join me in prayer for the quick recovery of my dear wife, who in her moments of calm in the Lord, is the sweetest woman I ever knew. I trust you will understand.

Here was the dark night of Cam's soul. Clearly he was profoundly concerned about the emotional and physical health of his wife. He was also concerned for the work in San Antonio. Much was at stake in his cry for prayer. Resting on Elvira's health was his dream of an expanded school, a hospital, the translation of the New Testament into Cakchiquel, the growth and spiritual development of the Cakchiquel believers, and an evangelistic outreach.

Cam and Elvira could have been tempted to lose confidence or faith in the God they both believed brought them to this work in Guatemala. This, however, was not their response. Whether or not they believed they were being tested by God or attacked by their soul's enemy is unclear, yet Cam's response in his general statement to Judge Scott was that God was teaching him some "special" lessons. From his response it is clear that one lesson he learned was his faith was rooted not in a personal ideology, but in God—no matter how dark the night of his soul seemed. And this was true for Elvira as well.

Elvira's response to what was happening is recorded in an amazingly strong and positive letter written to Mrs. Young just two days after Cam's letter to Judge Scott on March 9, 1921. She wrote passionately about the injustices ethnic peoples of Guatemala suffered at the hands of the Spanish-speaking populace and compared the racial harassment and social inequity of Guatemala's Indians to those of black people in the southern States.

Cam learned of Elvira's and Legters's safe arrival in New Orleans from Judge Scott in an April 1, 1921, letter written from Paris, Texas (home office of the Central American Mission. It would later be moved to Dallas):

> I have just received a message from your dear wife and Mr. Legters, simply a post card, stating that Mrs. Townsend is quite well and that she is hoping to see me soon. We are glad they have landed safely. We have prayed much for them. Our prayers have been particularly for Mrs. Townsend's [hernia] operation. We expect it to be a success so that she may be well and strong and able to return to the work to which God has called you both.

Fully confident that Elvira and Legters would arrive at their respective destinations, Cam left for a destination of his own: "I am leaving today [March 30] on an evangelistic campaign in the neighborhood of Comalapa where just now great interest in the gospel and persecution go hand in hand." Twenty days later, on April 19, Cam wrote a detailed report on his trip:

> I want to tell you about some of the things I experienced on my recent trip. In the weeks before I left, the Lord gave us five new [national] workers. I decided the best way to train them was to start an on-the-job training school. As a result, we left three weeks ago tomorrow for Cajawalten.
>
> When we arrived, the local people warned us not to have a service in their town. They threatened to shoot us if we did. But their bark was worse than their bite. We had a splendid service without any

"fireworks," except the flicker of the pine torches held by the attentive listeners and the beaming of their eyes as they listened to a message from the Word of God. The next day we reached Chimaltenango after speaking to a great many along the road. Two of the workers' wives came along and would speak to the women while the men worked in pairs and spoke to the men.

We reached Comalapa Friday evening just as the men of the town were coming in from their work in the fields. We all had great opportunities to speak to the men about their eternal souls. What a priceless moment this was! It seemed like Apostolic times. We stayed in Comalapa all day Saturday and Sunday teaching, holding Bible studies and doing personal evangelism. On Sunday afternoon, when I went out to do personal evangelism on the streets, such a large crowd gathered that a big drove of cattle couldn't get by. I was so interested in what I was saying to the crowd that I didn't realize what was happening until a big billy goat began to look at me with his head tilted in a very significant posture. When I understood what was happening, I quickly asked the crowd to step to one side and let the animals pass.

One day we separated into two groups in order to cover more territory. From time to time I would pair off with different workers so as to give each one some personal help and attention. When we got tired, we would find a shady spot along the trail, stop, study the Word and pray. After services at one *hacienda* we couldn't find a place to sleep, so we slept outside under a tree.

Early the next day we came upon a group of Indians who were pressing out sugar cane. They listened with great interest. Still further on we met a large number of men going to Guatemala City to find work. Others were on their way to the big plantations on the coast to work out their time. Practically all of them listened attentively to the gospel saying they had never before heard the things we were telling them. Some from Nepaj (four days journey away) were so grateful that they gave us a lot of *totoposti*. This is best described as cracked tortilla hardtack. It wasn't as stale eating as you might think. They had ground plenty of chile into it.

Cam's report continued with many more interesting encounters about holding services in towns, villages, and the countryside. He spoke about being "drenched" with blessing as one old man, overcome by the good news of the gospel, fell on his knees before Cam. Cam begged him not to do that and said, as he lifted him to his feet, that he and the others were mere men just like him, only saved by God's grace. He reminded the old man that if he would accept Christ as his Savior, they would all be brethren together. The old man replied that he understood perfectly well, but said since God had sent Cam and the others as messengers of peace directly to him, he wanted to honor them. At that moment, the old man quickly caught hold of Felipe's hand and kissed it. Cam concluded his report with a timeless challenge to all who wish to do the will of God:

> My eyes were opened as never before to the vastness of the field. If the number of our workers were doubled, it would take us six months to a year to cover the area we said we would be responsible for. Eight months ago we asked the Lord for ten [national] workers by January 1922. We thought with that number the field would be adequately covered. The Lord has given us the ten we asked for, and with the ten has come an expanded vision. He has shown us that at least twice as many [national] workers are needed, as well as more missionaries to train them. "His faithfulness reaches unto the clouds" (Psalm 36:5) and as the need, so shall the supply be.
>
> The task of getting the gospel in an adequate way to every ethnic person is tremendous. There is but one solution. I'm sure that it isn't man, money, surveys, nor talk. They all have their place, but if the basis of it all isn't fervent, believing prayer, they are all in vain. And prayer should not only be the basis, but it should permeate and vitalize the whole work. I long for the people at home, the believers here, the [national] workers and missionaries to be more faithful in wielding this great power that God has given them. I close with an example of how God can change events through prayer:
>
> One day we met an Indian on the trail who had drunk just enough liquor to make him loud and brash. When we greeted him it became obvious he didn't like who we were or the gospel we tried to share with him. In a brazen way he warned us not to come to his house.
>
> That evening, I called everyone together and quoted John 16:8, "When he (Jesus) is come, he will reprove the world of sin, and of righteousness and of judgment."

We made this FACT the basis of our prayer for the man we met on the trail. The next day, as we went from hut to hut through the valley, three of the workers came upon the man's house. When he saw them, he treated them in just the same mocking way as he had the day before. But in the middle of his mockery, his manner suddenly changed. To the amazement of the workers, the man became a humble, attentive listener. And what is even further amazing, the man gave himself with joy to what the men had to say. The prayers for this man had been answered. Our GREAT need is that expressed by Paul in Ephesians 6:19: "[Pray] for me, that utterance may be given unto me, that I may open my mouth boldly, to make known the mystery of the gospel."

When Judge Scott wrote Cam telling him of Elvira's safe arrival in the States, he also told Cam that because of his own failing health he would have to "lay aside the work." The treatment for his ailment was therapeutic hot springs at a health spa. It was common during the twenties and thirties for people to "take the waters" at hot springs around the United States. Cam and Elvira would themselves, in a few years, settle in Sulphur Springs, Arkansas, for that very reason.

Cam's April 25 answer to Judge Scott's April 1 letter expressed appreciation for his faithful service to the Central American Mission and a commitment to pray for his health. The letter also revealed something of Cam's reading interest in the twenties:

> I was sorry to hear of your poor health. I am praying that your stay at the hot springs will put you back in trim form. I am beginning to realize more and more how much we should take care of our bodies. They are, after all, temples of the Holy Spirit and we should keep them entirely for His service. Of course, this is often impossible when we are out on the trail. In these cases we just have to trust that He will overrule. But we should exercise all the wisdom He has given us in caring for His temple.
>
> On a trip to the capital last week, I read the life of Scofield by Trumbull. It was so interesting I could hardly lay it down. I even took it with me on the trail. I do thank God for Dr. Scofield. His reference Bible has been practically my only textbook. And I am almost glad that I had no other.

The schoolhouse is progressing rapidly. We hope to move in within a couple of weeks. It would have gone up much quicker if I had been here, but I didn't want to sacrifice the evangelistic work for it.

Within two months after the conference in Chichicastenango, Howard Dinwiddie wrote Cam telling him that on behalf of the Latin American Indian Mission, donated money had been sent to Robbie Robinson at the station in Panajachel for seven national workers. Clearly, he said, God was moving on behalf of LAIM.

Howard Dinwiddie was gifted with an ability to motivate and inspire people for Christian service, and then to organize them into a team. He was also something of a mission statesman and strategist as his April 30 letter to Cameron reveals:

Now, my dear fellow plodder, for the evangelization of the Cakchiquels, let me ask you to pray over one matter. Looking down the vista of the future, I am desirous that we should not make the same mistake that many mission agencies have made.

I trust you will not think me presumptuous on this point, but may I say that it coincides exactly with that of A. C. Moffatt of Korea. (I had a most inspirational time with him last Sunday in Detroit.)

The point I make is that it must be national believers who support and do the evangelizing among their own people. The example of this is Korea. Dr. Moffatt says there are thousands who are being evangelized in this way. He further believes the Korean Church is on the eve of reaching out into China. The heart of this great spiritual object lesson for the world is the teaching and practice that every believer must be a witness.

The Korean believers volunteer to give so many days for evangelizing at their own expense. Let us pray during these early days, when support of national workers is coming forward promptly, that it may not cut their nerve center of faith. At Chichicastenango, Mr. Herbert Toms and Mr. Paul Burgess were of one mind that the support of national workers should be secured from within their own national community. (Too many *ladino* believers and churches have looked to the homeland for financial backing.) Let us ask God for wisdom in this matter. I look forward to your own views on this matter.

With refreshment and encouragement from the Word and friends, and Elvira's improved health, Cam rose above his discouragement. In a matter of weeks he was once again in the arena where he believed anything is possible with God.

A Cakchiquel family of believers

Joyous Service

"**M**y days are so full of joyous service I hardly have time to write, but I want to share something of what God is doing." Thus began Cam's May 15, 1921, letter to Judge Scott. Clearly he was cheerful, optimistic, and expansive. Many other letters written during this period are infectious with his joy and delight in the variety of ministries that occupied his time. The irony is that Cam was facing several weighty issues that were anything but joyful.

Chief among these concerns was trying to develop the newly formed Latin American Indian Mission (LAIM). Howard Dinwiddie had asked for Cam's input on the formation of an American Home Council for LAIM and suggested Legters for this leadership role. Cam agreed. However, R. D. Smith continued to be troubled that LAIM would become a competing mission agency. He wrote Cam a letter that called into question the credentials and qualifications of those who made up the Chichicastenango Twelve. To Smith, Cam responded with both his visionary nature and his inborn diplomacy, smoothly handling the delicate matter:

> Dear Mr. Smith,
> I don't wonder you came to the conclusions you did in reference to our action in Chichicastenango. Naturally there was no way for you

to judge the special abilities of those who attended the conference. In one sense you are quite correct. All of us are fully conscious of our lack of ability. None of us is qualified for the enormous task we have set for ourselves, with one exception: we each have the vision.

Before your letter came last week, I was in Mr. Bishop's office in Guatemala [City] and saw a picture of the Bible Institute of Los Angeles in 1905 on his wall. Over the picture hung the motto, "Undertake Great Things For God, and Expect Great Things From God." I thought how marvelously that has worked for the Bible Institute. I don't think Dr. Torrey was connected with the Institute in 1905, but I do know some men of vision, prayer, and faith who were. It didn't take the Lord long to seek out Dr. Torrey and move the work along with Divine speed. Well, we have the vision of the Indians of Latin America hearing the gospel, not necessarily through one mission alone, or even a half dozen. We believe our prayers will be heard and the Indians will be evangelized. God knows where the men are who will do it. Perhaps He can use even our foolhardiness to get folks started.

Cam concluded the letter by assuring Smith there was no need for conflict between the board members of the Central American Mission and LAIM. In a follow-up letter to Dinwiddie, Cam urged they take up a special offering for Smith in order that he have his travel paid to come to Guatemala:

If it's the Lord's will for this work to go forward, and if this work is born of a God-given vision, it should be helped and received in the same spirit in which it was conceived, namely, that of cooperation. There is absolutely no need for conflict. To the contrary, there should be great mutual helpfulness. If this shall be the attitude of our mission, I can see no reason we can't belong to both organizations. We can just consider ourselves as associates in the greater work, i.e., the Latin American Indian work in general.

Cam's other concern, of course, was Elvira. By mid-May she was recovering in Chicago from her hernia operation on April 11. With her attending physician, Dr. O. T. Roberg, waiving his fee, Elvira's six-week hospital bill was $157.75.

Afterward, when she said she wanted to take part in a mission rally, Dr. Roberg said, "ABSOLUTELY NOT TO BE CONSIDERED FOR ONE MOMENT." Though this disappointed Elvira, she contented herself by talking to her visitors and nurses about the work in Guatemala.

Then to her even greater disappointment, Dr. Roberg gave instructions that she was not to talk about her work to anyone, to which the nurses from the Swedish Covenant Hospital jokingly responded that they would have to put adhesive over her mouth. Dr. Roberg reminded Elvira she had arrived for the operation at just the right time. He said, "With the seriousness of your condition, had you waited much longer there was the strong possibility you would have been useless both to God and man for the rest of your life."

Her one chance to speak publicly was immediately prior to her operation, when she was called unexpectedly to the platform of Moody Church in Chicago to give a short report on the work in Guatemala.

Discovering what many missionaries discover when they return to their home churches eager to share their experiences, Elvira found a polite indifference to the ideas of cross-cultural mission. While some were interested, she noticed not all shared her enthusiasm "for the things of the Lord." To a friend she wrote:

> I feel the awful coldness and indifference of the believers in the homeland. I was stunned to find so little interest among the Lord's people concerning him. They don't seem to take the time to commune and have fellowship, nor become really acquainted with their Heavenly Father.

While Elvira was learning to deal with the reality of certain believers' attitudes toward world missions, Cam was struggling with a different kind of reality. It was the reality all translators face: how to correctly translate the inspired text into an unwritten language so that new readers in that language can read with understanding. Cam also looked ahead for the funding of this new translation. In his trademark way of using words to involve people financially, Cam wrote:

Margarito Otzoy (a national translator) and I are working hard on the translation of the Gospel of Mark into Cakchiquel. It is the most delicate work I have ever done (even though Mark seems to be the easiest to translate). To be used as a transmitter of God's own precious Word that he has so marvelously preserved through all these years, makes me realize how careful one must be to get the exact thought [meaning] into Cakchiquel. We have to look to him for every word and he does not disappoint us.

Day after day we work in my little room off the corridor. Margarito and I occupy half the table, while the other half is covered with books. There are three Spanish translations, as well as two in English, one in Greek, one in Latin (the Vulgate contains some good notes), plus a translation of Mark in Quiché. This language resembles Cakchiquel. The translation work is slow. Sometimes we struggle all day just to find the correct meaning of a single word.

For example, I wanted to find the right word for "devil." I said the devil was the enemy of our souls. Was there such a word in Cakchiquel to express this idea? The word Margarito came up with was their word for "stink bug." I said it was a good word for the devil, but it wasn't quite what I was looking for. I am still asking the Lord for the right word.

Even though it will cost a bit more, I want the Gospel of Mark to be in a diglot style. That is, the Spanish text on one side, with the equivalent Cakchiquel text on the opposite page. I am wondering who the Lord is going to give the privilege of paying for this blessed work—giving the words of our Lord in their own tongue to 150,000 people.

By the end of May 1921, Judge Scott wrote Cam telling him he had benefited from his trip to Hot Springs. "I am again taking up the work of the Mission with renewed life and added joy." Cam also received a long and involved letter from Howard Dinwiddie relating that he was waiting to see how God was going to work out the details between the new LAIM and the board members of the Central American Mission.

Cam's response to Dinwiddie expressed his frustration with mission boards in general, who were afraid to accept the vision of "field workers." Then with words that were amazingly prophetic and insightful he wrote:

> My expectations for the foundation of the Latin American Indian Mission is that it would not be born overnight. The Lord has suggested to me that he is laying the basis for a deep-seated, permanent, extensive work in which spiritual people, both in the denominations and in the independent missions, will be linked together in a common task. My impression is that such an organization will far transcend the power and resources of both denominational and independent missions. In fact, such an organization would call for the exercise of the omnipotence of God himself upon which, ultimately, I rest my confidence.

Cam always encouraged national believers to assume responsibilities for their own church development. In two letters written on May 27 and June 20, 1921, to Dinwiddie, Cam wrote about this concern:

> You are right about national support for national workers and every believer a soul winner. I have been praying much over this matter as well as talking it over with the national believers. I believe funds that come from the homeland could well be used in training national workers. There are today between twenty and thirty nationals who could be immediately trained as prospective workers.
>
> My heart just burns to get the pioneering part of the work done, so as to be able to go to a more needy field with a few faithful workers. An American scientist told me recently that there are 200,000 Mayas in northern British Honduras and Yucatán who know little of the gospel. I'm sure the Lord will give me the desire of my heart, if it is from him. More and more I feel the call to devote my attention to the development of national workers.

While Cam delighted in the joys of an expanding work, Elvira was experiencing the frustration and pressure of not being able to fulfill her role. She was a skilled correspondent and scrupulous record keeper who acknowledged every letter and accounted for absolutely every monetary gift, no matter how small. Now she struggled to keep up with her correspondence while recuperating from her six-week hospital ordeal. Her June 14 letter to Judge Scott reveals this frustration, while also revealing her struggle with some unexpected ailments:

> Was glad for your good letter of the 6th. I'm sorry I let so much time go by without writing you. I will try to do better in the future. Looking over my pile of unanswered letters makes me wonder when I'll get through them, especially since I don't have a typewriter and each has to be handwritten.
>
> This past week was difficult for me. I suffered the entire time with severe attacks of chills and fever. But after taking a good bit of quinine, I was able to control it. I didn't know I had malaria in my system. Looking back I see I probably had it for several months.

On June 18, Elvira wrote Judge Scott again, this time to ask his blessing on her plans to leave Chicago for California. Her letter is notable because it's the first time she spoke about her "nervousness" as an emotional problem:

> You no doubt know that Chicago is intensely hot during the summer. This climate never did agree with me and it seems the hotter it is the worse I suffer from colds. With my nervous condition, I find it even harder to bear up. For some time I have been thinking that the California climate might be better for me. I have received two letters from family and friends there suggesting I come for a visit. The Townsend family would love for me to come. After praying over the matter, it seems to me this is what I should do. I would, of course, need the ninety dollars you have on hand for me from Moody Church. I will stay with the Townsend family until Mr. Townsend comes for me in August. He will want to have a visit with his folks and then present the work of the Indians of Guatemala to some of the churches in Southern California. We would then return to Guatemala in November via Chicago. It will be colder then and that should be good for my malaria.

After receiving both the encouragement and the ninety dollars from Judge Scott, on July 10 Elvira left Chicago on a train bound for Los Angeles and then to Clearwater, California.

To the south in Guatemala, an energetic Cameron Townsend was fully involved with executing Jesus' command in Matthew 28:19. In fact, Cam began a late June (undated) letter to Judge Scott with a part of that verse:

> "Go ye into all the world and preach the Gospel to EVERY creature." I have been traveling through the district where the Gospel has been preached in Spanish for over twenty years. I didn't meet a single Indian Christian. The first day I asked one Indian man if he knew there was a God. The man said yes, "I heard he had come to Chimaltenango." He meant that an extraordinary medicine man had made an appearance in that town and claimed to be a prophet. The medicine man was going about the whole district deceiving the Indians. I had great joy in telling the man I met about the true and living God.

Not all of Cam's experiences on this trip were successful, or pleasant. He reported that on two occasions he and his party were lost, once off the trail by five miles:

> About noon one day, after a long morning of hiking, we came to a small Indian village. We tried to buy something to eat, but everyone was afraid of us. I knew a little of their language and was able to quell their fears enough for one woman to sell us some tortillas.
>
> When I tried to share the gospel with them, most turned away in indifference. It was then I decided to be daring in an effort to gain their confidence. I noticed a woman toasting a large pile of flying ants caught just before their wings had sprouted [they look like termite larvae]. I knew this was purely an Indian delicacy but reasoned that if I ate them, the Indians would know I wanted to be one with them, to be like them, to appreciate the things they appreciated. So, much to their surprise, I purchased some and ate them with relish. I had found a "point" of contact and won their confidence.
>
> When we left the village that afternoon, we once again lost our way and had to return to that same village. We were all upset over this because it put us greatly behind our schedule. However, when we returned to the village, we were received this time with warmth and cordiality.

Two afternoons later, Cam found himself in a wayside shed with fifteen Indian travelers seeking shelter from a hard tropical downpour:

> As we all gathered around the fire, I took out my Bible, read some passages, and pointed out the way of salvation. To my surprise, one after the other took off their hats as I read the Scriptures.
>
> After awhile, it became apparent the rain was not going to stop. I was cold, hungry and didn't relish the notion of spending the night in a damp shed on an empty stomach. The problem was, I was twelve miles from Huehuetenango and the cheery home of fellow missionaries, Herbert and Mary Toms. It was dark and the trail was slippery and unknown to me. There were no travelers on the way from whom I could ask directions. But with the vision of the Toms' home in front of me, I decided to go, determined not to stop until I reached Huehuetenango.
>
> About 10:00 P.M. my efforts were rewarded. I found a policeman who led me to the home of the Toms. In spite of my remonstrances, Herbert and Mary got out of bed and welcomed me like their own long lost son. Before long Mary made me some hot soup, the kind I used to get when my mother wanted to baby me.
>
> With a warm body and a warm heart, I rolled up into a bed so soft that I hardly realized I was lying on anything at all. For days I had been sleeping on anything I could find—a brick floor, a stone bridge, a bench thirteen and a quarter inches wide, and a hammock that folded me up like a jackknife and was so short my feet hung out on the sides.

Throughout the month of July, Cam's work load increased daily. He spent the last week of June and the first of July attending to the physical needs of Cixto Waján, a national worker who had developed serious complications from malaria and pneumonia. In the July 6, *Central American Bulletin,* he wrote:

> You will be sorry to learn of the death of Cixto Waján. He took sick a month ago on his tip to Huehuetenango. We took him to the Treichlers'. They and I did all in our power to help him. A week

ago he went to be with him whose name he had announced to so many hundreds. He was one our most valuable workers. We feel his loss greatly. But he who raised him up from a life of drunkenness and gave him to us for a worker, also took him, and we look to him to raise up many more to take Cixto's place.

Immediately following Cixto's funeral, Cam presented himself for an interview with Guatemala's President Herrera. The object was to secure permission, letters of introduction, and a waiver of duty for the supplies of Dr. Craig Potter, of Johns Hopkins Hospital in Baltimore, whom Cam had contacted to conduct a medical and evangelistic campaign. Cam had scheduled the campaign to begin in mid-July. But because of the sudden death of Dr. Potter's father, the campaign was rescheduled for the end of the month. This created a problem for Cam. He had planned to leave for California to pick up Elvira and do deputation in August. In a letter to Judge Scott, he wrote:

If it had been possible, I would have packed and left for home when I had planned. Now my hands are so full of work, I believe the Lord would have me stay by the stuff a little longer. Dr. Potter, along with his mother, Dr. Marion Potter, who is also a physician, plans to be here until October. This means I will not be able to get to California until the first of November. Elvira is in good hands in California, and she can have an extended vacation.

In addition to arranging for Dr. Potter's visit, Cam faced the problem of growing tension between the Central American Mission board and LAIM. Abe Bishop, chairman of the Central American Mission conference who had severely criticized the new mission, was outraged with an article that appeared in the *Sunday School Times.* Allegedly written by L. L. Legters, the article gave the impression that Paul Burgess and Cameron Townsend were the only people who were interested in reaching the Indian people of Guatemala. In a letter written to Howard Dinwiddie and Cam, Bishop wrote:

When I read Brother Legters's article on Central America in the *Sunday School Times,* I sought to find whereby I could justify his blunders.

It did not occur to me that they would be repeated. The Indian problem is gigantic and needs concentrated action. My vision and that of Mr. Townsend speaks of cooperation, but not of separation.

Repeatedly you have told me that sound existing agencies would be recognized, strengthened and cooperated with. This is as it should be, and by the grace of God is what I am confident will yet be carried out. To separate the Indian work from the Spanish, at least in the territory in which Mr. Townsend and myself are working, would be like picking woof and warp apart. Such action would, in my mind, be deplorable and bring no end of dissatisfaction as well as danger to the whole work. I think it would please the Lord if you would take unto yourself dear Brother Legters and expound unto him a better way, a method more sane with a broader viewpoint.

Ever the diplomat, Cam wrote Dinwiddie and said that Bishop's criticism had given him a stronger desire to more carefully structure the new organization and overcome Bishop's objections in such a way as to win his confidence and the confidence of all concerned.

The allegations by Bishop over the *Sunday School Times* article took a curious twist when Dinwiddie wrote Cam the following:

There have been two attacks by Mr. Bishop. One on LAIM, and one on Mr. Legters in regard to an article in the *Sunday School Times*. Mr. Legters did not write such an article. He knew nothing about it until it was published. And he did not approve. This, and the unexplainable inability of Mr. Smith and others on the Central American Mission board to set dates when I could be present at their Council meetings suggest to me that the basis for confidence on the part of the Council is not strong enough for me to enter into a full-time relationship with them.

The first threads that would begin to unravel LAIM had just become exposed.

The Louise Heim Clinic under construction in San Antonio

Chapter Eight
The Circuitous Route

When C. I. Scofield, the brilliant Bible scholar, founder and first president of the Philadelphia College of the Bible, examined the state of world mission in 1880, he used Acts 1:8 as the model: "You will be my witnesses in Jerusalem, and in all Judea and Samaria, and to the ends of the earth." Most missionaries, he discovered, had by-passed "Samaria." They had gone "to the ends of the earth" (Africa, China, and the islands of the South Pacific), but the nineteenth-century churches had overlooked sending missionaries to Latin America—particularly Central America. In 1888 Hudson Taylor personally challenged Scofield to consider foreign missions, and Scofield determined to correct what he saw as a neglected field of mission service—Central America.

In the fall of 1890, out of his own home, with a few church leaders, Scofield founded the Central American Mission. And the rest, as they say, is history. The Central American Mission has had a long and distinguished ministry in Central America to the present.

Though Cameron Townsend did not always agree with Scofield's dispensational views, Cam loved his Scofield Bible and included Scofield among his spiritual mentors (the others being Hudson Taylor and Abe Bishop of his own Central American Mission). When on August 17, 1921,

Cam received word that Scofield had died July 24, a month earlier, he wrote a letter to Judge Scott:

> The *Sunday School Times* has just arrived with the sad news of the death of Dr. Scofield. A great Christian warrior has gone home. To those of us who haven't had a course in a Bible Institute, his notes and lessons are invaluable. What a vacuum there would be in my knowledge of biblical truth had I been without them these past four years. He was a man of God. He was in touch with mission history. I was refreshed in his knowledge.

Cam's letter also gave an update on the medical and evangelistic team headed by Dr. Craig Potter. The team consisted of the two Potters, three nationals, and Louise Treichler, who acted as guide and interpreter. Cam had asked Treichler to accompany the team, partly because she knew the country and spoke Spanish, and partly because he knew of her own interest in public health. He also hoped some of the national people themselves might be trained as paramedics.

Cam had secured letters of introduction from President Herrera to be given to the administrators of the many plantations the team would visit on their three-month summer medical campaign. Of that medical trip Cam reported:

> Many hundreds of ethnic peoples received basic medical attention for sore eyes and ears. Others were given medicines for a variety of ailments, and some received the benefit of minor operations. During the day, people flock to be treated. At night they come to hear the man, who had worked all day for their physical welfare, sing hymns and tell them of Christ who bore all their infirmities and who could save them from their sin. The effect is strong, and not soon forgotten.

Cam, too, never forgot that experience. Just weeks into the campaign the medical team was robbed on the trail by six men who stole most of their equipment. When Dr. Potter later departed Guatemala, he left behind a surplus of medicines. Cam used these as a base to establish a clinic, later named the Louise Heim Clinic, in honor of a former Sunday school teacher who had donated money for a clinic and home for Indian children to be built in San Antonio.

At the time Cam learned about the death of Dr. Scofield, he also received a report of what had transpired at the July 15–17 Central American Mission council meeting held at Moody Bible Institute. The principal agenda item, of course, was the formation of LAIM, the role Legters and Dinwiddie were to play, and the Central American Mission's disposition toward the new agency.

Attending that meeting was Luther Rees, one of three original laymen who met with Scofield to pray for the evangelization of Central America. When the Central American Mission was founded in 1890, Rees became the first president of its Home Council and was known as "an intercessor, a man of wisdom and seasoned experience." While he was willing to talk to Legters and Dinwiddie about LAIM, he considered a new mission agency to be "superfluous and counterproductive for the Central American missionaries to belong to two mission agencies." The board agreed, and recommended that LAIM be disbanded.

Dinwiddie told Cam that when Legters heard the decision of the Central American Mission he said, rather loudly, that sooner or later some of the Central American Mission missionaries would probably have to withdraw their membership. Then, as if to shrug off the Central American Mission's decision as being of little consequence, Legters made plans to make a survey trip to the state of Chiapas in southern Mexico.

Cam answered Dinwiddie's letter by return mail. He first assured Dinwiddie that he was unequivocally committed to the Central American Mission and its mission outreach. As far as Legters was concerned, he said:

> I regret that some of us spoke about our grievances too freely. And dear Mr. Legters went so far as to say some of us would have to withdraw, or something to that effect. Now Mr. Legters is one of the two or three men to whom Elvira and I are deeply indebted. You know, therefore, that I wouldn't criticize him unless I thought it was constructive. I am sure his remarks did harm. Therefore, if we really mean to inspire and gain the confidence of the established boards, we should, in the future, carefully guard against speaking in ways that might be harmful.
>
> Far from wanting LAIM to disband, I want to move ahead with confidence and a desire to make it work. There is a need to be met, and we have the vision for that need. What we must do is

to keep busy in such a way as to little by little gain the confidence of everyone.

Dinwiddie, who been planning a return trip to Guatemala (at Cam's urging) to help organize LAIM, had also written to tell Cam he was cutting his proposed trip to three months. Cam was less than pleased with this news:

> I know you plan to be here by the first of October. That is just about the time I plan to leave for California. I know also that you have a great many demands on your time. But I can't understand why you have to return to the States within three months. Why, we've simply got to have you for the next six or nine months. I'd like to go to Philadelphia just to tell your council so. A hurry-up speaking trip like you had last time would be fine but I am afraid that it won't do to get the machinery [for LAIM] in shape.
>
> On this trip you should master Spanish, help solve the problems in the different centers and out stations, and in every way devote your talents to the development of the work here. In this way you can show the world you really meant it when you offered your life for the Indians. My, I am so in earnest about it that I am hitting my hands together here at my typewriter. You should also plan the allocation of new recruits. In short, we have work to keep you more than busy until next June. I see this as more important than organizing home councils and raising funds! I give you Acts 16:9: "Come over to Macedonia and help us."

This response reveals Cam's extraordinary single-mindedness and practical idealism. It also reflects a character trait that those who worked and lived with him sometimes found troubling. His total dedication to the "work" prompted Elvira to write Judge Scott, urging him to use whatever influence he had to help Cam see the importance of returning to California for a rest:

> I received a letter from my good husband in which he tells me he will leave Guatemala the last week of September, or the first week of October. I do not think either Cameron or anyone else can realize

as I do the need for him to have a complete rest for at least six months. During the four years on the field he has suffered severe cases of dysentery, malaria, and flu. From an outward appearance, he would seem to be in good health. But I know he becomes so exhausted at times that at the end of a day it's an effort for him to move.

I know if I had used a bit more common sense I wouldn't be in the run-down condition I am today. I actually thought there was no limitation to my physical strength. With a heart full of enthusiasm and love for the people and seeing their deep need, I would simply go, go, go, just as happy as a lark, counting it all as the greatest privilege in the Lord that could ever come to a person. That's why my heart goes out to Cameron and for others who are in danger of the same thing happening to them as has happened to me.

It may be that Elvira's letter to Judge Scott was as much for herself as it was for Cam. Since leaving Chicago, her general health had deteriorated. She had healed from her hernia operation, but the doctors in California discovered a bowel infection, severe anemia, and a leaky heart valve. Quite categorically she said, "My physical condition is miserable."

Elvira's faith and the faith of those moving in and out of Cam's and Elvira's lives in the fall of 1921 seemed to be profoundly attuned to an inner assurance that no matter the physical afflictions, disappointments, or setbacks, they were in the will of God. She and Cam, like many of their colleagues, believed the only solution to life's problems was found in Christ. They were happy to be servants of a great God and tried to remain undaunted in the face of suffering. At the conclusion of the letter in which she spoke about her physical condition, Elvira wrote:

Were it not that I have Jesus, I would truly be discouraged. I have no plans for the present nor the future. I have him and that's enough. I am not anxious in this matter. I know God knows and he will direct all for the very best. I find these days that it is not health, strength, money, or popularity that counts. Rather it is being in the center of his will that means everything. I am happy to rest and be guided by him, moment by moment.

On September 28, 1921, Cam spent the day saying farewell to friends and giving final instructions to those who were to look after the various aspects of the ministry in his absence. After taking the "auto stage" to Guatemala City, Cam spent the night with the Bishops, and in the morning tried to book passage on the *Pacific Mail* for Los Angeles. However, all passages had been booked, and Cam decided instead to go to Los Angeles via Mexico.

Cam's diary and notes of this and other trips he took reveal his appreciation for natural history. Few would consciously ascribe the word "naturalist" to him, but in fact he kept detailed notes and accurate descriptions of the terrain over which he traveled.

His notes reveal that he did more than merely describe the landscape. He also struck a chord for the preservation of the environment. The word "ecology" was not part of the popular lexicon of the twenties, but Cam's notes reveal how pained he was when he encountered those who violated God's creation. Revealing a vision of a man having broad interests, Cam's diary portrays the quintessential missionary. His faith was completely integrated with his life. All activity, all awareness, was planned and directed toward a single purpose—that of honoring God by being a faithful witness, regardless of the circumstances:

Friday, September 30, 1921.

I had been sick with vomiting and diarrhea the night before but this didn't stop me from having a great time of fellowship. Before we left, we had a time of prayer. As we left, I realized it was four years (lacking three days) since I first arrived in Guatemala with Robbie [Robinson] to be a colporteur.

The three-hour trip was beautiful. We descended from the five-thousand-foot-high plateau on which Guatemala City is built, to the coastal plain. The prettiest stretch was crossing lake Amatitlán. Interesting to see the shores steaming and the beautiful hills that skirt the shoreline with the majestic volcano *Agua* towering overhead.

I went about the train distributing tracts (I had 800 specially printed for this trip). At Santa Lucia I got off the train for a quick look. There are great stretches of fertile lands generally covered with mighty trees—jungle penetrated only by cattle, although sugar cane and coffee plantations are numerous. Thousands of acres and untold water power are going to waste.

In spite of a heavy rain, I distributed tracts at all the train stations along the way. Toward the end of the trip, had a long talk with a Spiritualist. We reached Ayutla a little after 7:00 P.M. Went to the International Hotel. Pretty good place, even had a mosquito net. Food was poor, but the hotel was clean.

Saturday, October 1.
After breakfast I distributed tracts along the town's two main streets. Afterward I went to the bank and got some Mexican money. I then went down to the River Suchiate that forms the boundary with Mexico.

There was quite a troop of soldiers and three flat-bottomed boats. When I arrived at the customs office on the edge of town, the officials asked me to open my baggage. Fortunately I was carrying only the bare necessities of life. The Suchiate River is quite broad at this point, but not too deep. The man who poled the boat across deftly piloted around sandbars to the opposite shore. The Mexican officials showed little interest in my arrival, until they were going through my luggage and saw my tracts. When they discovered I was an evangelical, they became friendly. One man was particularly interested and directed me to the hut of a woman who was a believer. He said he would guide me after it stopped raining, but the rain kept up so I went on ahead of him. The woman received me cordially, and her sister soon had a meal ready for me.

They told me there would be no train until the next day. Trains from the border to Tapachula run only on Sunday, Tuesday, and Friday. I decided to go about the business of the gospel in the town of Mariscal. When I left Ayutla, I thought of taking a horse to Tapachula so as not to lose a day. I also thought it would give me greater opportunity to witness, since I believed the town of Mariscal to be more needy. But the rain made the thirty-mile walk [on horseback] impossible. In Mariscal, I was pleasantly surprised to find believers, and surprised still further to discover they were anxious for me to help them. I was happy to have been forced into giving them a day.

I easily secured a schoolhouse for a meeting and went from hut to hut inviting people to come to a meeting at seven o'clock that night. Even though the rain continued into the evening, a large crowd gathered. Several families came from four or five miles away. Everyone was soaked. Mariscal is a town of huts not more than three years old. The huts are made of split bamboo (the giant variety) with palm roofs.

Sunday, October 2.

After a good night's rest in a hammock, I had breakfast, then went to a place called "Buena Vista" from where some of the believers had come the night before. In order to escape the terrible mud, the deacon, Francisco Pérez, loaned me his horse and rode with me.

As we rode along, Francisco told me that during the Revolution, on the same lonesome road over which we were traveling, it had often been filled with hundreds of soldiers shooting birds, cattle, horses, anything that would serve as a target. He told me how men on the plantations had been shot, women raped, and cattle by the thousands killed for their hides. The aristocratic class had been ruined. In Mariscal, an old Italian man told me he had been threatened with death twice and was left without anything but his life. As I rode along, everything was so peaceful (except for a flock of parrots jabbering away in the gigantic overspreading trees) that it was hard to believe all he was telling me.

Reading Cam's record of this trip, it is easy to notice that he was in no particular hurry to get from point A to point B. His attitude is relaxed and cheerful with little evidence of stress or anxiety. Just as Jesus told his workers in Luke 10 to accept whatever circumstance they encountered, Cam did likewise. He ate whatever was set before him, stayed in the house where he was accepted, and took time ministering to and teaching those he met along the way.

To his surprise and delight, Cam met a young man from the town of Tapachula selling Bibles around the countryside. His name was Eulogio J. García Jacobo, and he showed Cam the way to the train station in Tapachula:

When we arrived at the train station (Francisco had returned home), Eulogio and I were met by a group of believers who took my luggage to their chapel while Eulogio and I went into the center of town to find something to eat. I was impressed with the town. It had tramways, electric light, and good buildings. A circus was in full swing.

In a fine big drugstore, I had my first real ice cream since leaving the States four years ago.

Eulogio invited me to speak at their church service that evening at eight. They had a large hall with a good number of believers. All listened attentively as I spoke from Romans 12.

Monday, October 3.
One of the elders slept at the chapel to see me off. He, with three other believers, took me to the train at four o'clock this morning. I was a bit sleepy. After the service last night, the elders told me a long story of how the work got started. It was after eleven before I got to sleep. The chief elder on his own initiative wrote a letter of greeting to send with me to the brethren in the States.

Second Class is less than half the cost of First Class, so I got a Second Class ticket. The car was crowded and the benches uncomfortable. All day long the train slowly dragged itself through the more or less marshy jungles. Every now and then we came to a large town. There are fewer plantations here in Mexico than in Guatemala. I was impressed with the great stretches of fertile soil going to waste.

A washout held us up for several hours and we got to our destination seven hours behind schedule. We were trailing an empty Deluxe Pullman. Since I had some extra money and enough experience traveling steerage for one day, I paid the five and half dollars to get a berth. Soon after I did so, a young Honduran, Professor Rogue Hernández, did the same. Except for the crew, the two of us had the car all to ourselves.

The sheets they gave me were very much out of keeping with the luxurious Pullman. They looked as though several parties had kicked them off as undesired allies of the tropical heat since last they had seen a washtub. I slept splendidly and woke just as we laboriously pulled into the town of San Gerónimo at 6:00 A.M., twelve hours behind time.

Tuesday, October 4.
After an expensive breakfast at San Gerónimo, we took the train that had just pulled in from Salina Cruz. On this stretch a few days before, the train was derailed by bandits who were about to rob the paymaster

and passengers, when troops happened along and their plan was frustrated. It was a comfortable feeling to have a number of soldiers on the train with us. The conductor told me there were holdups every day during the Revolution. So many trains were shot up and derailed there were heaps of wrecked cars and engines and the railroad companies were unable to continue their operations.

We finally arrived in a swampy little town where we changed cars for Tierra Blanca. Here we had to wait until two the next morning. I again bought a Pullman and passed the afternoon writing, reading and redeeming the time. I retired early and remained unconscious until I was awakened the next morning by the tossing of the train.

Cameron and Elvira in Clearwater, California

Back on the Home Front

The long, slow train that carried Cameron Townsend on his circuitous route through Mexico during the early days of October 1921 was a kind of metaphor for Mexico's own long, slow struggle to freedom. Assaults by Spain, France, the United States, as well as dictators like Porfirio Díaz, all had to be shaken off. The leftover effects of Mexico's sundry coups and revolutions were evident everywhere on Cam's trip.

Mexico was in a period of change. The revolution of 1914–1915 had inspired many Mexicans with a spirit of social consciousness and a profound desire to see the country emerge out of her past. To many Mexicans, this past was shameful and humiliating—particularly the war with the United States. Though Cam did not know it then, Mexico would, in a few years, play a pivotal role in Cam's life and mission outreach. And one of Mexico's great presidents would become his personal friend.

The slow journey gave Cam time to observe the countryside and to become acquainted with some of Mexico's national heroes: the Zapotec Indian, Benito Juárez, who became president and fought to abolish slavery; Miguel Allende, who championed the extension of human rights to the Indians and *mestizos*; Father Hidalgo, whose cry for freedom and ringing of the church bells is celebrated as a national holiday.

While Cam's train swayed and clattered through the landscape of contemporary Mexican history, history of another sort was being made. Unknown to Cam, Howard Dinwiddie reported to Elvira in a letter dated September 27, 1921, the results of a conference held in Philadelphia, in which representatives from six denominational mission agencies interested in Indian evangelism had met. The Central American Mission was there, as well as representatives from the Evangelical Union of South America. High on the conference agenda was the newly formed LAIM. Said Dinwiddie:

> After much discussion, the conference decided it would be better to change the name of LAIM and call it a committee. The reason is that the name "mission" has been misunderstood as being a competitive agency to other mission work. Also the word "Latin" preceding America was generally thought to have an element of offensiveness. The name suggested by the conference was the "Indian Mission Committee of America." That name met with unanimous approval. The new name will have the same objectives as those that were planned in Chichicastenango.

Dinwiddie concluded his letter by telling Elvira they had formed an executive committee consisting of Thomas C. Moffett, Secretary of the Indian work of the Presbyterian Board of Home Missions as Chairman, Dinwiddie as General Secretary, and Legters as Field Secretary. There were two others appointed: Mrs. Alfred R. Page, wife of a New York Supreme Court judge and active in the Reformed Church's Indian work, as Recording Secretary, and J. Harvey Borton, from the Society of Friends and Chairman of the Victorious Life Testimony, as Treasurer.

There was also news that Dinwiddie and Legters were planning to sail on October 15 from New Orleans to begin work in Guatemala. Dinwiddie expressed his disappointment that Cam was not going to be there when he arrived. As an afterthought he wrote, "Legters and I have just spent two weeks doing conference work in Rhode Island. Legters is going home to spend a week with his family whom he has not seen since July and will probably not see again until next June."

In a letter written to Elvira a day later, Judge Scott said he had heard about the development of the new organization in Philadelphia and that the six denominational leaders affirmed the vision that had been born at Chichicastenango.

Unaware of these new developments, Cam continued to record the events of his train trip through Mexico in his diary:

Wednesday, October 5. To Vera Cruz.
We traveled most of the day through swampy lagoons on every side. There was a large stretch of wonderful pasture where the grass grew thick and high, but not a steer was in sight. I was told that once thousands of head grazed these plains, but the rebel leaders, as well as those representing the government, had killed them and sold their hides to the U.S. For the first time in its history, Mexico is having to import beef from the U.S. On top of that, 38,000 hectares have been expropriated by the government.

The swamps make this an unhealthy place. There have been reports of yellow fever, but the government is waging a campaign against the disease. There are lots of mosquitos. Unfortunately the train doesn't travel fast enough to keep them from entering. If the other passengers fared as I did, several hundred bites were scored!

Thursday, October 6. To the Capital.
Left Vera Cruz at 6:30 A.M. for Mexico City. When I left the station, I dropped tracts out of the window to the men in the yard and people along the streets. A gust of wind carried one of my tracts far over the city. I watched it soar out of sight and prayed God would carry it to some person who would read it and find the Saviour. "The winds and the waves obey thy will."

There were six cars filled with passengers. I gave them all tracts. I might add this was an expensive proposition. While I was distributing tracts, a thief stole the Kodak camera right out of my overcoat pocket. What made it worse was that Dr. Potter had loaned it to me. I was chagrined to think that after nearly four years of traveling all over Latin America without being robbed once, I have in the past three months been twice the victim of thieves.

When Cam and his traveling companion, Professor Hernández, arrived in Mexico City's Central Station, he promptly went about giving out tracts. He and the professor then checked into the Hotel Regis. After refreshing themselves, the two men went out for a light supper and then visited Professor Hernández's friend in one of the city's residential districts.

Unfortunately, the remainder of Cam's Mexico travel diary is lost, but there is enough recorded to reveal the fullness of Cam's wonder, joy, and gratitude to God. The opportunity of seeing the great land of Mexico with such intimacy, as well as having been given a part in God's plans, were occasions for Cam's gratitude.

When Cam reached El Paso, Texas on October 15, he went directly on to Clearwater, California and the home of his parents. What awaited him was the sad news that Judge Scott had died and that Elvira's health had worsened. In the November *Central American Bulletin,* Cam wrote:

> Never has a death brought such a vacancy into my life as the home-going of this great saint of God. I never met Judge Scott, yet through his letters we had come to know and love him deeply. He was a wise and sympathetic counselor. His vision and love for the work was an inspiration to us all. It was through him that we as a mission were knit together.
>
> Treasurers of mission boards are often criticized by the missionaries, but I never heard anyone on the field speak about Judge Scott other than in terms of deepest love. Meanwhile let us be doubly diligent in prayer and sympathy for the work and workers so dear to God's heart.

Elvira also wrote a letter to the *Bulletin* expressing her response to Judge Scott's death:

> I think of the homegoing of our beloved Judge Scott as a graduation, not from one school to another, but a final one unto perfection and complete rest.
>
> [Judge Scott's] letters made me feel as though he was a father. They were always cheerful, inspiring, encouraging and at the same

time full of good advice and suggestions. There was never, never a word of complaint. His letters to us reminded me of the "rivers of living water." We will remember him always.

The man who succeeded Judge Scott as treasurer for the Central American Mission was Luther Rees, one of C. I. Scofield's friends who first met to pray for Central America. On November 14, Cam sent him his first report from Clearwater:

Dear Mr. Rees,

I almost addressed you as "Judge." It's been so natural to begin my letters to our mission parents that way. Judge Scott's homegoing has left a big hole in our lives personally and an even bigger one in our mission. But while the Lord tarries, his work will go right on, though the one who made it so much stronger and sweeter has been taken from us.

Since my arrival four weeks ago, my time has been filled with work and visiting. I accepted a carpentering job with my brother Paul (the skills will come in handy on the field). It's been good to be with my brother again. Both he and his wife would like to go to Guatemala. If they can sell their place, they will take a course at the Bible Institute of Los Angeles.

Elvira is a little stronger. We go to the doctors a great deal. They are trying to get to the bottom of her trouble. They have found a leaky heart. This scares us a good bit. Our one joy is the thought of getting back to the field soon. We have confidence the Lord is going to take care of the problem.

All the doctors have been kind. None has charged us even though they have given a great deal of their time. There will be a few bills, but we are sure [God] will supply as he has in the past.

We have had several opportunities to speak. The little Downey Presbyterian Church promised to send fifteen dollars per month—ten for a worker and five for an orphan. I asked them not to take up an offering and that's what they did instead. Last Thursday night I spoke to one hundred and fifty students at the Bible Institute of Los Angeles. Some expressed interest in the work.

The following months of November and December 1921 were times of struggle for the Townsends, as Cam's December 14 letter to Luther Rees reveals:

> Over the years I have shared with Judge Scott about Elvira's nervous condition that often explodes into violent spells. Her outbreaks have become worse since I arrived. Stella Zimmerman took Elvira home with her and spent several days in prayer for her. These past two weeks have shown great improvement. I can only trust. Do help with your prayers.
>
> This is the reason why I haven't written concerning deputation. It's hard to talk about the work when one's mate is in such a condition that his own life seems to be wrecked. If Elvira continues to improve, I do want to tell of the need wherever there is an opportunity. I believe God has given me a message. But I do not want to stay in the States any longer than necessary.

While Cam experienced sadness over the state of his marriage, he didn't allow this difficulty to cripple him from doing the will of God. For Cam, that meant not complaining or grumbling at God. While he was unsure why all this was happening, he was for the most part silent about Elvira's problem. When she lashed out at him in anger, he assumed the position of silence. He was in a desert experience and he believed the appropriate response was trust. Like many of the great saints of God, Cam was learning that a desert experience was essential for mature faith. Cam would one day discover an oasis, but for the moment he was learning the patience and understanding he would need to lead, counsel, and inspire the growth and development of Wycliffe Bible Translators and the Summer Institute of Linguistics.

During this time, Cam worked with his brother Paul on a room addition for his parents' home. He also wrote a booklet on colporteuring, designing it as a guide in the fine art of Scripture distribution, and busied himself with a number of local speaking opportunities. Cam's slow, folksy speaking style made him a charming one-on-one or small group story teller. Requests for him to speak came from as far away as St. Paul, Minneapolis, St. Louis, Baltimore, and Denver. Yet Cam was

never considered a dynamic platform speaker. And it was precisely because Cam recognized platform speaking wasn't his gift that he chose
the dynamic Legters to be the mouthpiece, spreading the challenge of
Bible translation to U.S. churches and Bible colleges. One of the favorite
stories Cam told was how he first got several important portions of the
Gospel of Mark printed:

> After I had translated several key chapters of the Gospel of Mark into
> the Cakchiquel language, I wanted to get them printed and into cir-
> culation. I contacted a printer in Antigua who gave me a price I
> thought was too expensive. I decided then to go to the only other
> press in town. But there was a problem. The owner of the printing
> business was a politician who ran the town, and through some un-
> derhanded political maneuvering had gotten his candidate elected as
> mayor. It was the mayor who ran the day-to-day printing operation.
>
> I went to the mayor's office along with the politician and told
> them what I wanted. The mayor said, "No, Sir, we won't print any-
> thing in the Cakchiquel language. That's perpetuating the Indian lan-
> guage, and we don't want that. We want to get rid of those languages.
> We want everyone to speak Spanish."
>
> I said, well, the best way to get the Indians to speak Spanish is
> to have a bilingual text. If the Indians first learn to read in their own
> language, it makes it easier for them to make the shift into learning
> to read Spanish.
>
> Before the mayor could answer, the politician said, "Mayor, of
> course, that's the best way for the Cakchiquels to learn Spanish.
> They'll learn Spanish better if they have a bilingual edition. Sure,
> we'll print it for you." And the amazing thing is their price for printing
> was much cheaper than the first printer.

Another of Cam's favorite stories had to do with the president of Guatemala, Carlos Herrera, before he became president:

> Carlos Herrera was one of the wealthiest plantation owners in Gua-
> temala. I met him first in December of 1917 shortly after I first arrived
> in Guatemala. When I asked his permission to speak to the men on
> his plantation about how they could find eternal life through faith in
> Jesus Christ, he said, absolutely no!

This was a staggering blow to me, because there were thousands of men working on his various properties. However, just about that time, he bought another plantation on which there was an established congregation of believers. But as soon as Herrera learned of its existence, he ordered his administrator, an unusually gifted Swiss agronomist, to get rid of the believers.

With great courage, the Swiss administrator told Carlos Herrera that the believers were his best workers and he could not, nor did he want to get rid of them. In fact, the administrator said if he were forced to get rid of the believers, he would resign.

Herrera did not want to lose such a capable administrator and agreed to give the believers a six-month trial. When the six months were up, Herrera was so pleased with the believers' work performance, he opened all of his plantations to our gospel workers. On one occasion the big machinery in one of his sugar mills stopped completely while three hundred of his workers listened to the message of eternal life.

In December 1920, while Cam was in California, Robbie Robinson had returned with his bride to work with the Central American Mission. They were assigned to work in the beautiful lakeside village of Panajachel on the shores of the spectacular Lake Atitlán. There Robbie soon established himself as a beloved friend to ethnic people. Tireless in his evangelistic efforts, he, like Cam, traveled on foot and horseback all over the highlands and into sections of the lowlands as well.

Robbie Robinson was ten years older than Cam. They had been friends at Occidental College and they had sailed for Guatemala from San Francisco in September 1917 to become Bible salesmen under the auspices of the Bible House of Los Angeles. Together they shared their dreams, together they ate tamales and rice, and together they got sick. They shared in the danger of the terrible earthquake in Guatemala City in December 1917. Together they were helpful in restoring order and essential services to a city nearly destroyed, thus endearing themselves to nationals and expatriates alike. For a fleeting moment they had shared a romantic interest in Elvira.

Robbie had served in World War I, and returned after the war to complete his degree at Occidental College. He graduated in 1919 and married Genevieve Harber. Ordained in the fall of 1920, Robbie served as pastor of the International Baptist Church in Los Angeles before joining the Central American Mission.

Like Cam, Robbie dreamed about developing a work among the Cakchiquels of Panajachel. He planned to build a home where ethnic people would feel comfortable and always welcome. And there would be a chapel where Cakchiquels could worship in their own language. Already, this project was underway. Robbie had seen one of his dreams realized: providing a motor launch to take the gospel to other lakeside villages. He called it *Las Buenas Nuevas,* The Good News. But Robbie's biggest dream was of a Bible school where Cakchiquels could be trained for the gospel ministry.

In March 1922, Cam returned alone to Guatemala from California. Elvira, still under doctors' care, stayed in Chicago to be with her family and take speaking engagements as her strength allowed. Cam had several large and consuming projects that demanded his attention. One was looking into the possibility of providing a home for young people who had the potential of becoming teachers and evangelists. He had long held the belief that nationals were better equipped to preach and evangelize their own people. This belief was strengthened during an impromptu gospel service that he and Silverio Lopes, a Cakchiquel gospel worker, had held, during which a young man confronted Cam:

The young man took me to task because I had not honored the "gods of the earth." As I stood there thinking how to respond in Cakchiquel, the young man suddenly snatched the Scripture portion out of my hand and called us liars. In a minute the whole crowd was upon us. Before we could disentangle ourselves from the crowd and run, we were hit with clubs and a shower of stones.

The mayor of the town put the main culprit in jail. Later I secured his release on the condition he listen respectfully to our message. Then, with the mayor in attendance and a large crowd, we told the old story. God gave Silverio great liberty as he preached. It was the same people who had first heard me speak, but they reacted much differently when they heard Silverio preach in Cakchiquel. They were transformed. The national worker had won the day.

In June, Cam was hard at work building a children's home. He was anxious for this to be completed by early July before the arrival of Jennette Tallet, a graduate teacher from Moody Bible Institute. Robbie knew how hard Cam was working, and wrote to invite him to Panajachel in June to spend a few days swimming and relaxing:

> We both need a time of fellowship and study. I am sure our time together will bring large dividends in our future service for our Master and Lord. And I am equally sure that you would enjoy yourself. The lake scenery at this time of year is marvelously beautiful. Furthermore, there are several items of mutual interest we could discuss that are important to our work.

In his journal, Cam described his visit with Robbie:

> When I received Robbie's letter, I decided to drop my hammer and saw and take him up on his offer. He told me Genevieve hadn't been feeling well for some time and he was taking her to a plantation run by an Englishman for a few days rest. He said he would meet me at a place called Guatalón after dropping Genevieve off at the plantation.
>
> I met Robbie on Friday, June 23. Together we traveled along the trail taking time to visit in several homes along the way to tell people of the Saviour's love for them. I marveled at his unending patience. That night we slept on the floor of a manor house. Both of us were tired and sleepy, but Robbie carefully explained the way of salvation to two men until late into the evening. All we had for supper that night was a small bowl of partially-cooked beans. We didn't even have tortillas. The beans kept Robbie from sleeping, but the next morning he was just as diligent in his witness to people he met along the way.
>
> We crossed the lake in a launch and arrived in Panajachel about one in the afternoon. After eating a hearty meal, Robbie showed me through his lovely little home, yard, and boat house. In every way, things seemed absolutely ideal. Robbie's heart overflowed with gratitude

to God for having given him and his beloved wife such a lovely place to live, and for the response of the people to their ministry. After the tour, Robbie suggested we take a rest. And then he said, "When we get up we'll go for a swim in the lake."

*An early photograph of Cameron Townsend
and Robbie Robinson, center, on their way to
Guatemala*

Chapter Ten

A Great Loss

Cam had the interesting swimming anomaly of being able to go faster doing the backstroke than he could the crawl. Since his friend Robbie Robinson swam best on his side, Cam decided to teach him the swift backstroke. For about ten minutes, the two men practiced their swim strokes in the cool waters of Lake Atitlán. Occasionally Cam would poke fun at Robbie for wearing Genevieve's swim suit. And, good-naturedly, Robbie would remind Cam that if he had remembered to bring his own swimming trunks, *he* wouldn't be borrowing his wife's suit!

In every way, it was a perfect afternoon of rest, fellowship, and enjoyment of God's creation. The lake shimmered in golden light, pristine and radiant in the long shadows of the late afternoon sun. And then in an instant, the idyllic afternoon was shattered. Cam was swimming on his back just off shore, and Robbie was about fifteen yards away doing the same. Without uttering a sound, Cam saw Robbie suddenly throw up his hands, shake his head, and slip beneath the waters. Later Cam wrote in his journal:

> Robbie came up quickly still struggling and shaking his head. I reached him just as he going under for the second time. I grabbed him but was tired from my long swim and couldn't hold him up and

he pulled me under. I was able to get my head above water for air just as he pulled me under a second time [Robbie's third]. This time we went right to the bottom to a depth of about eight or ten feet. As I gave a push with my legs to go back up, his arms suddenly released me.

It took every ounce of my remaining strength to swim back to shore. I lay exhausted on the shore and called for help. There was no one in the house except a cook. She immediately ran to find someone to help me. Robbie's hired man, the strongest and best swimmer on the place, had left about an hour earlier.

It took about an hour before men came with a canoe and we could retrieve the body from the lake. It was hard to find the exact spot. Finally we spotted the body lying among the weeds. We recovered the body with a rake and took it into the parlor. By this time, a large crowd had gathered. For two hours we worked trying to revive him. Finally the district judge who happened to be in town said, "It's no use. Look at the back of his head. It's like a strawberry." He pronounced Robbie's death as due to a cerebral hemorrhage.

Cam quickly sent telegrams to Genevieve and Ben and Louise Treichler. The Treichlers arrived at 4:00 A.M. Sunday morning. It took Genevieve a long, uncomfortable eighteen-mile muleback ride and a special steamer trip to reach Panajachel by 9:00 P.M. Cam's and the Treichlers' particular concern was how Genevieve would respond to the sudden and bizarre death of her husband of just over four years. In the eighteen months since they had been in Panajachel, everyone had been warmed by the freshness of their love for one another and for the people of the area. Now the tranquility of their life and their hopes and dreams of ministry together had been swallowed up in an instant. Cam continued in his journal:

All of us have been praying hard for Genevieve. This is so very difficult for us to understand. When Genevieve finally arrived, she couldn't have been braver. She displayed the strength of her faith that says, "Though he slay me, yet will I trust him."

We had a short funeral service in the home by the lake. Then friends, humble Indians, and principal men of the town carried the coffin a mile to the schoolhouse that the mayor had ordered prepared for a public service. About halfway there, we were met by a procession of school children. When we arrived at the schoolhouse, the whole town was there.

Everyone loved Robbie. Many were in some way indebted to him for some service or other. The town orator delivered an address. This was followed by two gospel messages and the story of Robbie's life. The people were surprised to learn that Robbie's father was seventy-two years old when he was born. Such a fact was almost beyond their comprehension. In their society, men are considered old by their late forties.

When Trinidad Bac spoke in Cakchiquel, he surprised everyone with his knowledge of the Word and oratorical ability. "The coming of Robinson," he said, "was the dawn of a new day for the Cakchiquel people." I was amazed to realize that these people had been turned from superstitious enmity to love and affection in a short year and a half. Trinidad Bac laid his hand on the coffin and said, "Robinson is not dead. He is alive. He is alive in heaven." He then explained how they too could live after their mortal bodies had died. A believer read a message Robbie had left on his desk written in Spanish that told about the glories of heaven and how all could find such glories if they accepted the love God offered them through his Son.

The inscription on the coffin read, "*W. E. Robinson, Portador de las Buenas Nuevas*" (Bearer of the Glad Tidings). This was the name of their launch and home. It was also the purpose of their lives: bringing the good news of God's love for all people.

Robbie was then buried in the family tomb of a woman whose life he had saved. It overlooked the lake he so dearly loved. A few weeks before he died, Robbie had talked with Genevieve about what he wanted her to do when he died. "At my funeral" he said, "wear white for the resurrection." She did.

Before Genevieve left Guatemala on August 11, 1922, she sent a short note to Cam and Elvira, "It is wonderful the way the Lord has kept and strengthened me. He has poured into my aching heart his love and peace which passes all understanding. The Lord has taken home to himself my dearest treasure. This earthly separation would be more than I could bear were it not for the sustaining strength from above and the promise that he will go with me all the way."

Genevieve never returned to Guatemala. Cam and Elvira lost contact, but they did learn that a few years later she remarried and had a family. For years after, on the anniversary of Robbie's death, an unknown hand laid a wreath of flowers on his grave.

Robbie's unexpected, painful death was only one of many obstacles for Cam to overcome in 1922. His return to Guatemala was also marked by a contest of wills.

Cam almost never held his ideas of dissent with rancor. Yet, if he was strongly convinced that his idea or course of action was correct—even if it differed from his colleagues or associates—it was generally a colleague who had to conform to Cam's program. Paul Townsend, Cam's younger brother, recalls the same was true in Cam's childhood: "He always took charge and planned things for all of us. He did have a tendency to manipulate and get the things he wanted. Once some friends asked us to choose a puppy from a litter. My choice was different from Cameron's, but Cameron got the one he wanted. It was generally that way. But it was always done with a smile. He was never harsh." Of Cam's strong nature, Evelyn Pike, Cam's niece, once commented:

> If Uncle Cam believed a certain course of action was God's will, he always brought to bear his relentless drive and singleness of purpose to bring it about. However, if a colleague or subordinate or member of the family happened not to agree with his particular proposal, idea, or course of action, family members and colleagues alike generally had to modify their position to conform to Uncle Cam's.

The battle of wills between Cam and the Central American Mission began earlier in January 1922, though at this point there was just a gentle posturing of views. On January 6, Cam wrote Luther Rees a short note in which he suggested several possible ideas for the work in San Antonio, one of which was that his brother Paul and his wife, Laura, who planned to come to Guatemala in the near future, could take over the Indian work:

> I can go back to San Antonio as soon as possible to prepare for the coming of the new workers and get my brother well acquainted with the work. Elvira will wait for me in Chicago. If the mission wanted, I could return next summer to do the proposed deputation work.

Otherwise I will leave for Guatemala from California. This will mean a sacrifice, but I believe this will enable us both to return to the field well fitted for all [God] has in store for us. We need your counsel.

On the face of it, Cam's request to return to San Antonio was responsible enough. Besides attending to the mission churches, there were buildings to be built, a translation to be completed, journals to write, nationals to train (there were eleven or twelve nationals directly connected with the work in San Antonio), and more. He also needed to find a replacement for Coronado Estrada, the principal worker Cam had left in charge of the San Antonio work, who was ill.

But Cam was not at all pleased with the response he received. Unknown to Cam, the Central American Mission board members were being criticized by home churches and constituents for not providing enough firsthand reports and accounts from field missionaries. And since Cam was already home and a young enthusiastic, first-term missionary with slides and an exciting story to tell, he was their natural choice to send out on "official" deputation. Luther Rees, assuming Cam would comply with the board's wishes, had already sent out his name via the *Central American Mission Bulletin,* suggesting he would be available to speak in the Denver and Colorado Springs area. When Rees received Cam's letter telling him he wanted to return to the field by March, he responded with the following memo:

I do not feel your proposal to return to the field in March would be wise. As I wrote you before, I believe the Lord will care for the work until you return after having done some deputation work. We can ask Brother Bishop to put another national worker in San Antonio to replace Coronado Estrada.

It is most natural for the need of the field to be on your heart. But we believe the greatest need at this time is for someone who is acquainted with conditions on the field to do deputation work. And the Lord has seemed to open up the way for you to do this.

Cam's reply to Luther Rees was to assure him that if indeed the Central American Mission board was concerned with the need for deputation, he was happy to do his part. He reported he was, in fact, busily engaged in Southern California speaking in a variety of churches. However, his desire to return to Guatemala by March overshadowed most all other concerns. The following letters and memos reveal his diplomatic self-confidence and stubborn pragmatism:

> Word has come directly to me from Coronado Estrada that he cannot take care of our work in Guatemala after February. I should therefore return immediately. I have written asking Coronado to wait until March. A steamer sails March 17 [from San Pedro, California]. Mrs. Townsend will remain here doing deputation work as opportunity offers. This will allow time for her complete recovery so that, in the long run, it will neither be loss of time nor money. She is much better, but my folks want her to stay with them as long as she will. She is happy with these plans. I am sure she would be in no condition to return by June. I am also convinced that she will recover faster if I am not here.[1] Dr. Wilson is also of the same opinion. I am sure this is the course of action I should take. Should I not just go ahead and book my steamer passage for March 17?

First and foremost, Cameron Townsend was a classical missionary. He considered it illogical for a group of council members sitting in the Central American Mission's home office in Paris, Texas,[2] with little firsthand information, to make decisions that, he felt, would hinder rather than help the work.

Besides trying to convince the council he should return with all haste to San Antonio, Cam had two other equally burning convictions that the council opposed. One had to do with the nurse, Signe Norrlin. Cam was incensed to learn that even though she had been tentatively accepted to work in the San Antonio clinic, her final acceptance was held up because it needed the approval of one council member. On January 19, 1922, Cam wrote to Luther Rees:

> You say that the applications for Miss Norrlin can't be acted upon until Mr. Smith returns, which I learn won't be until next June. This seems lamentable. Dr. Kelly has offered to give her six to eight months of special training that would prepare her so much better for the field. Miss Norrlin is willing to take this training, but it all depends on the action of the council. If at all possible, I wish you would act quickly on her application.

The other issue had to do with Cam's brother Paul and his wife, Laura. Cam was convinced they both could play an important role in building the work in San Antonio. Paul was a gifted carpenter and all-round handyman, and Laura had a special way with children that would be useful in running the children's home. In addition, both could teach.

On January 28, Cam received two letters. One was from Luther Rees concerning the question of Paul and Laura going to the mission field. Rees wrote:

> In connection with the application of your brother Paul Townsend and his wife, we have encountered a difficulty. The medical certificate signed by Dr. Salisbury recommends both of them as being physically fit. But R. D. Smith tells me Dr. Wilson has examined Mrs. [Laura] Townsend and says that because she has asthma, poor circulation, heart trouble, and numerous other ills, this makes her a great risk on the mission field.

The other letter, from Mrs. R. D. Smith, was all business. At issue was Cam's insistence that he return to the field in March. With the tone of a mother to her recalcitrant child, she wrote:

> Dear Cameron,
> I have been thinking over the matter of your returning at once to the field. While I appreciate the urgency you have about returning, I believe the council will not be happy. I feel it is due them and the work of the Mission as a whole, to say nothing of the immeasurable benefit it will be to you personally and your work to carry out the original program the council set out for you.
> It seems to me you are leaving Mr. Rees in the lurch by rushing back to the field. He has a number of openings for you. You have your excellent slides and he has put the notice in the *Bulletin* of your availability.
> Our experience with missionaries is that they all feel the responsibility of their work on the field and all long to be back doing their work. However, taking everything into consideration, both on the field and here at home, I feel strongly that two months at least ought to be given to deputation work. I say this because of the importance of keeping faith with the Home Council and the constituency. I am

convinced that two months at home would mean more to the work in the end than it could possibly mean on the field.

Now Cameron, I hope you won't feel unkindly toward me for not agreeing with you about this matter that I know is pressing hard upon your heart. But these are my true convictions, and I believe they are what the council will feel also. No doubt you will hear from Brother Rees how he feels about it. Assuring you of my sisterly interest and regard, and praying that you may have the Lord's guidance, which you may have, if your will is entirely submissive to his, I remain, ever cordially yours.

Clearly Cam was in the grip of an intense dilemma. Did he acquiesce to the council's request, or did he try to point out that there was—from his point of view—a higher law at work? He did, after all, have Mrs. Smith's prayer that the Lord would give him guidance. And it was common knowledge that God's ways were not always clear even to a group of wise councilmen. Cam tried yet again to persuade these men of his deep conviction that it was imperative he return to the field by March. From Clearwater, California on February 6, 1922, he wrote:

Dear Mr. Rees,
It is hard to know what to do. A letter has just come from Mr. Bishop saying he is at the point of another breakdown and that I am greatly needed on the field. I think it is improbable for another national to go to San Antonio and replace Coronado. Remember he has to handle over a hundred dollars every month, sometimes more. Mr. Bishop just gives him the money you and we send for the San Antonio work. He then pays the eleven or twelve workers and cares for the home, school, and other things. I hesitate to trust this responsibility to anyone other than Coronado. However, he continues to write that he must quit.

I am waiting patiently for God to open the way in one direction or the other. Elvira has decided to enter the Bible Institute here after I sail. If her health were to greatly improve, she could return to Guatemala in July or August. However, only God can bring this about. It seems as if she will need another year to fully recover and find herself.

I do not know if she will agree to stay here if I go East. The door to her going back to Chicago for a protracted stay seems to be closed. Should sufficient funds come in by the twentieth and Elvira is willing to remain here at the Institute or with my folks, I shall be glad to go to Denver, Kansas, and St. Louis, drop down to Texas where I have been invited, and then sail from New Orleans. This trip could be made in a month and I still could get to Guatemala by the last of March. I will ask Elvira and then write you. Of course, it would be fine for her to go along and I could stay in Chicago if a place were to open up for her to stay. I will send you a telegram if we are definitely led.

I am just as busy as can be these days. I have spoken in thirteen different churches, besides the Institute and at Occidental College. I could keep busy with two or three services a week for several months right here in California. I feel I am too young for it, however, and the results so far make one believe that I can do more by prayer and hitting the work hard on the field. Also, I feel ashamed to be here when Abe Bishop desperately needs a rest, and he could do deputation so much better.

After that somewhat convoluted and desperate letter, Cam wrote Luther Rees on February 11, with a surprisingly candid insert from Elvira:

No letter has come from you since I wrote you last Monday. Since that time we feel we have received definite guidance from God. Elvira will write the next paragraph telling how this guidance came about.

Cameron wants me to explain, and I believe God wants me to as well. You know about my health problems and of the various doctors' opinions of my condition. I have to tell you I don't agree with them that I have a problem with my mind. My problem pure and simple has been selfishness. This has led to some of the other problems I've had.

The paragraph continued with a litany of self-flagellations and a repetition of victorious life clichés. Then after making her case that she go to Chicago to see her parents, Elvira continued: "Cameron feels he is needed in Guatemala now more than at any other place. And since his main work will be translating the Bible, I say a million times over, 'Go.' I know how much that precious Book means to me, and my heart aches for the Indians who have not had the opportunity to read it for themselves."

After this impassioned plea, Cam continued to pile reason upon reason why he should return to the field by March: Abe Bishop's ill health, the training of new missionaries, the matter of finances (it would cost more for him to go East than it would for him to sail directly from California). And, after all, wasn't he doing enough deputation work right in his own back yard? Making his case, Cam ended his letter to Luther Rees:

> These reasons seem conclusive to me, especially now that Elvira has guidance along the same line. The month between now and March 17 when the boat sails from here can be a very profitable time for me. Calls to do deputation work here are numerous. I am learning to print on the Multigraph machine, which requires time. I could not do the other preparations required for my leaving if I am going about from place to place. I believe also that God can raise up someone else to do the deputation work.
>
> Please write your opinion on these matters as soon as possible and join us in prayer that God may supply the needed funds.

For two anxious weeks Cam waited for a reply from Rees. None came. On March 1 Cam wrote again:

> I have been hoping to hear from you. But no word has come from my letter to you of some two weeks ago. I trust your silence means consent to my returning directly to Guatemala this month. To me, God's leading has been very clear. Up until Saturday night, the way was closed financially. However, after we had made my return a matter of prayer, a poor man at the Central American Mission prayer meeting who, as far we know has never given to our Mission, offered to pay my way back. Yesterday was the deadline for making my reservation and for holding my berth on the steamer *Venezuela*.

Since no further word has come from you, I made the necessary deposit, and unless some unforeseen circumstances arise, I will sail on the 17th and arrive in Guatemala on March 25 or 26. Elvira will go East soon after I leave.

The Children's Home in San Antonio

Chapter Eleven

Unexpected Supply

With a gigantic splash, the SS *Venezuela* dropped anchor in the warm-water port of Manzanillo, Mexico. The date was March 21, 1922. After four days at sea, Cam looked forward to stretching his legs and posting his first letter to Luther Rees since his departure from California:

> So far I am grateful to the Lord for giving me a chance to rest before plunging back into the work. There have been several good-humored parties aboard ship. On Sunday I was invited to speak twice.
>
> I was sorry you didn't answer my telegram in time for me to have received it before leaving. I telegraphed immediately after Dr. Brainerd gave his prognosis on Elvira's condition. She has improved steadily since January. I was anxious to have the opinion of a specialist as to whether she would ever completely recover. Mrs. R. D. Smith and others urged me to consult Dr. Brainerd. He is the foremost authority on nervous and mental health problems in Southern California.
>
> We weren't able to have the consultation until my brother-in-law offered to pay the bill. After going over Elvira's history, Dr. Brainerd spent two and a half hours with her. His conclusion was that Elvira's problems were emotional, not mental. He said he felt this was

brought on by her physical ailments and the nervous strain of the terrible earthquake she experienced in Guatemala.

Now that there are no serious threats of earthquakes, and she is over her hernia problem, he saw no reason why she shouldn't return to the field in July. I asked if the strain of the work would undermine her health. Without a moment's hesitation, he said "no." I then asked about Elvira doing some deputation speaking. "If she enjoys it," he said, "it will not hurt her." I therefore have left the slides with her.

You have never written to me saying specifically that Elvira cannot return to the field in July. However, several others have told me that the Mission has taken such a stand. Now that the doctor has given his approval, I wonder if Elvira might not return with [our new school teacher] Miss Tallet? I am writing to ask for the Mission's ruling on this matter.

Also, I wish that mission action could be taken soon on Miss Signe Norrlin. Mrs. Louise Heim, an old Sunday school teacher of mine, has given $1500 (she gave $1000 some time ago and has now given additional $500) to build a hospital for the indigenous people. We will not only need a nurse, but also a carpenter to build it. Therefore, I do hope my brother Paul is accepted.

Unknown to Cam, Luther Rees had written a response to his telegram neither encouraging nor forbidding them to return. He also reported that they were "holding in abeyance Paul's acceptance," adding the news that a self-supporting doctor had volunteered his services. Unfortunately, Rees's letter arrived in Clearwater the day after Cam sailed for Guatemala.

In the letter, Rees gave his blessing to Elvira to do as much deputation as she felt she could do. He also suggested she take part in a missionary conference to be held in Chicago at the Moody Church, May 31 to June 4, where the missions committee was especially pleased to hear Elvira had slides to show.

Cam was happily looking forward to returning to San Antonio and establishing a hospital. And though Rees informed Cam of the volunteer doctor, neither Rees nor the Central American Mission Board shared Cam's enthusiasm for the hospital. In a March 30 letter to Cam, Rees wrote: "In my letter that reached California after you sailed, I advised caution about undertaking the establishment of a hospital. Invariably, the expenses in maintaining such an institution are considerable. We need to be careful about starting programs unless we are sure we are doing it in faith."

Cam arrived in Guatemala on Sunday, March 26, 1922. He took the morning train to the town of Escuintla where he was met by a group of believers and, from there, rode the twenty-five miles to San Antonio on muleback. Along the way, he and his little company held services on two plantations. Several days after settling into his cornstalk house, Cam took a quick trip to Guatemala City to see Abe Bishop.

After receiving Rees's letter, Cam wrote a five-page report on April 5, responding to Rees's caution about the hospital project, providing information about Cam and Elvira's finances, and updating Rees on the current work:

> I am grateful to God for *don* Coronado and his wife who faithfully managed the affairs during my absence. The little cornstalk house looked quite forlorn, but after a couple of days of house cleaning, it now looks more like home.
>
> Margarito Otzoy [co-translator and school teacher] is hard at work translating the Gospel of John into Cakchiquel. He is learning to run the little printing machine quickly enough to handle all our printing needs. This will be a great help to me. It's our hope to use this to print the translation of John. As far as I know, this will be the first translation of the Gospel of John into any indigenous language in Guatemala. The printing press was a gift from Mr. and Mrs. Woodsum from Riverside, California. I have set it up in one of the tiny rooms in the cornstalk house.
>
> When I was in Los Angeles, I met Dr. Burrells of the Bolivian Indian Mission. He had translated the Gospels into the Quiché language. During our conversation, I discovered that he, like me, believed indigenous peoples can be taught to read their own language more easily and more quickly if the translator approximates his orthography as closely as possible to the alphabet of the national language. In our cases, of course, this is Spanish. Any Cakchiquel who can read Spanish should also be able to read the translation.

After a discourse on linguistic similarities between Quiché and Cak-chiquel, Cam candidly discussed Elvira's health and their shortage of money.

Cam's letter also revealed his seemingly contradictory views on how mission workers should be financed. Throughout his career he believed that when in need of money, he should ask the One who owned the cattle on a thousand hills. Cam's mission heroes were those who be-lieved that God—as promised in the Scriptures—would supply all their needs. Frequently, Cam would refer to Hudson Taylor and George Müller's writings and suggest these be required reading for all new candidates—"So they [can] better understand what it means to work with a faith mission."

At the same time, Cam also believed that God worked through his people when specific needs were presented to them. While some may have considered this to be double-talk, Cam did not:

> I felt terrible having to leave Elvira without money. When I expressed my concern, she insisted she would be all right. My folks will, of course, continue to do what they can for her, as they did for both of us when I was there. The only money that came directly to us during our time at home was from the Moody Church. That was last January. This meant we found ourselves uncomfortably dependent on my relatives, none of whom are well fixed.
>
> Most of the contributions that came in as a result of deputation were designated for the work. Thus, after our traveling expenses were paid, there was little left over for clothing and other supplies.
>
> As yet my things haven't cleared customs. I have no idea how much it will cost to get them out. God has been faithful in the past, and I am confident He will supply the funds.
>
> You may think God didn't provide more because he didn't want me to return. But all the money that came in, came in after I had told him I was willing to return to Guatemala from Los Angeles. Since nothing came in for me to go East, I believed that door was closed.

This was a natural lead-in to Cam's belief that the Mission should care for its elder workers—a subject few organizations, if any, had before considered:

I know you have many burdens, but when I arrived yesterday, I found Mr. Bishop in an absolutely broken condition. He was unable to do anything. He and Mrs. Bishop plan to go to California in June, if the Lord sends in the needed funds. The problem is, they have no relatives where they want to go. They no doubt will look to the Lord much more trustfully than I did. But I do hope the Mission will be just as faithful in helping in their needs as God makes it possible.

I believe that missionaries on the field should be cared for out of the General Treasury. I believe also that missionaries who must return to the homeland and are in need of a rest should be given financial help from the Mission.

Yes, I do agree with you that we should stick to our mission policy of keeping evangelization in the forefront. There are always strong pulls toward getting one deeper into medical and educational work. While they are good, they are apt to hamper our energies in preaching the gospel. However, this problem of just how many other things one should do has been one of my greatest problems of late.

I took your letter about the hospital as a caution. I now wonder if I should ask Mrs. Heim permission to spend the $1500.00 she gave to put up a simple little orphanage or children's home and clinic instead of the hospital. I think she would give her consent. I could easily set aside a room in the children's home to receive emergency cases. Miss Tallet has already been appointed for the children's school, and if Miss Norrlin is accepted, she could look after the clinic.

I feel confident the Lord will guide you about my brother and his wife and Miss Norrlin. We have a great need for their talents and gifts here on the field. With much love and prayers.

Just after Cam sailed, Elvira received a twenty-dollar check from Moody Church. Shortly after that, she received a fifty-dollar gift from Grace Woodsum (who, with her husband, had given Cam the printing press), and a surprise ninety-dollar gift from the Moody Church Sunday School. Believing this unexpected supply of money as a sign from the Lord, Elvira made definitive plans to travel to Chicago. Cam, though, knew nothing of this.

Also unknown to Cam was Howard Dinwiddie's activity on behalf of the work in San Antonio. During the very time Cam was wondering how to pay his customs fee, a check for $162 was on its way to Guatemala. When Dinwiddie had spoken at various churches and presented Cam's vision for the work among the Cakchiquels, five individuals responded with monetary gifts.

In addition, Dinwiddie recommended to the Central American Mission Board that Cam and Elvira change their base of operations due to the malarial conditions in and around San Antonio. Luther Rees agreed with Dinwiddie and suggested that while an "Indian center and the national workers remain in San Antonio, the training school and any other such facility be transferred to more healthful climate." The place suggested was Panajachel in the highlands.

Dinwiddie also suggested that a translation committee be formed of missionaries from other mission agencies to oversee and interact with Cam's Bible translation project. Such a committee had been suggested by L. L. Legters during the famous week at Chichicastenango.

While Cam was moving ahead with his plans to develop San Antonio into a mission center, he received word that Mrs. Heim was unwilling that her $1500 be spent on anything other than a hospital. However, she was warm to the idea of a children's home. She promised $2000 toward a children's home building. That's all Cam needed. Immediately he pushed himself and his workers to complete the building in readiness for the arrival of Jennette Tallet and Elvira in July.

When Elvira left California for Chicago in April, she sent letters and reports to Luther Rees and Cam telling of the people she had met and witnessed to along the way. Her letters pulsated with excitement as she wrote about the warm reception she received from the people in Gering, Nebraska, and St. Louis, Missouri. In Gering she spoke to a full congregation of the local Methodist church. And in St. Louis she was given the entire Sunday morning service of the Rock Hill Presbyterian Church. In the evening she showed slides to a group of young people.

In a remarkable way, the traveling, interaction, attention, and affirmation she received from people seemed to energize and clear away Elvira's depression. When she reached Chicago and was met at the train station by her parents, both were astonished at her vitality and shining good health. Elvira's mother, who never believed her only daughter was physically strong enough to be on the mission field, gave Elvira her blessing to return to Guatemala. Gone was Elvira's palsy-like twitching and any sign of her nervous disorder. Later, when she met Dr. Roberg (who had operated on her hernia), he, like her parents and friends, was astonished at her positive attitude and all-around good health. He pronounced her in perfect condition and cleared her to return to Guatemala whenever she wanted.

Both Cam and Luther Rees were also aware and pleased with the "new" Elvira. In several letters to Cam, Rees commented about the change in tone of Elvira's letters. Cam, of course, was aware of this change too and mentioned it in a letter on May 16 to Howard Dinwiddie:

> You will be glad to know that God has turned our darkness into day. Every letter from Elvira shows that the cloud has been turned inside out. For this we praise and thank God. We thank you also for your constant prayers on our behalf. The last letter I wrote you about Elvira was very uncertain. At that time everything before me was complete darkness, except that I knew God would one day work out this darkness for his honor and glory.

One disruptive note in Cam's letter was the news that Jennette Tallet had to push her arrival date to August. Cam wondered how he would manage without her help. His work load included overseeing ten Cakchiquel evangelists who were conducting Bible studies and teaching workshops. There were also two Spanish-speaking evangelists and two Cakchiquel elementary school teachers. One doubled as Cam's co-translator and the other as a printer of lesson material and gospel tracts. Cam was also hard at work on translation and the children's home building. Besides serving as an orphanage for children whose parents had died from malaria, tuberculosis, or other diseases, this building would also provide room for students who came to the school from a distance.

In addition to heavy field work responsibilities, Cam wrote copious letters, reports, and articles. He wrote booklets on mission histories, papers on mission apologetics, and short stories about life in Guatemala. In one article, Cam wrote about how to respond to "enemies"—those who might criticize or try to discredit the work: "Although you might encounter bitter enemies of evangelical work, make it a rule never to miss an opportunity to be kind to them."

Cam was also deeply concerned that his colleagues be sensitive to those who held opposing theological views. In an editorial published in the *Guatemala News* he wrote:

> The first impulse of many expatriate missionaries in Latin America is to correct what they feel are mistakes in the established church. I feel it would be much better to dwell less on the "errors" of the established church. What the church in Latin America needs is not correction and discussion over the usually debated doctrines, but a living reality of the great fundamentals all Christians hold in common. Such doctrines as God, sin, repentance, reconciliation, brotherhood, charity, spiritual ideals, and heavenly hope. It is precisely these fundamentals the world strives for and wants. The world is nauseous with those who engage in religious bickering. One finds rest and satisfaction in the fundamental doctrines. I have one word for all missionaries. Understand and preach Christ's conception of the fundamentals. When that happens, differences in theology will take care of themselves.

Though many of his fundamental contemporaries felt it necessary, Townsend believed that peace between religious groups was not won by polemics. Repeatedly he stressed the importance of love toward one another. Cam had seen leaders become filled with bitterness, using brutal tactics with each other. Whenever Cam encountered them, he tried to be faithful to his life principle: "By love, serve one another."

Cam not only looked for ways to reach out and show practical kindness to those who opposed him, he also championed the causes of his friends. His letter to Luther Rees regarding Abe Bishop's financial need displayed his gift for seeing beyond his own agenda. After several letters on this subject had passed between Rees and Townsend with little result, Cam wrote to the Central American Mission constituency, saying:

> Our brother [Abe Bishop] has to lay down the sword. The expense of keeping up the work will continue. He trusts in his God to continue to supply his needs. A few contributors give sufficiently to support their workers entirely, but there are several workers who must be supported by general contributions. Humanly speaking, these contributions will stop now that Mr. Bishop is unable to write reports

about the work. But our God knows these needs and will touch the hearts of his children to supply all.

Do pray, dear friends. As you dwell close to His great heart in prayer, you cannot forget these "other sheep" for whom He died. Should any of you be led to give toward our brother's work, please send your offerings rightly designated to the treasurer of our mission, Luther Rees.

On Friday evening, June 2, 1922, Elvira was one of the principal speakers at the large missionary rally at Moody Church in Chicago. It was a strong, clear, coherent message that outlined the missionary challenge and opportunities for service in Central America. Elvira concluded her message with the following:

> When we speak to indigenous people, they always have one special prayer request. The request is that we will keep our message simple and clear so all may understand and believe. When our teams go out to evangelize, the people often ask, "What sin have we committed that you never came before?"
>
> I ask you people here at Moody Church to pray for Mr. Townsend as he is right now translating the Gospel of John into the Cakchiquel language.

On July 8, Elvira sailed for Guatemala aboard the SS *Saramaca*. Her health was good, her spirits high. The Sunday before she left she gave a final report and was overjoyed to hear three thousand people at Moody Church sing a compelling "Blest Be the Tie that Binds." Several young men spoke to her and said how much her message had inspired them to consider full-time mission service. She left Chicago feeling cared-for and warmed by the support of family and friends. She was eager to return to Guatemala.

Overloaded with work, Cam was anticipating Elvira's arrival. Cam reported to Rees on the good progress of the children's home building but said he was extremely busy trying to look after Bishop's affairs. He was having particular difficulty trying to balance his books. "This," said Cam, "will be a job for Elvira." Cam also wrote that he was looking forward to "saying goodbye" to the kitchen, because there were eleven people eating their meals in the little cornstalk house!

With his responsibilities and the details of daily living, Cam's work load was extended futher by attending to the carpenters. To Rees he expressed his frustration that this was keeping him from the translation desk. Soon, he hoped, his brother Paul would be accepted and given the oversight of the building project.

Aware of the heavy load Cam was carrying, and fearful he might tax his wife with too many heavy responsibilities, Luther Rees wrote Elvira a cautionary note just before she left: "As you again take up the work on the field, I pray you will be careful not to overdo and bring about a repeat of your past physical condition. I know it will be difficult to obey this injunction when there are so many needs. But your experience has taught you that becoming ill interferes with your service. The better part of wisdom is to consider one's strength."

Elvira was touched by Rees's concern. But she shared her husband's vision, and to a large degree, his practical idealism. It was an idealism that accepted suffering, discouragement, even fear and ill health as part of one's calling. They were, after all, in the service of a great God. They could do nothing less than serve and live as his ambassadors, ill health notwithstanding.

Signe Norrlin, top center left; *and Alicia, an aide,* top center right; *with children at the Home*

Fellow Dreamers

It wasn't just a car; it was a Ford. A Model T Ford—the most popular car in the U.S. in the mid-1920s. Although Henry Ford mass produced these remarkable little vehicles at a price most American families could afford, not everyone had money left over to buy gas. This was the case for Paul and Laura Townsend when they, and their car, arrived by boat in Guatemala in October 1922.

Paul and Laura were finally accepted by the Central American Mission to work in San Antonio. Cam and Elvira met the boat with high excitement. Not only was the station at San Antonio doubling its expatriate help, they were getting a car as well. After all the hugs and greetings were over and the Model T off-loaded, Paul said, "Cameron, I hope you have money to buy gas for the car. We spent almost every cent we had just to get here." Cam smiled and said, "Sorry, Brother, so did we."

But one thing Paul Townsend did have in abundance was raisins: wonderful, plump California raisins. Just before Paul and Laura left California, his uncle gave Paul several large cartons. "This will be our gas money," said Cam. "The people here love raisins. We will sell them along the way for less than they could buy them in the market." Years later when Paul reflected on that incident, he would smile and say, "I was glad for a generous uncle who loaded me down with more raisins than I thought I could ever use."

Looking back on what he claimed was the first missionary car to Guatemala, Cam said:

> The old Model T saw service not only in Guatemala but in El Salvador as well. The car was eventually dismembered and its motor bequeathed for use in a new and larger launch on Lake Atitlán. However, not all missionaries welcomed this car. Some thought mules were the preferred method of transport. But with new and better roads, I knew a new day had come. Soon the old hold-outs were making use of this cheaper and more efficient mode of travel.

Besides the car and the raisins, Paul Townsend brought his carpentry tools. With the help of several nationals, he immediately set to work on the children's home building. Already, the outside walls and the roof had been completed, but nothing had been done on the inside. Only days after Paul was at work on the inside rooms, Cam asked Paul when he expected the building to be ready. In a letter to his parents, Paul wrote:

> Cameron had made up his mind the building would be ready at a certain date. I said I didn't think it would be ready by then. But as usual Cameron had his own agenda. He began telling the people all over the area that if they wanted to send their children to school, the building would be ready to accommodate them at the time he had specified.
>
> On the morning of that date, they came in droves. The only problem was we didn't know what to do with them. The building was designed for about thirty-six children. Before we could stop them from coming, we had fifty children in an unfinished building.
>
> In spite of not having specific training to run a children's home nor all the domestic help we needed, Laura and I felt we were functioning rather well. Then one day an Indian man who lived in the mountains some distance from the center came to see us. With hat in hand he asked us to forgive him for the difficulty his children had caused us. Laura and I looked at each other in bewilderment. We had no idea what children he was talking about. As we talked further,

we discovered his children had not been at school for two days. With trying to get everyone settled and into a routine, we simply hadn't missed the two children who became homesick and decided on their own to walk back over the mountain to their village. Fortunately, shortly after that, another expatriate staff joined us, and the school and home began to function very well.

By January 1923, the San Antonio center purred with the precision of a well-oiled, nicely tuned engine. The new nurse, Signe Norrlin, assisted by a young Cakchiquel woman, was, in Cam's words, "Doing much good healing bodies and opening homes to the gospel." Dr. Charles Ainslie, of the Presbyterian Hospital in Guatemala City, volunteered his services one day a week. He had also given the little clinic a supply of drugs and other medical supplies.

Jennette Tallet, who was now in charge of the children's home, was becoming a surrogate mother to the young girls there, although in three months' time she would leave the home in the hands of Laura and Paul to take a position in Guatemala City.

And Paul, too, was doing more than driving nails, as Cam disclosed in one of his letters:

> Now that school has begun, everyone is busy. We have two national teachers to teach over forty children. Of these, fifteen are boarders. Two are Quiché and the remainder are Cakchiquel. They come from nine different towns. Just last week we picked up another little girl all covered with sores and her feet filled with jiggers. She is the daughter of one of the men who works for us from time to time. Her name is Bonita and she is as cute as her name implies. Brother Paul has taken a special interest in her. Whenever he isn't working on the building, you can be sure to find him helping to care for Bonita in some way.

While Cam reported that smooth rapport existed between the workers and staff and how pleased he was that each had found his niche, he also showed concern that support money for the students wasn't coming in. In the report, Cam wrote, "While our work systems go smoothly, we do want your prayers for the support of the children. Money has been promised for only six. But I believe our Father will supply."

For the next five years, Cam would, as he said, "labor against tremendous obstacles and constant financial shortages." One of the central obstacles Cam faced in the twenties was bringing the vision of the Chichicastenango Twelve into full reality. While he reported that all was going well in San Antonio, implementing the vision on a larger scale was not as successful. In Cam's mind, the man most gifted to implement this larger vision was his friend Howard Dinwiddie.

Dinwiddie, Cam, and Legters formed a unique triad in the Chichicastenango vision. Each was different in temperament and style. Yet each shared a profound interest in missions and the fulfillment of the Chichicastenango meeting mandate—though it was largely Cam who sought the dream's fulfillment. To that end, Howard Dinwiddie, using his twin gifts of inspiring people for missions and organizing them into productive work, had incorporated the old LAIM into the new Indian Mission Committee of America (IMCA) with its own home council.

On the heels of organizing IMCA, Dinwiddie organized a sister organization called "The Pioneer Mission Agency" (Legters was appointed field secretary). The function of the Pioneer Mission Agency was to assist all evangelical mission societies in investigating and locating new fields for mission service. This agency was also designed to raise prayer and financial support and receive and forward monies for individual missionaries and their societies.

In the midst of this mutual activity, friendship among these three men flourished. On one of his first trips to Guatemala, Dinwiddie and Townsend had hiked up the volcano *Agua* and experienced one of those lovely moments when two hearts bond through shared experiences and youthful idealism for a common vision. For months and years after that experience, Cam would often conclude his letters to Dinwiddie with, "Your fellow mountain climber and dreamer." Recalling that moment, Dinwiddie noted:

> We talked all night about the great need for the long-neglected Indian peoples to have the gospel in their own tongue. At dawn the two of us stood on the rim of the crater of the ancient volcano and saw the glory and transformation of a new day.
>
> As the sun rose in flaming tropical splendor above the silver rim of the far distant Atlantic, its rays touched the ancient Indian altars on the volcano's crest where for centuries sun worshipers had prayed

to the sun god. Those rays also touched a man, an Indian descendant of those ancient sun worshipers who had allowed the true Light of the World to enter his heart.

As the Indian man stood there, the clouds thousands of feet below were warmed and lifted by the sun. In a few moments, through the rose-colored mist that hung over the volcano's crater, the man was surrounded by a seven-fold rainbow. We took this phenomenon to be singularly prophetic for the task God had laid on our hearts during the night.

Soon the men would realize that there was a hard price to pay for pursuing their dreams.

During the months Cam was in California (October 15, 1921, to March 17, 1922), some in the Central American Mission began to change their political mood toward Cam's leadership—and toward several members of the Chichicastenango Twelve.

Tension pervaded after the conference when Legters and Dinwiddie were guests in the Bishop home. Bishop, along with others in the Central American Mission field leadership, downplayed the importance of working exclusively with Indian minorities. Just before his return to Guatemala from California, Dinwiddie had written Cam: "I am finding a very different atmosphere here. For reasons that are not clear to me, I have found in your absence a spirit of disaffection toward you (I hope this will soon be wiped out). While some have shown friendliness, many others display a spirit of skepticism about our dreams and the vision that was born at Chichicastenango." Dinwiddie concluded this long letter with: "May God bless you, my dear fellow worker. He has called us together. May we each in loving trust and faithful prayer fellowship, apply one to the other the fullness of all God would have us to give in his great task of reaching the hidden peoples of earth with the gospel of our Lord."

In the ecclesiastical and secular world, there is sometimes little difference in politics, and soon that "loving trust" would be tested. Thus without Cam's moral support and enthusiastic spirit to carry the day, the flame that burned in the hearts of those interested in Indian work began to flicker.

While some in the Central American Mission suggested the "bottom had dropped out of Indian work," Cam did not. Numerous letters passed between Cam and Dinwiddie. After many letters, Cam, believing fervently that true friends spoke with candor and love to one another, wrote:

> I can't reconcile myself to believe that our vision cannot be realized as we planned. If, however, I am mistaken, I'll be happy to be straightened out. I'll be glad to partnership with you in every way I can. But if not, I can't see my way clear to go on in a very poor attempt to carry out the Chichicastenango plan. If it was poorly planned, let's discard it and get a new plan in which we can all work together. Believe me, I want to cooperate, especially with the one I love as I love you. I anxiously await your suggestions. I hope also it will mean that you can cut loose from your home responsibilities and spend most of your time with the *Indians* on the field. This is what is needed.
>
> Your fellow mountain climber and dreamer.

A modern writer once said, "There is a profound moral difference between the use of force for liberation and the use of force for conquest."[1] Cam believed he knew the difference. He sought to use candor and persuasion to liberate, to serve, and to inspire faith in the vision he believed God had given him. But not everyone shared his emotional commitment to the dream in 1922–23—or even throughout much of his life. His closest friends and colleagues sometimes bristled when in contact with Cam's single-mindedness.

The Treichlers, hosts of the first Chichicastenango Conference of January 23–25, 1921, did not want the responsibility of a second IMCA conference when the agreed-upon time arrived for the annual meeting. Experiencing mission burnout, the Treichlers were to soon leave the field. During this time most Central American Mission missionaries were concerned with the upcoming evangelistic campaign to be held with Costa Rica's Henry Strachan and Argentina's Juan Varetto.

So it was with some difficulty that Paul and Dora Burgess hosted the second conference in Quezaltenango February 5–12, 1922. And though Paul Burgess pronounced the effort worthwhile, he also said, "Neither the attendance nor the spirit of the gathering soared to the level reached at Chichicastenango."

Although Dinwiddie received yet another plea to join Cam on the field, his enthusiasm and dedication to Cam's vision seemed to shift in favor of the Central American Mission leadership position. In two separate letters, both written on September 9, 1922, he gave his reasons for not joining Cam:

> You speak of your conviction that I should come to the field to organize the work there. Frankly, I believe if I had come, the suspicion and jealousy that has been aroused [because of our association with the IMCA] would have created such deep feelings between the two mission organizations that future cooperation would have been impossible.
>
> I have been active as the executive secretary for the Home Council of the IMCA and have had good fellowship with the Texas members of the Central American Mission Council. Because I have such a good working relationship with them, I believe many of the mistaken reports about the IMCA have been allayed. This, in my view, would have been utterly impossible had I gone to the field as you wanted.
>
> Why can't you, my dear Cameron, give me the credit that I give you of seeking earnestly to know the will of God as we go through these perplexing days? Can you not, even now, though you do not understand me, be one who stands with me? I have not stood aloof from you even when I have not understood some of the things you have done.
>
> I have tried to bring the board into harmony and to build up confidence and cooperation that I believe is essential for the ongoing of the work. We must in every way clear up any suspicion or mistrust that may exist between the two agencies.

Though the at-odds tension between these two men was strong, and their diverging visions a complex web, their public lives and the content of their letters suggests these were men who shared a spiritual vision that was sharpened by conflict and deepened by mutual friendship.

Like Cam, Dinwiddie had stated repeatedly that his vision was for unreached peoples, particularly ethnic peoples. Also evident was that these two men shared the mind-set of the builders of those soaring medieval cathedrals: all for the glory of God. Self-glory was irrelevant.

All that mattered was a life poured out for the glory of God and the blessing of others. And this was the common goal of Townsend and Dinwiddie.

But now these two men, who served God with the highest of motives, had shown their humanity. They were in conflict. How was this to be resolved? For Cam the answer was simple. It was his personal credo taken from Philippians 1:27: "Whatever happens, conduct yourself in a manner worthy of the gospel of Christ."

For Cam that meant writing Dinwiddie an apology and admitting— while still holding to his original position—that perhaps he was wrong in his judgment. A month later, on Oct 6, 1922, he wrote:

> Your letter arrived last week and I want to answer immediately because I fear you may believe our friendship has become weakened (on my part). Nothing could be further from the truth.
>
> Some of us who have lived so long in Latin America forget that when we speak frankly, it sometimes hurts our best friends. And I consider you one of my best friends. Thank you for the room you have given me to feel such friendship toward you.
>
> Of course, I understand that God's plan for you may not be to send you personally to the field. However, I continue to believe that God could use your organizational gifts splendidly here on the field, even if it were only for a couple of years. If, on the other hand, God has other plans for you (and surely he is greatly using you in your present field), this demands care in deciding how he is leading.
>
> We shall continue to love you and no longer look to you for help in our problems here as we had talked about after the Chichicastenango meeting. I confess this is a bitter disappointment to me, but I do understand and I will have no more to say about the matter. Once again, be assured of my love for you. I will appreciate any friendly criticism, and under God's hand, I know I will profit from it. What is friendship for if not to help one another out of one's mistakes as well as to give an encouraging word?

In late 1922, Elvira was in the hospital again with further medical problems. By March 1923, she and Cam had accepted the Central American

Mission Board's decision to assign them to work in Panajachel's cool and more healthful area, but she would not be able to join Cam for six months. Assuming responsibility of the new work meant leaving their cornstalk house in San Antonio behind. "It was hard to leave," Cam said, "but anywhere with Jesus."

*Students at the Robinson Bible Institute with A. E. Bishop,
Elvira, and Cameron,* middle row, left to right

Chapter Thirteen
Winds of Change

C ameron Townsend liked the small rituals of eating, talking, and good fellowship. He was famous for saying, "We put as much pie as we can in pioneering." In later years, he used these rituals to build goodwill among his host country officials, friends, and SIL members. He took seriously the scriptural injunction to be hospitable and to extend unconditional love to all. Cam also believed that all missionaries needed to give, as well as receive, hospitality. A practical way to do this, he believed, was to have a retreat center where people from diverse missions could relax, eat good food, and enjoy the restorative powers of God's beauty in his creation. And Cam knew just the place—Panajachel.

To his dismay, not everyone on the Central American Mission Council agreed with Cam's ecumenicalism. Lewis Sperry Chafer, newly elected executive secretary, responsible for the general direction of the mission, was one of these. On April 25, Cam wrote Chafer a lengthy letter expressing how pleased he was over his recent appointment and included a routine report of his work. It was a warm, informative, four-page, hand-written letter—the kind of report he had written for over three years. But, knowing how Chafer felt about fellowship with missionaries and believers other than Presbyterians, Cam added:

I wonder what you think about developing a conference and recreation ground for missionaries at Lake Atitlán. Local missionaries have pledged about three hundred dollars toward such a project. However, I know of at least two council members who believe it should be developed for the exclusive use of Central American Mission personnel. These council members believe if other mission agencies want to develop a conference ground, they should develop it on the malaria-infested Lake Amatitlán. They are afraid if we let in missionaries from other societies, even for recreation and conference purposes, they are apt to run off with our work. I may not be well enough taught on "separation," but I can't understand why I should hold myself aloof from fellow believers in recreation and conference just because they believe differently on non-essentials. Also, if I can't fellowship with other brethren, I don't think it's right for me to deny them such a beautiful place the Lord has given me.

If our mission holds the balance of power on the property, I see no danger of getting in people who will teach false doctrines.

At a little over five thousand feet, the sub-tropical town of Panajachel nestles on the shores of Lake Atitlán and is set in a blue-green tiara of rolling mountain ridges accented by three volcanos. Cam knew the area well. Part of his reason for visiting his friend Robbie Robinson in June 1922 was to implement plans to move the small Bible training school he had started from San Antonio to Panajachel. But with Robbie's sudden and tragic death on the very weekend of Cam's visit, plans for the Robinson Bible Institute (as they were now calling it) were suspended until the Central American Mission could find suitable leadership.

The person the Mission decided was most qualified to get this project off the ground was Cameron Townsend. With Paul and Laura Townsend settled in San Antonio, as well as Signe Norrlin, Jennette Tallet, and several nationals in leadership, the Central American Mission leadership determined the work in San Antonio was in good order. Cam's gifts were needed more in Panajachel.

Cam had several reasons for expanding the Bible Institute: to keep faith with supporters who had sent money specifically for such a school; he now had qualified expatriate help in Archer (Archy) Anderson; and there was urgent need to train the young national men who had responded to the call to ministry at the Victorious Life conferences led by Dinwiddie and Legters.

Clearly Cam believed it was fatal to stand still. He had a vision and energy for ministry, and he had an independent and innovative mind. The three Central American Mission board members (Rees, Jones, and Chafer), who visited San Antonio in February 1923, observed this in Cam and recommended that he take charge of commencing work with the Robinson Bible Institute. Cam accepted the challenge even though it meant he would have to go without Elvira.

Elvira continued to suffer with health problems, and in April Cam wrote Lewis Sperry Chafer concerning her surgery: "April 26 (noon). Elvira was operated on at seven this morning for removal of cystic ovaries. Her trouble was much more advanced than Dr. Ainslie had thought. This accounts for her very poor health. However, we are thankful that the operation was successful and believe in time Elvira will be restored to full health."

To Howard Dinwiddie he wrote:

> The hardest part is that I will have to go to Panajachel alone. Elvira is in the hospital here and Dr. Ainslie says she shouldn't go up for at least six months. In fact, he says she must have a year's complete rest and recommends she return to the States for it. The problem is, I don't know where she could go. If she returned to Los Angeles or Chicago, she would be kept too busy. I have arranged for a room in a boarding house here in the city, but today I decided to write you to ask if it would be possible to get a room for her at America's Keswick and how much it would cost. Both Elvira and I feel it would be an ideal place for her. I'm sure you will try your best for me. If Elvira can be restored to health, our lives will be much more useful to those we serve. Please pray for me.

While Cam cared for Elvira, he also had responsibility for Panajachel and San Antonio. In fact, the Central American Mission council officially recognized Cam as the director of all mission activities in these two places. On May 2, Chafer wrote telling Cam of his authority to represent the council on the field. They would rely on Cam's judgment regarding any decisive step taken on behalf of the mission. Chafer also admonished Cam about his workaholic zeal:

I feel it necessary for me to send this kindly word of caution. You two men [Cam and Archer Anderson] are undertaking too heavy a schedule. When you interpret for Archy three hours a day and then teach an hour yourself, and I dare say add much more to the hours of the day with other duties, you are overtaxing your strength. If you continue, this will result in your incapacity at a time when it will be most painful for you and distressing for us all. I also fear you are not eating as well as you might. With all you are doing, you need nourishing food. Please take time to rest. These are absolute laws and neither you nor Archer are exceptions. If you want to do God's will and God's work, it must be done in God's way. Even the Lord said, "Come ye apart and rest."

In another letter from Chafer, dated May 7, Cam received his answer regarding non-Central American Mission missionaries participating in the common conference and using recreation grounds:

The report of your work is most encouraging. I cannot tell you how greatly you have entered my life and how delighted I am at every remembrance of my acquaintance with you. Now a word to answer your letter of April 25 in which you ask about developing a missionary resting place to be shared with other missionaries in Central America. I fear if a property were open to such groups as Pentecostals, Friends or Adventists, there would be very little fellowship of the kind you are thinking about. Of course, if the conferences were combined with the Presbyterians, there would be no doctrinal disagreement.

But it would be impossible for you to sit down and have a Bible Study with such groups, without, in my opinion, much unpleasant discord. I know this is a rather delicate situation. My own policy has always been, in such matters, that it is easier to keep out in the beginning than to get out after one has gotten in.

I am not assuming to give direction in this matter, I am merely stating my own experience. I personally would never, under any condition, undertake to fellowship with any missionaries other than those of the Presbyterian mission. Of course, if you mean just social interaction, you might get along. But since your project anticipates a certain amount of combined study of the Word, I believe it would be impossible for you to have fellowship. This is not merely a matter of theory. It has been tried hundreds of times, and always ends in failure. I shall be glad to hear more from you regarding this matter.

Before Cam left California for Guatemala in March 1922, he made arrangements to have a motorcycle and sidecar shipped to him. In one of his earlier, less stressful letters to Chafer, he exulted over the arrival of this exciting new mode of transportation and made particular reference to trying to get any customs duties and tariffs canceled. Since money was always scarce, suspending customs duties on goods and equipment used for "ministry purposes" became an imperative for Cam.

On June 7, Cam wrote his parents about a trip he took with Archy Anderson on this new motorbike. While he had praised the bike for being, "surer than muleback," it turned out that this bike was just as irascible as the four-footed beast which has become a metaphor for stubbornness and unpredictability. What was supposed to be a happy, carefree day of exploration and visitation turned out to be an exhausting and frustrating two days and a night of trying to get the motorcycle to work.

As recorded in Cam's letter, the trip became notable for more than just the misadventures of two men and a machine's capricious intake valve; it became, for Cam, a never-to-be-forgotten study between two kinds of hospitality. One host provided polite care, but with a sterile correctness. The other provided grace, warmth, and practical love. True hospitality, Cam learned, gives something more enduring than the basics for physical sustenance. True hospitality is an almost sacred gift of one's presence, the gentle art of "being there."

In 1923, many of the coffee and banana plantations in Guatemala were owned and operated by Germans. German nationalism was as strong in many plantation manor houses as it was in the houses of the rising middle class in Germany itself:

> We struggled all morning with the motorcycle that ran for a few miles and would stop. I would work on it for a bit, get it running, only to have it sputter and die a few miles down the road. At noon we were trying to climb a steep grade when the bike quit for good. About three miles back we had passed a flour mill operated by Germans. We returned to the mill to ask for their help.

All afternoon we worked but couldn't get a spark. Since we were stuck, there was no alternative but to put up for the night at the flour mill.

After being shown to our room, we were invited into the parlor. As I grew accustomed to my surroundings, it seemed we were in a little bit of Berlin rather than being in Guatemala. A big picture of Kaiser von Hindenburg hung in the hall where we placed our hats. In the parlor, directly over our host's big chair, was yet another portrait of Von Hindenburg.

In front of where the "lord of the manor" sat was a table with a bottle of whiskey and several bottles of some other beverage. At the other end of the table sat the lady of the house quietly knitting, hardly acknowledging our presence. On one side of the table sat a handsome young man with big brown eyes that looked as if they had been mellowed by some sad experience. I discovered he had been in Guatemala for a year but took no interest in the day-to-day operations of the mill. Nor had he taken time to learn Spanish. He had tried to help us fix the motorcycle but gave up an hour before supper and took his pretty black horse for a ride. He didn't go far, but spent most of the time circling the yard making the horse prance with different gaits. All the time I kept wondering what brought him to Guatemala, and what was the story behind such melancholy eyes and the faraway expression on his face.

On the opposite side of the table sat another young man dressed in a German uniform. He had a scar clear across the back of his head where some allied shell had gotten him. Unlike the other young man, he had a big friendly smile over his face. But like his friend, couldn't speak either Spanish or English.

Just before dinner was announced, our host, a tall, dignified man with a military bearing, stood and raised his glass. The two men also stood and raised their glasses. At a nod from the "lord," they each drank to one another's health. We then marched into the dining room behind our host, his wife and four-year-old son, and the other two men.

Soon after supper, we dismissed ourselves and went to bed. After breakfast the next morning, we again tried to work on the motorcycle, but with no better success. I ended up breaking the timing gear which left us no alternative but to start out walking the thirty miles to San Antonio to order new parts.

We left everything at the flour mill except what we would need on the trail and started out on foot for San Antonio at one-thirty in the afternoon. Our host heartlessly let us start out without any lunch. After a several-mile climb, we came to another large plantation.

The owner was Swiss and a young German couple was in charge. They were entirely different from our host the previous night. They expressed warm interest in us personally and in our mission work. After giving us large cups of coffee and cake and making sure we were well rested, they wished us Godspeed and gave us two good horses to ride the twenty-five miles or so to San Antonio.

About 3:00 P.M., a hard tropical rain came. We had raincoats, but on horseback, this didn't give us the protection we needed. Around five-thirty, the rain cleared and we were able to get dried out before nightfall. After leaving the town of Itzapa, we decided to take a short-cut, but the horses had never been this way before and had a hard time picking their way over the trail.

Archy's horse seemed less afraid of the trail so I gave him the lead, but we both found it hard to keep on the trail. In spite of this, I thought everything was going well until we started down a steep gully and came to a place where the trail ended at a stream. Archy flicked on his weak flashlight, and there looming before us was a ten-foot washout. Archy's horse was standing right on its edge when suddenly and without warning the horse reared and whirled around on his hind legs, just missing tumbling into the great hole with Archy on his back.

We calmed the horse down and both of us led our horses across the stream. As we were going up the other side, Archy unexpectedly called out, "I've fallen into a ditch." I looked around, and sure enough he was out of sight. Fortunately his horse stood perfectly still while he scrambled out. There were no further incidents for the re-mainder of the trip. We arrived in San Antonio at ten-thirty to a happy welcome from Paul and Laura. We were safe and sound, but very, very tired.

Difficulty with his motorcycle did not dampen Cam's enthusiasm for this machine. In fact, he was nothing short of an evangelist in his belief that the motor bike was an aid for ministry. Even Elvira was caught up in Cam's belief in this new mode of transportation, in spite of a three-month convalescence in the Presbyterian Hospital in Guatemala City. In a post-script to one of her later letters, she wrote, "Last Sunday, Paul and Laura Townsend, my husband and I ran out with the motorcycle and held three services in two different towns. We were able to help a husband and wife reconcile their differences and distributed tracts in ten towns along the way."

And in a not too subtle postscript to a letter to L. S. Chafer, Cam wrote, "If brother Paul had a light model motorcycle, he could reach many of the congregations around San Antonio without being away overnight!"

In the summer of 1923, Cam's work with what he called the "Cak-chiquel Department of Central American Mission" was extremely pro-ductive. The officers listed on the minutes of this newly constituted department consisted of chairman and dean of the Robinson Bible In-stitute, Archy Anderson; executive secretary, William Cameron Town-send; superintendent of the San Antonio Station and treasurer and editor of *Cakchiquel News*, Paul Townsend; and recording secretary, Elvira Townsend.

The Bible school had seventeen full-time students. Signe had twenty-one children well under her control in the children's home in San An-tonio. And Paul, Laura, and Archy had given themselves to serious Spanish study. Archy, in fact, could now lecture without Cam's help.

In addition, Cam and his co-translators had completed translating the Gospel of John into Cakchiquel. In a bulletin entitled, "St. John Pub-lished in 1923," Cam wrote:

> In 1923, the entire Gospel of St. John in a bilingual edition came off the press. This time two Cakchiquel men did the printing on the Woodsum press [mimeograph machine] as well as the binding. After this publication, we determined to wait until the whole New Testa-ment had been completed before doing any more printing. One rea-son for this decision was because there was opposition from certain *ladinos* who were out of harmony with the idea of specialized Indian work. Some Indian leaders who, due to their knowledge of Spanish, meager as it was, found it convenient to have the Scriptures only in Spanish so that the rank and file of the believers would have to

depend upon them for an interpretation. We felt the latter would have less ground to stand on if our translation were as near perfect as possible before being published, and if the whole New Testament came out at once.

Even some of our fellow missionaries thought we were using our time and money foolishly. Finally, the advisability of our work was questioned by two leaders at home who at that time were on the council of the Central American Mission. I am glad to say, however, that the rest of the council backed us to a man.

The other good news is that the representative from the American Bible Society is enthusiastic about publishing all four gospels just as soon as they are completed.

Cam's work expanded but never fell into the rut of routine. In the summer and early fall of 1923, he increased his pastoral activity among many Indian congregations. His letters reveal a growing number of ethnic people turning to faith in Jesus Christ and requesting baptism. Thus the question of the proper scriptural mode for baptism came into focus when these believers formed their own Indian congregation in a new area. Archy strongly supported the Baptist position of immersion. A lifelong Presbyterian, Cam had been sprinkled as an infant and had not allowed this issue to dominate his thinking. Further, his position was always one of "working together without friction." In a September 11, 1923, letter to Luther Rees, Cam wrote:

> Elvira and I are giving messages in Cakchiquel and finding the Gospel of John a big help. There is no getting around it. The Cakchiquels are so very different from our Spanish-speaking brethren. They have a different language, different customs, and they demand a different kind of treatment from those in our Spanish-speaking churches.
>
> With regard to the question of baptism we have agreed to let each believer make his own choice. I wish the same arrangement could have been made for all the congregations in our area. I am told those who want to be immersed have to make other arrangements in some other area or in another church. Why not permit the believers to receive their rite of baptism here among us in their own church rather than going off to some congregation in another town?

> Some Baptist missionaries could be asked to officiate. If this were our position, the issue of mode would never become a point of division. I suggest we pattern our mode as they do in Moody Church, or the Church of the Open Door in Los Angeles.

While Cam actively supported the concept of unity in diversity, he still held strong personal convictions about baptism, as this letter to Chafer shows:

> Archy and I have agreed to put the question of baptismal form up to the applicant and follow his desires. Archy, however, will only immerse. Since I was myself baptized as an infant, I have come to the conclusion that baptism is for believers, and have decided to be baptized as an adult believer. And since studying the question, I have come to the conclusion that the biblical mode for baptism in the New Testament is by pouring.
>
> However, when I made my decision to be baptized in this mode, I found it difficult to find anyone who would accommodate me. I asked Fred Lincoln who was visiting here. At first he hesitated, but said he would take a closer look at the Scriptures. After spending half the night examining the various scripture passages on baptism, he was convinced I held the correct biblical view and baptized me in Guatemala City on Friday.

Little did Cam know, following his baptism in September, that he would soon encounter another baptism—a near baptism of cold steel and a hot bullet.

*The early morning moon setting over Lake Atitlán,
Panajachel*

Chapter Fourteen

Facing Battles

Cameron Townsend and Rev. Dudley, a newly appointed Presbyterian missionary, rode their horses over a wooden bridge. They were about to enter a high point of a boxed-in canyon when they heard it: an excited war whoop. The two men reined in their mounts and turned toward the frenzied yelling.

Stunned to silence, they saw five drunken horsemen racing toward them. The lead man held a flashing machete raised high in the air. Another rider clutched a revolver.

To gain firsthand field experience, Dudley had accompanied Cam to outlying ethnic congregations to preach and perform baptismal services. The men had just left the town of San Martín on their way to the town of Chimaltenango and ultimately to San Antonio, when the five drunken, disheveled men on horseback began to heckle them:

> From what I could tell, the men had been celebrating for at least
> four days and nights without sleep. The only thing that kept them
> going was their booze. When they first rode up they just made a
> general nuisance of themselves. I tried to explain who we were, but

they were in no mood to listen. They rode with us for about a mile laughing and brandishing their liquor bottles while cutting in and out with their horses.

Finally, one of the men went with us while the four men dropped behind and began putting their heads together. I knew they were up to no good. We had just entered a deep canyon, and I knew there was no way to escape them. The one man who rode with us kept telling us that he was a brother and that we were all friends.

When the other riders returned, the drunkest of the men came up on my right side, slid off his horse, and pushed his machete into my face. The one with the drawn revolver came up on my left and aimed his gun also at my face. The man who had gone with us, raised his liquor bottle and said, "Hey Gringo, we want you to drink with us. If you don't drink, we will kill you."

I said, "I thought you told us we were friends—brothers." At that point, he hung his head in mock contrition and said, "I am a brother of deviltry."

After we talked for a few minutes, the man brandishing the machete began to side with us and put away his weapon, as did the man with the revolver. But the man who had gone with us, slid off his horse, grabbed his friend's machete, and waved it in front of my eyes. "You have insulted me by not taking my liquor," he said.

I said, "If I invited you to my house and served you something you didn't like, what would you do?"

"To be courteous, we would accept it," said the man, "but when no one was looking, we would throw it away." Since I still had the cruel-looking machete pointed at my face, and saw no moral infraction here, I said, "Good, give me the bottle." I took it, poured out some rum in my hand and said, "Health!" and then threw it on the ground. Dudley held out both hands and I poured out a much larger amount than mine, and he too threw it on the ground.

This seemed to satisfy the men. Two immediately rode away, while the other three rode with us for about another mile and then left.

Two weeks after this incident, Cam and his brother Paul met the gunman again—this time, however, under very different circumstances. They held a gospel meeting in his home.

Cam's battles were not only physical, but sometimes theological. A conservative Christian, he occasionally spoke out against theories and beliefs emanating from "modernism" that robbed the Bible of its unique position as the inspired Word of God. While deeply concerned about the preservation of orthodox doctrine, Cam never shielded himself from seeing human need. He helped people at their most fundamental level. Throughout his life, he made it a practice to drop what he was doing and give his help to people who requested it.

The morning after Cam returned to San Antonio, the gardener and his wife, a humble Cakchiquel couple, came to him in some distress. Through the woman's tears, Cam learned that their teenage daughter had run away from Antigua and gone to Guatemala City. They feared the worst and asked Cam's help in locating her. He related:

> I was still quite tired from my trip, but this was an urgent matter. And since we had just put in new front springs on the Model T, I drove the couple to Guatemala City. The couple had the address of an inn where they believed the daughter was living. When we inquired at the inn, the proprietor said he didn't know where the girl might be, but I didn't know whether to believe him or not. I told the couple to stay at the inn and watch to see if the daughter might return while I attended to some errands. When I returned later that afternoon, the couple told me the proprietor of the inn had remembered a place that had offered their daughter employment and took us to a cheap hotel in the center of the city.
>
> The proprietor of the inn and the poor mother and father went inside. In a short while they emerged with the daughter beside them. What a shock! Instead of an innocent barefoot Indian girl, there stood a made-up young woman in clothes that were obviously designed to allure men in off the streets. I noticed she even wore a much-prized wristwatch.
>
> It turned out the daughter was living with a man and didn't want to leave. With the mother imploring her daughter to return home with them, we went inside to talk to the man who had given the girl "employment." When I spoke to him, it was obvious he had coerced the girl into prostitution. I had prayed with the girl's mother and father before we began looking for her and continued to pray

silently while speaking to the man and exhorting the girl to return home. The mother, of course, was weeping copious tears. In the midst of my long conversation with the man, God seemed to touch his heart with compassion, and without a struggle or harsh words, he gave up his hold on the girl. It turned out to be a happy ending to a situation that would only have ended in utter ruin for the couple's young daughter. We returned home praising God for answered prayer.

Through this incident, Cam experienced the joy that came from being God's instrument. Another joy he knew was the joy of receiving from others. Those dedicated to being God's instruments were an extension of the kingdom of God, and they brought joy to others. Howard Dinwiddie was such a person. His letters were filled with encouragement and he held out an enlarged vision for world mission to Cam.

Dinwiddie's schedule took him to England for a Victorious Life Conference and then to Ecuador for a fact-finding tour of the Amazon. Traveling left little time for his usual correspondence with Cam. But on September 11, 1923, Dinwiddie wrote a letter from Quito, Ecuador, that Cam never forgot:

My dear Cameron,

You will be pleased to know that through a most providential means I was able to enter fourteen of the seventeen sections of this country. As for travel, take the worst roads you have ever seen in Guatemala and multiply them by ten, and you will have some idea of the road conditions under which we had to travel.

There are no missionaries in ten of the seventeen areas of the country. I found only two tiny beginnings of a gospel work among the ethnic peoples of the Amazon. The Christian and Missionary Alliance is doing a fine work, but my heart bleeds to see the vast areas of people that have never yet heard the Gospel.

The most difficult and dangerous part of the trip began when we left Ambato to cross over into the headwaters of the Amazon valley by way of the River Pastaza. Here many ethnic groups in the dense jungle are engaged in almost incessant inter-tribal warfare. Their savagery against one another is frightening. At the same time, I am always saddened when I realize the impact "civilization" has upon these jungle people who seldom see sunlight. The history of Spanish colonization is filled with blood and oppression. They have every reason to fear those who come in from the outside. Yet, I believe the God who has guided us thus far will continue to be with us through the multiplied and hidden perils of the Amazon jungles.

This letter played an important role in Cam's later decision to approach the Ecuadorian government asking that SIL personnel be allowed to work with the ethnic groups of Ecuador's Amazonian jungle. Dinwiddie never knew how prophetic his words about the hidden perils of bringing the gospel to Amazonia were to become. Among these people groups were the Auca Indians, known as *Waorani*, meaning "people." In January 1956, the Christian church was galvanized by the news that five young American missionaries to the Aucas had been speared to death on a remote river sandbar in Ecuador's Amazonian jungle.

As the work grew, challenges remained in Cam and Elvira's marriage. Both were committed to living what Elvira called the "victorious Christian life," both were risk-takers, and both shared a passion to bring the gospel to disenfranchised peoples. Yet for all their common togetherness, there was also division. Cam and those closest to Elvira hoped her general health, nervousness, and angry temperament would change after her operation in Guatemala City. They did not. Cam, however, continued to believe all her outbursts were the result of her deteriorating health.

In late September 1923 Elvira was faced with the loss of her mother. She wrote L. S. Chafer of her mother's unexpected death, expressing her keen sense of loss. Elvira had enjoyed an intimate and ongoing correspondence with her mother, and the loneliness of that loss seemed to smother her. And though her brother, father, and many friends continued to write, it was never quite the same.

In addition to losing her mother, a month later Elvira received a second shock. In a letter from board member Luther Rees, Elvira found herself the object of an official, but kindly, reprimand for the embarrassment to the "work" she was causing by her too frequent outbursts of temper against Cam and her difficult disposition toward fellow colleagues. The October 3 letter read:

Your physical condition has given us all great concern, and there has been much prayer for you. But information has reached us from a variety of sources that your condition is still causing considerable embarrassment in the work. There is a difference of opinion as to the extent to which you are responsible for your actions. Let me say at once that not a single word, not the slightest intimation of this has come either directly or indirectly from your husband.

Our information is that the present situation cannot continue without serious injury to the work. It seems the enemy is getting the victory in your life. I believe, from past letters, this was your own diagnosis. It is not in my heart to scold. I cannot know the conflicts and trials you have had to bear. But [God] knows and I plead with you to let him give you the victory in this. Don't pity yourself because of your infirmities. I pray that his power may rest upon you. You will need much grace for the future, as some may not be as patient as they should be with you. But remember HIS GRACE IS SUFFI-CIENT.

In the letter Rees admitted he was, perhaps, unwise in writing these things. He ended with a commitment to continue praying for her and offered to help in any way he could.

The block that seemed to keep Elvira from freely and joyfully entering into a happy intimacy with Cam was created, in part, by her cultural background and upbringing. Her answer to Rees's letter on October 13 was polite in tone, and for that time period, amazingly open about why she might be experiencing interpersonal difficulties with Cam and others:

No, I do not think my problem has been altogether the result of my illness. I do not mean to boast when I say that my life in my home, in the office, among my friends, and in Moody Church had always been in harmony with my testimony. When I left for mission service over six years ago, my older brother said, "Elvira, when I become a Christian, I want to live a life like yours." When my best friend learned I was going to work for Mr. Allison in Guatemala, she said, "I hope he isn't a cranky old man, but if he is, there is one thing in your favor. You can get along with anybody."

I do not mention these things to try and justify myself. I know, as well as does my Lord, whom I have seriously grieved, that I am not worthy of a single word of commendation in my actions ever since my marriage.

I know you and others are probably asking, "But why?" I don't know if I know myself. It's hard to explain, but I'll try. Our home in Chicago always had everything in order. I never knew anything at home but the most scrupulous neatness. Even with my father's limited income, our home was always inviting and well kept.

However, for the past four years I have had to fight an all-out war in order to live in a fashion that is at all appealing to me. I cannot stand dirt, disorder, and unsystematic living. Further, I have never understood why, just because we are missionaries, we are often made to live our lives in such conditions. I admit I have nagged when I have wanted things to make our home nicer and wasn't able to get them. I know I have been guilty of having a bitter spirit. Most of the time I have done this out of frustration over our living conditions. Please understand I am not speaking out against Cameron. He is a good husband. However, I have spent a good deal of time in his folks' home and have to say that the way he was brought up was very, very different from the way I was brought up. I therefore do not in any way blame Cameron for the differences in the way we see things. I do know many of my demands are selfish and must yield to God in these matters. I do earnestly pray that my life will be one that is marked by the fruit of the Spirit. With kind Christian greetings, and again thanking you for praying for me. I am, sincerely yours in Him, Elvira.

In the latter days of 1923, Cam seemed to be fighting for a new sense of perspective for himself, Elvira, and his growing responsibilities with the Mission in San Antonio, Panajachel, and the new area of Sololá ("Weeping Willows"), located on a ridge almost seven thousand feet above Lake Atitlán.

At the end of October, Elvira's health and emotional problems had come under the direct care and supervision of Dr. Charles Ainslie and his wife, Ruth. These two gracious servants of God agreed to have Elvira live with them in their home in Guatemala City.

October's end brought a letter from L. S. Chafer that caused Cam great consternation. It said that since Archy Anderson was doing such a fine job at the Bible Institute in Panajachel, the council had decided it was a poor use of personnel to have two missionaries living in that immediate area (even though the council had earlier asked Cam to make such a move). The postscript said a fuller explanation was on its way, but Cam did not wait for the explanation.

Incensed over this decision, Cam told Chafer that he had been given both the responsibility and authority for the Cakchiquel work and believed it was incumbent on him, as a servant of God, to determine the direction of the work. Now the council, miles away, with little firsthand knowledge of the field, had rescinded his field authority without due process. He lost no time in letting Chafer know how he felt. On October 26, 1923, he wrote:

> Dear Mr. Chafer,
> I am writing this from Guatemala City. We came here yesterday. My sister-in-law, Laura, is going to have an operation tomorrow morning. Elvira is boarding at the Ainslie home while the doctor studies her case.
> Now about the matter you mentioned in the last paragraph of your October 12 letter. The letter you said was coming regarding the council's new direction for me has not arrived. It seems from your letter that the council does not want us to work in Sololá or Panajachel.
> Do you realize that we moved all our belongings to Panajachel in March and that we spent considerable money and a lot of hard work fixing up the house? Furthermore, if we don't live and work in Panajachel, where do you plan for us to go? We have turned everything in San Antonio over to Paul, Laura, and the others there who are carrying on the work very nicely.
> Do you realize also that Archy Anderson has his hands more than full with the responsibilities at the Bible Institute every other month and conference work on the off months all over the Cakchiquel area?
> We have been working out what I consider a fine plan for the overall work here. Brother Paul is to look after the work in San Antonio in a pastoral way. I am to open up the field of Sololá. Archy is to have five conferences every other month and is looking after the Bible Institute, which is a growing work. I am to deal with

national workers who are going out to all of the fields and continue work on the translation of the Scriptures.

The move you and the council propose would likely destroy the unity of this plan and split us up just when we are getting along so beautifully. I point these things out for your consideration. I am willing to be moved wherever the Lord would have me, but I would rather have the calls from the council a little less erratic. I do not want to move backward. Also, I want to be in a place where the demands for me to speak Cakchiquel are greater than they are in San Antonio.

I would like to work in the three different towns that make up the Sololá area for several more months to fully open up this area, be of help to Archy, and to exert an influence in the Bible Institute. If at the close of this time the council feels that Archy or someone else can attend to the work without me, I would then rather settle in the town of Comalapa. I have spoken to Elvira and she is willing to go there just as soon as she regains her strength.

I have discussed some important matters in this letter. I realize you have a difficult job, and I don't want to make it harder. At the same time, we must express ourselves clearly and at all times seek the greatest good for the work.

I want to ask you an important question which I hope you will answer. The question is this: Are there any other large faith mission agencies whose work on the field is directed by its home council? And are there any mission agencies who are doing a substantial work whose missionaries are themselves not organized on the field, and are not being directed by those on the field?

My belief is that the Home Council should direct everything at home, but the various field organizations, now piloted by our general secretary, should have the ultimate word of authority on the field. I beg you to work out some such plan. I have written to the other council members about this. I now, after much prayer and study of the problem, make a formal protest directly to you. It is a protest from which I can not retract. Yours in real love and earnest prayer, Cameron.

Surveying the San Antonio area

Chapter Fifteen
Forging Field Policies

It was May 1924. In New York harbor, Lewis Sperry Chafer stood on the deck of an ocean liner that would take him on a trip to England, Scotland, and continental Europe. As the gangway was pulled away and the big tugs began to maneuver the ship out of its birth, he opened a telegram. Believing it to be a message of good will for his trip, he had put it into his coat pocket to read at his leisure. The telegram was from Cameron Townsend. As Chafer read the message, his face turned white and he felt sick to his stomach. Townsend had tendered his resignation from the Central American Mission. Of that moment, Chafer wrote:

> Had the telegram reached me ten minutes earlier, I am not sure but what I would have abandoned the ship. But then it was too late. I called back over the water to Mr. Smith with instructions for him to wire certain things to Mr. Rees and then went to my room and prayed. I don't know when I had a more difficult burden to carry. This stayed with me during the voyage. But when I reached England, God gave me the assurance the problems could be solved without my assistance. I am now rejoicing that it has indeed been adjusted.

resignation

Cam sent his resignation for two reasons. One was his difficulty with Article 3 of the Central American Mission's "Principles and Practices" for field missionaries, the last sentence of which read, "The missionaries are members, not agents of the Mission, and the direction of the work at home and in Central America is recognized as being under the executive council." When dealing with individual missionaries and public relations, Cam conceded that the "final" word should be the responsibility of the home council. He had urged them to work out those details. But the field work was a different matter:

> I believe the missionaries on the field should have general supervision of the work in their respective fields as well as the final word in all matters touching the ethnic church and general planning of the work. I believe also the allocation of missionaries and direction of expatriate workers should be done in cooperation with the field organization and the field organization should act as advisers to the executive council.

Particularly puzzling now to Cam were those early letters from Chafer, on behalf of the Central American Mission Home Council, giving him authority to act as director of all mission activities in San Antonio and Panajachel. Chafer had specifically urged him to "claim this authority," and the council would depend upon his judgment when decisive steps had to be taken.

The second issue that troubled Cam was the council's decision regarding Elvira's direct involvement in Panajachel's mission work. After Cam opposed the council's response to his decision to move to Panajachel, Chafer, on November 8, 1923, wrote a response:

> The council's desire is to help you in every way. We have no notion of directing as to where Mrs. Townsend should go. Because of the living conditions in San Antonio, we thought it best for her to remain in Guatemala City and continue her treatment under Dr. Ainslie. We want you to know that we have not at any time intended to disturb your work. This is in your hands. We are greatly pleased with the division of the work as you have outlined it. The council is with you, heart and soul. Be assured of our unbounded affection and love and prayer for you on the part of all of us in the council.

However, in another letter, the council seemed to give Cam authority over Elvira's situation with one hand, and take it away with the other. Chafer wrote:

> We know Panajachel is most restful and attractive. We wish we were free to encourage you to remain there indefinitely and make it the center of your work. The council is aware that they have given you as much latitude as possible in working out this problem. You are very much in our hearts and in our prayers, but we are counting on you to avoid allowing any difficulties with Elvira to be repeated in Panajachel that occurred in San Antonio. For medical and other reasons, the council advises that Elvira not be involved with any direct ministry.

In yet another letter, Chafer pointedly urged Cam to conform to the council's wishes. Based on Cam's report that Elvira was doing well, gaining weight, and contributing to a happy home life, Chafer responded:

> Cameron, I am happy for the report that Elvira's condition is much improved and that you say she is happy in Panajachel. I know both of you have lived and worked under great difficulties and extreme conditions and you now feel these will be reversed at this new location. However, the council still hesitates over allowing Elvira to remain at Panajachel. We feel it would be much better if she were located in an area outside the work. You could then go out alone to the various mission stations. We must have much greater assurance that there will never again be a repeat of her problem. You know our love for you is great, but you must cooperate with us in protecting the testimony of the mission field.

During Chafer's overseas trip, Luther Rees assumed Chafer's duties as General Secretary. Attempting to forestall Cam's resignation from the mission, Rees began a vigorous correspondence with Cam throughout the month of June. Most of those letters are lost. However, in one letter from Cam to Chafer dated June 19 and another to Rees dated June 24, the Central American Mission proved to be patient with Cam and his unwillingness to compromise his idealism. The first letter read:

> I have been praying much about what you have written about my
> directing the Cakchiquel work. I think I can tell you that what you
> desire has been arranged. As you say, we must work together without
> friction. Last week we all got together here in San Antonio and talked
> it over as a group—Paul and Laura, Signe Norrlin, Archy Anderson,
> the Beckers, Elvira and myself. Our aim is to have a close fellowship
> with one another in the work, and have in place a system in which
> you, as general secretary, can work more satisfactorily.

In his letter to Rees, Cam wrote:

> I can't tell you how much I appreciated your last four letters. Your
> encouragement means much to me at this time. I feel, as you do,
> that God has brought us together, and I hope I can continue to work
> with the Central American Mission. I think Paul and Archy sent you
> a copy of the agreement we drew up (as the Cakchiquel Department
> of the Central American Mission). If this is endorsed by the council,
> there will be no need for me to resign. I am beginning to realize the
> mistakes I have made in dealing with new missionaries. I have
> pushed them forward too fast. Some, I discover, don't need to be
> pushed as much as I thought.
>
> As to the matter of a field organization, I know that distance makes
> it difficult for us to get together. But I do urge the council to take
> steps toward establishing a field secretary even though such a per-
> son's authority would be limited and subject to the appeal of the
> council. At the same time, I understand the difficulties you and others
> have mentioned. I guess, therefore, I will have to withdraw from the
> strong stand I have taken on this matter. I do feel, however, I must
> continue to petition you on the matter of recognizing our Cakchiquel
> Committee, and if you can go further, to encourage its growth into
> an all-Indian committee.
>
> On another matter, Elvira's health has greatly improved, and I
> don't think allowing her to participate in a public service now and
> then would hurt her. I wish the council would permit it.

The matter of health—Cam's this time—soon was of concern to the
workers of the newly formed "Cakchiquel Department." While in Panajachel in November 1923, he came down with a severe case of mumps.

So severe, in fact, that Archy, who sat up with him all one night battling his temperature of 104.2, joked later that he was thinking about a funeral sermon for him. Cam's sickness was so grave that a rumor had spread throughout the area that he had died. Cam recovered after a month's struggle against the debilitating disease. Dr. Ainslie considered Cam's run-down condition severe enough to recommend that he and Elvira return to the States for a year's rest in order to regain their strength. Cam's immediate response was an emphatic *no,* as to do so would mean giving up his language study and the translation work.

Paul and Laura had also been sick. Paul's illness was severe and prolonged enough to require a week's hospitalization. When the Mission council reviewed Paul's condition, they considered reassigning him to a more healthful area of the country. Cam's concern grew. To lose Paul would seriously hinder the work in San Antonio.

Besides battling illnesses and nursing a broken foot (due to a high-speed motorcycle accident), Cam, from 1924 to 1926, became entangled in yet more policy issues. Abe Bishop, elder mission statesman for the Central American Mission in Guatemala, strongly favored integrating congregations of Spanish-speaking *ladino* and ethnic believers. He did concede, however, that the "Indian" church indeed had special needs and in a July letter said that in some instances, two chapels—one for *ladinos* and another for the Indians—might be advisable. If this were the case, he suggested, men from both congregations should be selected as elders. But, generally, he opposed the notion of separate churches. "After all," he reasoned, "the scriptural notion identifies the Church as one body, a 'new man' composed from two discordant elements—Jew and non-Jew. And because of Christ's sacrifice, all barriers to fellowship and ministry were abolished."

Cam continued, nevertheless, to press for separate congregations for ethnic believers. For almost three years, this issue was vigorously debated by the Central American Mission council and became known as the *"Ladino* Indian Question," and by some as "The Townsend Proposal." At first glance, it appeared that Cam was a segregationist. But his argument for separate congregations was always linguistic and cultural, never racial. He reasoned that as long as the ethnic church was considered an object for expatriate mission work, there would be little opportunity for the church's religious growth or self-assurance. He wanted the ethnic church out from under the control of the aggressive

Spanish-speaking *ladino* community. Then it could gain enough breathing room to define its own religious and cultural life. Cam took Moody Church as his model. They had an English-speaking congregation and also sponsored an Italian congregation with Italian-speaking pastors and elders.

The heated debate had each side vying for its own turf. The result was three years of infighting and open suspicion of others' views, taking a serious physical and emotional toll on Cam and many of his colleagues.

During this time Cam wrote an insightful biography of Antonio Bac, the man he called the "great Cakchiquel evangelist." When he wasn't writing, translating, or preparing long letters for the council, Cam occasionally took time to explore and identify new verb forms in Cakchiquel. He also studied archaeology on an amateur level. On August 15, 1924, he wrote the Smithsonian Institution in Washington D.C.:

> Six years ago I wrote to tell you of a hill in Western Honduras, three days by muleback from the ruins of Copán. When I was there, I found the hill full of fossils. At that time, I sent you two of the smaller specimens with a description of the hill and surrounding district (also rich in fossils). I wonder if you ever sent anyone to study that field? I believe it would be well worthwhile.
>
> Recently, while traveling through the mountains between Santa Catarina Ixtahuacan and Santa Lucia Utatlán in this state, I came across a ledge of rock about sixty feet high at the center of which were carved in figures about eight inches high and in a straight line, some interesting characters. I enclose them for your consideration. I had to climb a tree to be able to read them clearly. The place is inaccessible except by ropes from above. Can you tell me the significance of these characters?

About a month later, Cam received a reply from the Smithsonian acknowledging his letter and the receipt of the specimens. As to the significance of the strange characters, the Assistant Curator of Old World Archeology said, "The characters are Latin and are meaningless, possibly the name of some ambitious man who hoped thus to immortalize himself by such an inscription."

Especially encouraging to Cam at this time were letters from home. His father and mother were faithful correspondents who missed both sons more than they liked to admit. Occasionally, however, their true feelings leaked out. Cam's deaf father, who always signed his letters "Father Townsend," ended his September 14, 1924, letter with:

> It will be nice when by God's grace we all arrive in our eternal home nevermore to part. There will be no sickness or sorrow nor deafness there, and nothing to vex us. In the meantime, we can't tell when Christ will return for his people. When he does come, may he find us all ready and watching. May God prosper all you do in your labor of love, and grant you every needed blessing.

Cam's mother's letters reveal that she shared a common faith with her husband, but held sometimes opposite theological and cultural views. While Cam's father appeared to be more serious in his faith, his mother frequently found something humorous about those who took themselves too seriously, as this paragraph in her November 9, 1924, letter shows: "It may not be biblical to have bobbed hair, but it sure is convenient. It hasn't been so very long since George Washington and his gentleman friends were going around with their hair tied at the back. Just think, Cameron, how you would look with your hair tied back that way! Goodbye and may God keep you both. Your mother's prayers."

If ever there was a time in Cam's life when he needed his mother's prayers, it was now. At the end of November 1924, Cam received a short notice from Archy Anderson that he was resigning his post as dean of the Robinson Bible Institute. Cam informed Chafer:

> Archy advised me a week before he planned to leave. When I asked him to reconsider, he said it was too late, that he had already agreed to teach at a new school in Huehuetenango. I had to insist, almost roughly, for him to agree to finish out this year's work, and then he stayed for only two more weeks.
>
> I am not objecting to his move. It may be of the Lord. But I think he should have stayed with us until someone else was in place, especially now when we are starting new classes in January. I think this all could have been avoided had we had better management

here on the field. Archy left in the best of spirits. He roomed with us for the last three months and seemed to enjoy himself greatly. I love that fellow, and pray that the Lord might teach him steadiness from Mr. Toms. Archy is a remarkable teacher. I wish some of his teaching skills would have rubbed off on me, but they didn't. In the meantime, I am busy with language work. The Gospel of Luke is just about ready for its first revision. This whole process of translation becomes more and more interesting as we move along. It would go much faster if you could send someone to fill Archy's shoes at the Bible Institute, thus freeing me from the day-to-day administrative details.

Cam's translation work was bound to his vision of making the Scriptures available for the Cakchiquels. Only well after the task had begun did both Cam and Elvira realize the complexity of the language they had chosen to translate. Without realizing it, they were following in the footsteps of some of the greatest translators in history—like Jerome, Erasmus, Wycliffe, Tyndale, Luther, and Cloverdale who often worked in the thick of some kind of theological or political controversy. Like Cam, the heart of these and hundreds of other unnamed translators was their commitment to the "work of God, to which nothing ought to be preferred." Likewise, Cam was convinced of the extraordinary power of the "Book" to change and enrich individual thinking, as well as the thinking of entire nations.

The year 1925 began well enough. On January 8, Cam received a warm affirmation from L. S. Chafer on the publication of the Gospel of John in Cakchiquel by the American Bible Society:

This translation of the Gospel of John done in diglot is truly amazing. I feel unable to express adequately just how I feel about this fine work. It will be a great advantage for the Indian believers and preachers to have an accurate translation of God's Word. I appreciate the thoughtfulness that went into the design and printing of this valuable Book. I showed it to Mr. Bishop and he was filled with wonder and delight. May the Lord guide you and your co-workers in every step you take. You are in our prayers.

This encouraging word and the drive to "do the work of God" kept Cam going through the dark months of 1925. During this time the controversy continued over who had authority over the field—the executive council or a field organization. And still awaiting official ratification was the forming of the Cakchiquel Department. There was also the shortage of money for Cam and Elvira's personal support. At one point in early 1925, Cam wrote that they were down to eating nothing but tortillas and beans.

But then came two surprise letters. The first, dated January 13, 1925, from L. L. Legters, had far-reaching effects for Cam, forming the beginnings of Wycliffe Bible Translators and the Summer Institute of Linguistics:

My dear brother Townsend,

You have been much on my mind, and I have been wondering how you are getting along and what you are doing. I have sent you a questionnaire asking you to tell me your needs and the needs of the Indians of Guatemala. Please write fully, as I would like to use it for publication.

I have just returned from a trip to South America [Peru and Brazil]. It was some trip. We carried our own food and were in the wild interior for more than five months. Time after time I wished you could have been with me.

Since my return, and without solicitation, the Lord has given me the support for five men for the work in South America. I wish you could write me once in a while and let me know if in any way I can be of assistance to you. It may be that the Lord could still use me in some way to help send in funds and interest people in working among Indian peoples.

I am trying to raise a fund that can be used for the publication of books. I believe one of the great needs today is to get information before people, and the best way is through readable books. I leave on Friday for a six-month speaking tour in St. Louis, Los Angeles, and up the Pacific coast to find men and money for Indian work.

The second letter came at a time when Cam had no money to buy food, and nothing with which to pay the national workers. Cal Hibbard, archivist for the Townsend papers, friend, and personal secretary for Cameron Townsend, notes that:

> This letter is one of two "famous" miracle letters Uncle Cam often spoke about to illustrate how God provided in a time of great monetary need.
>
> Uncle Cam was in the habit of paying his national workers a month in advance so as to avoid a situation where he might come to the end of the month and not have money to pay the workers. On this particular occasion, Cam came to the end of the month with no funds to pay the workers for the following month. He told the workers that the next day would be their last day of work. However, on the day he told them this sad news, the enclosed letter arrived.
>
> What is remarkable about this letter is how it was addressed. It simply said: "William Cameron Townsend, San Antonio, Central America." As Cam looked at this letter, he was amazed it had reached him. There are many towns in Central America with the name San Antonio, and several in Guatemala. God's hand was clearly in this matter since it arrived on the very day it was needed. When he told this story in later years, Cam said, "This was the first time this man had given a monetary gift to the work. It proved once again that God can and does provide for his children."

The letter and gift were from A. E. Forbes, a ninety-year-old man from St. Louis, dated February 1, 1925: "Dear Mr. W. Cameron Townsend, I am enclosing a check for $500. I managed to scrape together this amount for your work. I have lost money for the last four years, but the Lord's work comes first, since everything I have comes from him."

Soon after this came, so did the news of Lewis Sperry Chafer's resignation as general secretary of the Central American Mission Council. Though still a member of the council, Chafer's energies moved toward establishing what was to become Dallas Theological Seminary.

Replacing Chafer was Karl Hummel who was, in Cam's words, "a prince of a fellow." There is no evidence of Hummel's personal thoughts on Cam, but within weeks after taking over his duties, Karl wrote a letter to the council to answer Cam's persistent correspondence on the issue of who should have final authority. Among other things, he wrote, "I deplore some of the statements Cameron Townsend has made regarding the right to have final authority on the field."

Cause and effect are difficult to determine, but it appears the months of struggle took their toll on Cam's physical health. At the end of May 1925, no longer able to hide his run-down condition even from himself, he returned, without Elvira, to his parents' home in Southern California.

The Townsends on furlough in California

Chapter Sixteen
Harmony at Last

The pressure of day-to-day duties, the infighting around his plan for a new field organization, and the weight of responsibility for developing new geographical areas of ministry all suddenly crashed in on 29-year-old Cameron Townsend. Elvira was convinced he should leave when she saw him nodding off to sleep in the saddle of his horse during a short trip. Dr. Ainslie and Paul were also aware of Cam's emotional weariness, and they all shared a common concern for him to, in Ainslie's words, "slow down and get as much rest as possible."

Elvira immediately wrote Central American Mission's new general secretary, Karl Hummel, of Cam's departure for California in May 1925, and asked him not to book speaking engagements for Cam during his time in the States. She informed Hummel that Signe Norrlin would move from San Antonio to stay with her at Panajachel, also informing him that she planned to continue translation work along with assuming Cam's responsibilities. Cam, too, wrote Karl of his "sudden departure," saying he was emotionally and physically fatigued and needed a couple of months to regain his composure. Elvira would not join him in Santa Ana, California, until the end of August.

If Cam thought problems wouldn't follow him to California, he was mistaken. Mail came with the same regularity and emotional impact in

California as it had in Guatemala. And Karl Hummel lost no time in exercising the full weight of his position as secretary to pursue the question of a field organization. On June 17, 1925, he wrote Cam an uncompromising and somewhat condescending letter on the question of "final authority":

> The question of "final authority" is at the crux of the difficulty currently facing our mission. You must constantly keep before you, Brother Cameron, not other missions, but rather the way *our* mission was raised up of God. It was not started on the field by Hudson Taylor or George Allan, but had its birth in Dallas. God first raised up the council, and then the missionaries. It's evident neither can get along without the other. But I am sure you will recognize the order the Lord has established for the Central American Mission.
>
> You say the missionaries must have the authority [on the field] for decisions that directly affect them. On the other hand, the council members feel they are the custodians of the policies and principles established by our founder Dr. Scofield and [other] Central American Mission founders. The council feels, therefore, they must have the right to maintain this [historic] order.

The day after receiving this letter, Cam was hit on yet another front. This time it was the question of separate Indian and *ladino* congregations. On July 18, Cam wrote a six-page letter to the council in an attempt to clarify his position and correct what he felt were "inaccurate" statements people had made on this issue. First he corrected the notion that he favored completely separate congregations. Cam's proposal was for the church session in each town to have its separate department of Indian elders to manage their own affairs. He further proposed that this department should meet regularly with the *ladino* department to consider their mutual interests.

Cam's detractors had accused him of introducing disunity and division, and of trying to create two classes of people. But, over all, Cam wanted unity and equality. To achieve this, he wanted to develop two departments in one local church congregation. With bold uppercase lettering, Cam again stressed that he made this proposal on the basis of LANGUAGE, not race:

When we are talking about fellow believers, the issue of *race* hardly enters into this question. We should constantly endeavor to work toward the elimination of any racial bias. But in our attempt to reach the ethnic peoples, we must be sensitive to reaching them in their *own mother-tongue language.* When the first century church council met in Jerusalem to consider those non-Jews who were coming to faith in Christ, they agreed that the non-Jews did not first have to become Jews before they could enter into fellowship. In the same way, the ethnic Christians do not have to give up their unique cultural identity and become *ladinos* in order to become "good" Christians.

So passionately did Cam feel about this issue, he once again considered resigning. In a letter to his friend Luther Rees, Cam wrote:

The reopening of the Indian question by Fred Lincoln and others creates continual uncertainty and difficulty, plus it is wearing and causing me no little worry. I gave my life for Guatemala's Indian peoples and I don't want it to be worn out by endless discussions. I may be a misfit, and my presence in the work may be causing trouble, but why did everything go so nicely when Mr. Bishop was in charge of the *ladino* work?

Everything worthwhile costs, and reaching the Indians with the gospel is costing, but it must be done. I do not believe we can go back on our arrangement without losing efficiency. I would rather go to some new field than have this happen.

Not mentioned in this letter to Rees was the legislation concerning Cam's authority. Cam had been given authority by Bishop, but it was not being recognized by his colleagues. Yet, Cam pushed for all Central American Mission missionaries to have the right to vote on proposed changes in the mission's by-laws and constitution. In this way, reasoned Cam, the missionaries would feel more like members of the mission. This important concept was one Cam incorporated years later in the formation of Wycliffe Bible Translators and the Summer Institute of Linguistics.

When Cam encountered a problem, he faced it directly, almost physically. There was something profoundly elemental in his character. He knew what he wanted or what needed to be done to accomplish his vision. There was little need in his mind for philosophizing. His home-spun logic and faith in God were enough to push him through to a conclusion of his ideas.

However, when others held an opposing view with equal conviction, sometimes Cam gained the advantage by threatening to resign. This proves a difficult strategy if both sides play by those same rules. And this is exactly what happened over Cam's desire to have an ethnic and *ladino* department in a single church, each being meaningfully minis-tered to in their respective languages.

On October 8, 1925, ten of Cam's colleagues, led by Fern Houser, signed the following petition and sent it to Karl Hummel:

> The plan to develop separate churches is bringing in its wake the difficulties we feared and worse. We cannot understand how you dear brethren can be so deaf to our repeated warnings and appeals and have completely ignored us in making your decisions.
>
> We can ill afford to lose such valuable workers from the field as the Lincolns [they had tendered their resignation as of October 27] and some of the very best in the mission [who vigorously opposed the "Townsend Proposal"]. This issue has become acute and unbear-able. At a meeting on the third of October in Guatemala City, the undersigned missionaries, along with all the principal national work-ers connected with the work of the Central American Mission, dis-cussed the Townsend Proposal. The result was that all of the workers have threatened a strike. They said if Brother Townsend returns and continues to separate the Indians from the different congregations, thus making two congregations, they will refuse to continue in the work.
>
> The Indians themselves do not want to be separated from the *ladinos*, nor do the *ladinos* desire to be separated from the Indians. All of us are united in our feelings on this matter, and we send this as another PROTEST in the hope that your eyes may be opened to see the danger ahead if these conditions continue.
>
> Unless you brethren of the council take a definite stand and revoke your permission and recognition of this movement by not later than the middle of December, we will act on our own responsibility. This is in no way intended as a slight or depreciation of our dear brethren

who are seeking to reform this department; but on the other hand, if they are willing to stand for and practice what the Gospel teaches, viz., unity and not separation, we shall enjoy sweet fellowship.

Clearly, this issue had an injurious effect among the missionaries of the Central American Mission. The work in Guatemala was not in disarray, but Cam believed there was a spiritual schism and a disturbing lack of community among his colleagues. This issue, like no other, had galvanized the missionaries and created rivalry. Instead of working toward a common cause, the preoccupation was to protect their own turf. Rev. R. R. Gregory, who spent thirteen weeks in Central America during this difficult period, observed:

> The outstanding impression I received during my thirteen weeks in Central America was the lack of cooperation among the missionaries. Each was working in his own little field as if he were independent of the other missionaries of the same mission. My impression was that I was dealing with many different mission bodies instead of one whose central office was in Dallas.
>
> For there to be unity and greater efficiency in the work, I suggest a forum whereby the missionaries can get together to discuss their problems, and reach consensus. If this is not done, individuals will continue to harbor misunderstandings. Such harboring is deadly to mission work.

Cam agreed completely with Rev. Gregory's assessment. He pushed for a conference where missionaries and council members alike could participate in frank discussions about the issues of concern. Cam recommended this conference be held outside of Guatemala—preferably in Dallas—and to Karl Hummel, he wrote:

> It would be wise to have as many as possible attend an open discussion about our problems. The Indian-*ladino* issue should not sidetrack us from the main responsibility of our work. You understand that here on the field some of us get into a rut. We overemphasize our own problems and fail to see the other person's point of view. At least this is true for myself. For this reason, I hope we can have these discussions in a more neutral place like Dallas.

Both Cam and Elvira were proud to be associated with the Central American Mission, its members, and its ministry among the people of Central America. And they longed for a restored peace and unity among the membership and council. This desire for solidarity, Cam's basic dislike of "domestic" quarrels, and the combination, perhaps, of his physical illness and emotional burnout, prompted Cam's letter of concession. The letter, dated November 28, 1925, is remarkable for its brevity:

> Dear Karl,
>
> Out of love and deep appreciation for Mr. Rees and others of the council, and in hopes of relieving the tension on the field, I want to state that whatever the proposed delegation to the field may decide regarding the *Ladino*-Indian question, I will stand by your decision. Praying for closer fellowship in our mission.

During the endless debates and misunderstandings over the "Townsend Proposal," Cam himself remained remarkably composed. He had left the field because of physical and emotional exhaustion, but in his letters he vigorously attempted to refute misunderstanding between his colleagues, and he continued his lifelong practice of focusing on issues, never on personalities. In the large body of his life's letters, there is no hint of personal attack or resentment leveled against a colleague.

Many years later, when Cam was coming under personal attack by the religious right for offering hospitality to missionaries and religious workers from non-evangelical denominations, Marjory Nyman, a long-time Wycliffe member, asked him how he could be so calm and composed in the face of such bitter personal criticism. With a whimsical smile, Cam said, "I rest and have confidence in Psalm 119:165 that says, 'Great peace have they which love thy law: and nothing shall offend them'" (KJV). And this peaceful presence was especially evident in both Cam's and Elvira's correspondence during these difficult months.

The Central American Mission council finally agreed to a special conference. This conference would be a forum for missionaries to freely voice their concerns. But rather than a Dallas meeting, the council sent a special delegation to Guatemala to deal with, among other things, the Townsend Proposal. Cam and Elvira, Karl Hummel, and fellow council member Rev. H. MacKenzie from Toronto, Canada, sailed from New

Orleans on December 19, 1925, and arrived in Guatemala two days before Christmas.

The first hints of the meeting's proceedings came from Elvira on January 15, 1926, when she wrote to a friend in Dallas: "We arrived back in time to have a lovely turkey dinner with Paul and Laura and Dr. and Mrs. Ainslie. It is good to be back in Guatemala. In some ways, it seems like my very own country. I haven't been home to Panajachel yet. Cameron and Karl Hummel are out on an evangelistic tour. I am here in Guatemala City waiting for his return."

Other than that, no further letters supply the exact details of those special meetings beginning on January 1. At January's end, Cam wrote a general letter telling his constituents that a new working agreement had been reached:

> In most of the territories where we were working, we were responsible for only the ethnic minorities who for so long have been neglected. Other Central American Mission missionaries of the Guatemala City Center were responsible for most of the *ladino* or Spanish-speaking peoples. Now, under a new system agreed upon in this last conference, Elvira and I have the responsibility for the Indians and also the Spanish-speaking peoples in the territory assigned to us.
>
> This means added responsibility as the two groups of people must have their separate pastors, elders, and chapels since they each have a distinct language, customs, and social standing. We covet your prayers for these two groups of people.

It appears that Cam indeed won his original proposal. But it wasn't until the five-page, legal-size *Report of the Deputation to Guatemala Representing the Council of the Central American Mission* was printed that the full story of what had transpired was recorded.

Both expatriate workers and ethnic and *ladino* workers attended the meetings that began with a New Year's Eve watch night service. Devotional and prayer meetings Friday through Sunday followed. Then came the formal business meetings.

The council met with those of opposing views on the Indian-*ladino* issue, finding two equally divided groups with strong and sincere opinions. As the team from Dallas listened and asked questions, they identified several areas of misunderstanding and guided the groups, suffering from strained relations and personal prejudices, into concili-ation. This resulted in an agreement allowing the missionaries freedom to pursue different policies and methods within their own assigned dis-tricts. Cam's "field organization" idea was reintroduced and after thor-ough discussion, unanimously accepted.

These members of the first 1926 field organization (which continues to today) included: Fred Lincoln, field chairman (after he withdrew his resignation); Fern Houser; Herbert Toms; Abe Bishop; and Cam Town-send. Regarding this, page three of the report reads:

> It is the hope of this deputation that Mr. Karl Hummel's present visit to the other four [Central American] Republics may be the occasion of bringing similar organizations and plans of cooperative working among the smaller groups of those fields and of imparting to the missionaries there the same inspiration and hope that manifestly came to the missionaries in Guatemala through the adjustments and new arrangements.

These "new arrangements" also included a field superintendent to over-see the entire field work. The superintendent was to give leadership in unifying mission policies and methods, and stimulating and strength-ening expatriate missionaries, national workers, and national churches.

The report concluded with great praise and thanksgiving to God. Reconciliation and unity of purpose had averted the division. In his March 1 letter to Luther Rees, Cam wrote: "I suppose you have heard all about the conference. We praise God for the outcome. In every way, God wrought miracles. It now seems like a great calm after a bad storm. Everything is so very peaceful. How blessed it is to be able to work together when there is harmony among our fellow workers. Praise God there is harmony at last."

In America, 1926 was a year of "firsts." Clarence Birdseye and George A. Hormel revolutionized the American palate by introducing frozen vegetables and flavor-sealed canned ham. The first commercial postal plane took flight from Dearborn, Michigan, with Charles Lindbergh on subsequent mail planes. Richard Byrd and Floyd Bennett made the first overflight of the North Pole. For $75, people in New York could make a three-minute transatlantic phone call to London. And Lee De Forest demonstrated that sound could be attached to a motion picture.

In the summer of 1926, Cameron Townsend wasn't too interested in the motion picture industry. He was, however, captivated by the growing field of aviation; and when he learned that five U.S. Army planes, on a good-will trip to South America, were to land in Guatemala City, he was among the welcoming party and introduced himself to Major Herbert Dargue, the commander.

Among the first questions Cam asked was whether planes could be used to reach isolated Indians in the jungles of South America, and how much it would cost. Major Dargue said he saw no reason why planes couldn't be used for such a service. Later he sent Cam a detailed report and estimate of the cost of purchasing and operating a plane. Now Cam would need to consider finding a pilot. Of this Paul Townsend wrote: "L. L. Legters had just returned from his famous trip to Amazonia and was telling Cam that the only way to reach the isolated jungle peoples of Amazonia was by airplane. The two men knew of a biplane they called 'The Bird.' They talked about exchanging some property I had in Long Beach, California, for The Bird and teaching me to fly."

Like many of Cam's ideas, using planes, along with having radio contact with translators living among remote ethnic peoples, would have to wait. Not until 1946, with the birth of Jungle Aviation and Radio Service (JAARS), would this idea be fleshed out. Yet the faith and the imagination for this significant support ministry was born in 1926.

Cam's other dream was to one day work in that formidable area—Amazonia. In August 1926, Cameron Townsend received the Pioneer Mission Agency's report of Legters's second exploratory trip into Brazil. Clearly the report had a profound effect on him:

> My heart burned within me when I read Mr. Legters's account of his trip to South America. How I would like to go! However, one can't be in two places at once, and there is still much to do here. Our frontiers seem to lie to the north in Mexico. And, God willing, just as soon as the Cakchiquel New Testament is completed and published, I expect to make an exploratory trip among the Lacandones in southern Mexico. They are reported to be quite wild and some say even dangerous. Nevertheless, they too must have the gospel.

"Pathfinder and Missionary Explorer," L. L. Legters

Chapter Seventeen
A Formidable Challenge

Leonard Livingston Legters isn't listed among the names in National Geographic's index of early twentieth-century explorers of wilderness areas. Yet Legters and the party that set out on June 7, 1926, into the wilderness of Brazil's Mato Grosso State (today called Xingu National Park) seeking to locate ethnic people groups, were pioneer explorers in a sea of unknown dangers.

In the the January 1966 issue of *National Geographic*, Harald Schultz described the upper Xingu region as "the last fortress of primitive man." Schultz observed, from the comfort of a DC-3, the area that Legters and his party explored on foot, muleback, and bark canoe. He reported:

> We are flying toward the remote heart of Brazil, the upper Xingu region. Far to the south, the Mato Grosso [meaning "thick forest"] Plateau gives rise to five major rivers. Trickling across vast savanna, coursing through stands of towering forest, gushing into foaming rapids, they finally merge in the lower jungle to form the Xingu River some one thousand winding miles from its confluence with the Amazon. The immense wilderness separating these rivers is the hidden world ringed by once dreaded tribes: Chavante, Tshikáo, Tshukahamae, Cayapo [and more].[1]

Until 1961, Xingu Park was a vast, unprotected area of 8,500 square miles, home to at least sixteen of Brazil's ethnic peoples. In 1926, the Brazilian government hadn't fully addressed the needs of its many ethnic tribal peoples in this vast Amazon area. As late as 1935, the Amazon was referred to by explorers and others as the *terra viridis incognita*, "the green unknown." This unknown area excited land speculators, rubber, oil, and diamond hunters, as well as travelers like British explorer Colonel Fawcett and his son who, in 1925, vanished while searching for a "city of crystal" in the "green unknown," somewhere near the headwaters of the Xingu River.

Undeterred, Legters took his own seventeen-year-old son, David, into this very area just a year later. Unlike Fawcett, Legters's epic journey over rugged land, deep jungle, and long meandering rivers was in order to eventually give tribal peoples the opportunity to learn about a heavenly "crystal river": "the river of the water of life, as clear as crystal, flowing from the throne of God" (Rev. 22:1).

Legters called himself a "pathfinder and missionary explorer"—in the manner of the Scottish explorer and his missionary namesake, David Livingston. His trip plans began in 1924. Legters received an official invitation from the founder of Brazil's first Indian Service, General Marshal Cándido Mariano de Silva Rondón, to visit the Xingu River district.[2] "This area," said General Rondón, "holds one of the greatest opportunities for Indian work in the state of Mato Grosso."

Because he had been denied governmental permission to conduct a language survey[3] of eastern and northeastern Bolivia, Legters accepted General Rondón's invitation to identify the specific Indian groups living in the headwaters region of the Xingu River. With his son, David, W. E. Halverson, missionary with the Inland South American Union, Jauaquin, a guide provided by the Brazilian government, two men to care for the mules and oxen, and seven other Indian men who came along as canoe makers and rowers, Legters's party was complete.

On June 7, 1926, they began the trip from Corumbá, a frontier town straddling the Bolivian-Brazilian border. The party journeyed up the Paraguay, the Sao Louronco, and Cuyabá rivers to the capital of Mato Grosso, Cuyabá City. "This," said Legters, "was the staging area from which all expeditions into the geographic heart of Brazil began":

After buying supplies and organizing our train of oxen and mules, we started out for the Xingu country three hundred air miles to the northeast. But our foot trail was much more circuitous. The first obstacle was a twisting rugged trail set between rough hills that led to a pass a thousand feet above sea level to the great plateau of South America. We first traveled two hundred and twenty-five miles northwest to the government Indian post at Simón Lópes. From there we traveled due east for over a hundred miles to the Xingu River.

By canoe or open boat, river travel in the Amazon is beset on the smaller tributaries by encounters with overhanging saw grass and thorny branches, as well as gnats, mosquitos, ants, and chiggers. This was not new to explorers. One early oil explorer to the Amazon wrote that he had battled malaria, yellow fever, snakebite, wild animals, and *curare*-tipped (poisonous) arrows from hostile natives.

Legters and his party experienced similar physical discomforts and hazards of jungle travel. He wrote about hiking over the small trails made only by wild animals or "wild Indians." Wrist-thick vines and heavy undergrowth made it impossible for the pack animals to get through. The only solution was to hack through the thick curtain of jungle. But it was the rivers that presented the most formidable challenge:

> When we came to rivers that were impassable because of large boulders, we unpacked the animals and carried the cargo across on our own backs while the animals were led across one at a time, scrambling and falling over the rocks as they battled the swift currents. At one crossing, the oxen fell and were injured. Several mules were also injured. One mule lost his balance and fell backward to the bottom of a deep ravine. As our cargo mules fell one by one and were made useless, we put the cargo on our riding mules and we walked. After a very long journey, we finally reached the headwaters of the Xingu River where the Indians made our canoes.
>
> The Indian men were expert craftsmen. They knew exactly the right kind of tree from which to make our bark canoes. After cutting the shape of a canoe onto the bark while the tree was still standing, they drove bamboo wedges between the bark and the body of the tree until the entire piece was pried loose from the tree.

Carefully the men placed the canoe-shaped bark into a specially prepared cradle and placed braces on the inside to keep it from warping. The men then built a fire inside the bark to dry and soften it. When the bark was sufficiently softened, the men bent and molded it into the required shape. After letting the bark canoe cool for a day, we were ready to resume our exploration.

At this juncture in their journey, the Legters party was reduced from thirteen to seven. Fearing Indian hostility and those *curare*-tipped arrows, one Indian helper deserted the party. Five others returned to the government post at Simón Lópes with the injured animals. So began their perilous river journey on the Xingu River. Legters recorded that after shooting ninety rapids, only one of the canoes made it back on the return trip.

Three and a half months later, Legters and his party ended their expedition where they had begun. After making contact with over a dozen different tribal groups, Legters returned to Corumbá on September 26, 1926, exhausted and trail-weary, but with enormous drive to tell American Christians of the opportunities for a gospel witness in Amazonia.

For a man untrained in cultural anthropology, Legters produced a thorough report touching on a wide range of topics, including locations of the different tribal groups, detailed accounts of their everyday routines, nutrition, death rituals, animistic and spirit worship, and gift giving. In one jungle village three-hour's walk from the river, he was given special flutes and rattles and told not to let the women see them—whenever the men of the village played these long four-foot flutes, the women hid inside their huts. Legters also wrote about social and kinship groupings, described flora and fauna, and commented on the keen intellect and physical prowess of the ethnic peoples he met:

The Indian men I met were masters at memorizing the details of their world. They have keen vision and seem to me to think more logically than most people I have met in solving problems and surviving in their environment. Most people in the west think being able to trade and make money is a mark of intelligence. If this is the mark of intelligence, then the Indians lose. But look at what they accomplish with what they have! With stone axes and crude tools they clear land and plant manioc. They hunt large and dangerous game with

> bows and arrows. From grasses and bark of trees, the people weave
> sleeping hammocks and other useful household objects.
>
> I was also impressed with the physical development of people we
> met. The nomadic [Nambikuara] are sleek and agile, broad shoul-
> dered and narrow hipped. Others have splendid chests with muscles
> on their arms and legs that stand out like whipcords. When they row
> and pole their canoes, their movements are made with the utmost
> grace and beauty.

He also wrote about the large number of Indians who had died or were dying because of exploitation by outside influences. "Anyone wanting to serve these people," Legters said, "must not come out of a sense of pity or sympathy, but from a true heart of love and appreciation for them as people." And as an afterthought, he added, "And they should know how to swim. The men in one tribe, apparently, often swim under passing canoes, tip them over and kill the people."

Throughout Legters's report, there appeared a curious reference to "wild" or "hostile" Indians. Most of the details of these encounters, however, were omitted or only briefly mentioned. But one story, later told by his son David, was more complete. This encounter occurred while David and Legters were visiting the Kaipau people. The party's guide and rowers, knowing the Kaipau's reputation for savagery, chose to stay with the canoes on the river's edge. Not knowing that among tribal Indians of Amazonia it is generally understood that anyone coming into your village making a noise cannot be an enemy, Legters and his son entered the village quietly. However, when the Kaipau saw them, they greeted them with a display of excited yelling with everyone interrupting everyone else while frightened children clung to their mothers' bare legs.

Legters approached the village chief and presented his gifts—an axe, decorative items, colored ribbon, fishhooks, and other things. He had learned that in this ritual of gift giving, not the gift itself but the act of giving was important. Gift giving built trust and relieved tension. During this exchange, Legters noticed they were surrounded by brightly-painted warriors who carried five-foot arrows and wooden spears. The Kaipau chief accepted the gifts, but then pointed to the full packs Legters and his son had strapped to their backs and began beating his chest and sounding a wild war whoop. Immediately the warriors surrounded them with menacing looks and began to yell and rattled their arrows against their spears.

Needing to act quickly in what he knew was a serious situation, Legters recalled that besides gift giving, dancing was the most effective way to relieve tension. To the surprise of everyone, including his son, he suddenly darted from his son's side, broke out of the circle of warriors, and began, at full volume, a series of piercing yips. "Eee-ee, yee-ee, ee-ee, yee-ee." Ever serious, Legters's action was completely out of character. The Indians watched in wonder as Legters clasped his hands behind his back, bent over like a question mark, and began a half-stomping, half-hopping dance around the village fire ring. With his knees coming up to meet his chin, this former missionary to Oklahoma's Comanche Indians was doing a Comanche rain dance.

As soon as they overcame their sudden surprise, the chief and the village men followed suit, yelling and expertly imitating Legters's strange hopping and stomping rhythm. The dancing finally came to a halt when Legters could no longer find breath to fill his enormous lungs. But whatever tension had been there before was now gone. The chief opened his arms and welcomed the men from the outside. Clearly, anyone who could produce such yells, hops, and howls was a friend!

When he returned to the U.S., Legters was more determined than ever to "find men and money for mission work in South America." And he once again sought out his friend and colleague, Cameron Townsend.

Aware of Legters's new vision for a gospel work in South America, Cam began reading information on Brazil and wrote Legters that, while "his heart burned within him when he read the report of his trip, he still couldn't be in two places at once." Besides, he still had a New Testament to complete, and developments in San Antonio required his attention: a Mrs. Greenleaf had contributed five hundred dollars for the installation of an electric plant in San Antonio, and the school there needed help.

Knowing of Cam's commitment, Legters challenged him to explore the possibility of expanding the work into El Salvador. A group of Philadelphia businessmen had promised Legters that if he determined there was a need for a gospel work among indigenous peoples in that country, they would commit to financial support. Acting on Legters's urging and with the blessing of the Central American Mission, Cam, along with Elvira and Anne Edson, a visitor from the U.S., drove from Guatemala to El Salvador in April 1927. Cam left Elvira and Anne with friends along the way while he surveyed western El Salvador, often accompanied by American Baptist missionaries in the area. After a two-week survey, Cam wrote a report to Karl Hummel in Dallas. The report said it would be unwise to begin a work in El Salvador without the cooperation of the American Baptist Mission and others there. From his survey of the various ethnic groups in that country, Cam determined there was, "no great need for a specialized work among the Indians since most, if not all, were rapidly being absorbed into the Spanish language and *ladino* culture, with the exception of the Pipiles where the Baptists had responsibility."

It appeared to be an almost bland survey report. Yet, like most doing language and linguistic survey work, Cam had harrowing incidents to relate. In a letter to his parents, Cam told how he repeatedly dealt with car trouble on the drive from Guatemala to El Salvador. First it was a bad battery. Then the car wouldn't climb the steep grades and had to be pushed up the hills. Even after coasting down the hills, the car just sputtered and "gave up the ghost." Then Cam found a Chinese Salvadoran mechanic who got the car working again:

> I don't know what the mechanic did to the car, but after he fixed it, the car ran with great power—alas, only for a few blocks and then quit again. I examined the engine and discovered he had left a connection undone. I fixed this and all was well again.
>
> Since this was Thursday of Holy Week [Easter], we were in a hurry to get into Indian country before Friday when we knew it would be dangerous to travel. About five-thirty in the afternoon, we were on a bad piece of road when suddenly we came upon about twenty men all brandishing their long machetes. When they saw us, they tried to direct me to take a side road, and ordered us to stop. When I didn't, they became angry and started shouting. At this point, I gave the men as much room on the road as I could and stomped on the gas pedal hoping and praying the car wouldn't cough, sputter, and die as it had so many times before. Thankfully the car responded quickly. As I sped past the men, the leader landed three quick blows on the car with his machete. One of the blows left its mark on the

windshield, right where Anne was sitting. It's remarkable the wind-shield didn't break. After this manifestation of fanaticism, we were rather nervous until we reached the city of Sosonate and put the car in a garage.

With the survey trip to El Salvador behind him, Cam was increasingly concerned that he wasn't spending enough time on translation. In June 1927 he wrote:

> With the exception of Revelation, the first draft of the Cakchiquel New Testament is completed. However, in translation this is just the beginning. We must go over and over the translation many more times before we can give it to the printer. Some of the Gospels have been reworked six and seven times.
>
> It has been almost five years since we first published the Gospel of John. I had hoped we could have more published by this time, but many other mission matters have intruded on my translation time. Up until now we have done well to get a week a month set aside for translation. The national translators, however, are working con-stantly. We feel an urgency to get the translation completed, but we also realize the work of translation must be done well, so we plod on.

Cam also wanted to take the gospel to Mexico. Earlier in 1927, after holding a series of meetings in Chichicastenango, Cam wrote Legters a lengthy report outlining his vision and plans for Mexico. He then added:

> As we stood preaching to the Indians in the plaza of Chichicas-tenango, I thought of you and of the big plans we laid six years ago in that town. Evidently we didn't lay our plans according to the Lord's will. But the vision we were given for Indian work still burns in my heart and in the hearts of many who were there then. How I wish we could talk and pray together over this part of the task that is weighing heavily on my heart. I may be a dreamer, but nevertheless I believe it's necessary to have a vision.

A month later, Legters responded to Cam's letter:

> That vision we all had in Chichicastenango was no wild dream. I
> believe God gave us a view of his will. I can see why some of it
> was not carried out. When I see you, I will explain why. But one
> reason is that then as now we must have people with a dogged
> determination to stay by the task until it is finished. It means plodding,
> plus brilliant plans and a vision.
>
> I have learned one lesson during these last years. It is one thing
> to find the will of God. And it is another matter to know the right
> time to carry out that will. I think there was a failure to know the
> right time. One cannot say it wasn't God's will because things didn't
> move at once. It was indeed his will. I am fully convinced that what
> we did in Chichicastenango was most certainly the will of God. I
> believe God's time for the Indian is drawing near.

The log cabin in Santa Ana, California, where the team finished translating the Cakchiquel New Testament (left to right: Elvira, Trinidad Bac, Joe Chicol, and Cameron)

Chapter Eighteen

A Most Significant Moment

The Great Depression of 1929–1938 threw millions of people in the U.S., Canada, Europe, and Latin America into a time of disorder and chaos. At its depth—1933—over sixteen million Americans were unemployed. When the Wall Street stock market crashed on October 29, 1929 (known as Black Tuesday), it triggered economic and political nationalism in Guatemala and other parts of Latin America. Many anti-American and socialist sympathizers used this dark time to accuse the U.S. of being a neo-imperialist power bent on the exploitation of Latin America. Guatemala's rising middle class had only to point to the Monroe Doctrine and the presence, since 1912, of U.S. Marines in Nicaragua.

In 1928, a year before the crash, there was already great unease in Central America. Cam and his brother Paul wrote frequently to their friends, parents, and the home council in Dallas about the disturbing anti-American rhetoric fueled by Mexico's president, Plutarco Calles, who was hostile to the clergy and the church. Even some groups in the churches founded by the Central American Mission were caught up with this sentiment and began clamoring for self-determination. One of these groups was the Cinco Calles Church (Church of the Five

Streets) in Guatemala City. A group of women in the church collected money to start their own evangelical hospital because they felt the existing Presbyterian hospital did not meet all their needs. The elders, however, vetoed this, and the women submitted to their decision. Another group of men, headed by a man named Gregorio Morales López, took this as an affront to their democratic rights and also felt there was a disparity in wages between the North American and Guatemalan missionaries. When ownership of the chapel properties was denied, they felt further deprived of their rights and wrote a strong open letter of protest:

> We are well acquainted with the infamous way our Guatemalan missionaries are treated. It is quite different from the North American missionaries who receive good salaries that permit them to enjoy life without much struggle. We are also up in arms about the way the women were treated. When they did not protest and obeyed the elders of Cinco Calles Church (who obeyed the instructions of their "Lords"), we decided to champion their cause.
>
> The "Americanized" elders and the *gringo* pastor of Cinco Calles Church tried to silence us, as they had the women, but they did not realize they were dealing with men who would not retreat, even in the face of threats and persecutions from the "lily-white" reverends. Even though we fifteen men and two women are victims of dismissal, we will not give up our convictions.
>
> Now, we, along with a group of believers from Cinco Calles Church, are raising our voices in protest against the impudent maneuvering of a hypocritical "Beneficent Society" made up of "North-Americanized" ones who, in their imperialistic way, seek to deprive the national churches of their real estate. We believe their promises of protection of properties and evangelical chapels obtained by money from Guatemalans are hollow.
>
> Protest, Sirs! Protest in the face of such lies which these North Americans seek to put over on us. If you don't, you will have no voice or voting privileges. Today these modern fighters are still victims of dismissal, a weapon they use to frighten and control us. Now is the time to open your eyes. Open them now because you too could be the next victim of dismissal.

Undoubtedly this was a letter with uncomplimentary generalizations.

Karl Hummel wrote a general letter to the constituents of the Central American Mission asking for concerted prayer regarding this antiforeign spirit in Central America:

> We [on the council] are praying much about the political unrest in Central America. Letters from Honduras tell us the anti-American spirit is as high there as in many other areas in Central America. The Townsends write that the town of Panajachel has boycotted their services because they are foreigners. Paul reports that most of the Indian church remain faithful, but that the *ladino* churches are embracing the anti-American spirit in large numbers. Our prayer is for the Lord to overrule so the gospel may not be bound. The situation calls for more and better-trained national workers.

Training nationals had always been part of Cam's agenda. Earlier he had written that the Lord had been impressing on him a greater emphasis on training national workers "in the Word and methods of the work." But the pressures and responsibilities of his own work often left the actual implementing of such training low on his list of priorities. Now this overt anti-American prejudice galvanized his thinking and caused him to write to a Mr. A. H. Stradling:

> At our last Field Committee meeting we extended a call to the [Herbert] Tomses and Archer Anderson to open the Central Ladino Bible Institute and a Normal School in Guatemala City. The Lord seems to be guiding us to put our first emphasis on the training of national workers. Since you left Guatemala, the antiforeign and, more especially, the anti-American spirit have grown tremendously. Our national brothers must come to the front and bear more responsibility for the ongoing of the work, but to do so they must be trained. With trained nationals, we expatriate missionaries will have more time to train teachers and workers and open up new fields. Just as soon as the translation is finished, Elvira and I intend to go to a new area. I have been most interested in the Lacandones in southern Mexico and the Petén area of northern Guatemala.

By the beginning of June 1928, Elvira had returned to Panajachel with her brother Carl Malmstrom, who, through the Central American Mission, had come to act as dean of the Robinson Bible Institute.

Elvira returned to a climate of anti-American feelings that spread throughout the Cakchiquel area. This had devastating effects among the churches. In 1928, Cam had over a hundred congregations under his general supervision plus a large staff of national workers to supervise. He also had responsibilities for the preparation of the new Bible and Normal School, called the Latin Bible Institute, opening in January of 1929 in Guatemala City. Herbert Toms and Archer Anderson had agreed to run the school.[1]

Thus with the weight and responsibility of the work growing daily, Cam was finding less and less time for translation. By the spring of 1928, he decided if he was ever to complete the New Testament, it would have to be done away from the distractions and demands of work on the field, and Cam once again sought an economical place to stay in the States. His friend Luther Rees suggested Sulphur Springs, Arkansas.[2] Rees had been to a Bible conference there and recommended it as a place where Cam might find solitude. Cam warmed to the idea until he realized Arkansas was in the South. In 1928, the southern states did not treat blacks with respect. There was, in fact, a law on the books of Sulphur Springs that forbade blacks from sleeping there overnight. This posed a problem as Cam planned to bring two dark-skinned Cakchiquel-speaking men for translation work: Chema (Joe) Chicol and Trinidad Bac.

As was often the case, Cam held the minority view. While he favored taking these two Indian men to the States, Bishop and Toms both opposed the plan, saying the two men would be "spoiled" for Indian work if they ever got a taste of the "good" life in the States. And Karl Hummel, the Central American Mission's ever-pragmatic secretary—always considering the corporate picture—also objected:

> I hardly know what to write concerning your suggestion that you come home to finish your translation work. I will be interested in the field committee's opinion about this. Mr. Rees and others on the council have read your letter, and the opinion is that the disadvantages of coming to the States with two national helpers would be far greater than any advantage you might gain. Personally, I feel bringing

two men to the States is a serious responsibility. It would involve expenses that would hardly be justified. It seems to me that no matter where you were it would be a physical and mental impossibility to give undivided attention to the translation work.

If the field can spare you to come home, I should think it could spare you to go into seclusion on the field just as easily. Of course, if you are not well down there, this is a different matter. I am rather surprised that the altitude of five thousand feet at Panajachel is affecting you. Personally, I would happily exchange a home in California for a residence on beautiful Lake Atitlán.

For several weeks, Cam accepted Hummel's direction not to take the two nationals to the States. Yet, during this time he grappled to find the Lord's direction for the situation. On July 24, he wrote:

In spite of the overwhelming objection from our colleagues to taking the two men to the States, I still feel the Lord is leading me to go, but as yet the way hasn't opened. Elvira agrees we should go, provided it is to California. And California seems to be the best option. It would be cheaper, and my folks would welcome us with open arms. If I can secure free passage for the two men [I would take this to be a sign that the Lord wants us to go].

Concluding that letter, Cam added what seemed to be an afterthought about his other vision:

I am enclosing a copy of a letter from Major Herbert Dargue who commanded the Pan American goodwill flight to Guatemala. As you will see, the letter explains in great detail the type and cost (with the spare parts) of aircraft he believes would be best for reaching the remote areas of Mexico and Guatemala. I have written before about my visionary idea for evangelizing the Lacandones, who, as you know, live in a wild part of Mexico. Perhaps it's only a vision, but I just can't help having them.

On August 28, Cam wrote Legters telling him he had secured a fifty percent discount for Trinidad Bac and Joe Chicol on the steamer. He said he felt this was God's leading and had made immediate plans to go to California, despite the "many criticisms" from those on the council and his colleagues on the field. There was also a sad note to Cam's letter that told about the unexpected death of Trinidad's brother, Antonio Bac—a man for whom Cam had high regard:[3]

> Antonio Bac is at home in Glory. Almost immediately after hearing your message in Panajachel, he took his thirteen-year-old son and a sack of gospels and headed for the jungles near the coast. After giving out all his gospels and hiking over very difficult terrain, he returned home only to begin yet another evangelistic trip within a few days. He had contracted a bad case of malaria in the lowlands but thought he could fight it off. He fell several times on the trail and after reaching Chimaltenango, decided to return home. He got as far as Itzapa where he died. Before he died, he continued to exhort the brethren and sing hymns. He was truly a marvelous evangelist. The church has lost a vibrant warrior. I am praying for the Lord to give us more workers just as vibrant. The young lad who accompanied Antonio on his second trip also fell ill with malaria, but has recovered. We expect to sail [for California] on the *City of Panama* the day after tomorrow.

By mid-September, Cam, the two co-translators, and Elvira were settled into a routine of New Testament translation in Santa Ana, California. Elvira typed rough-draft copies of completed chapters; Cam struggled to conjugate Cakchiquel verbs and render scriptural metaphors into relevant Cakchiquel equivalents. One difficult passage he and his cotranslators struggled with was 2 Timothy 3:16:

> We were struggling with the part of the Scripture that says, "All scripture is given by inspiration of God." We tried several different ways of translating this, but the men were never satisfied that it communicated well in Cakchiquel. I consulted the Greek and said, "How about translating it 'all scripture is God-breathed?'" "No," they said, "that doesn't sound right." Then I suggested using "God's breath." The men liked this and we agreed to use this phrase. But I wasn't entirely convinced it was as accurate as it should be. Then I began to read other portions of Scripture where I noticed that when God

spoke in creation it had the same connotation as God's breath. And so we left it that way: "All scripture is God's breath."

Though Cam was busy translating, he also pursued the airplane dream. Once again, not everyone shared his dream. When Karl Hummel received Cam's letter with the copy of Major Herbert Dargue's letter, he replied:

> It is possible that using airplanes to reach the remote missionary stations may happen in the future. However, at present I must confess I would rather go overland, even if I had to walk. I have no desire to go up in a plane. When Mr. Butler said he thought a plane would help him greatly in his work in Honduras, one of the older missionaries, Miss Gohrman, thought this was a sure sign he was backsliding. She said she had known Mr. Butler for many years and considered him to be one of the most efficient and dedicated evangelists she had ever known. She said that as he traveled the countryside, he never missed an opportunity to give out a tract or speak a personal word to someone along the way. Miss Gohrman said that if Mr. Butler were to use an airplane, it would hinder his ministry. How could he give out tracts from an airplane?

Cam responded on October 27, 1928, a month later, clarifying his position on the use of airplanes to Hummel:

> I should have written before now, but I haven't been doing much writing. We spend five hours a day translating. After that, I relax by working a little in my father's garden, or visit friends and relatives.
>
> I'm afraid I didn't make myself clear on the issue of airplanes. I don't recommend their use for all ordinary missionary work. An airplane would certainly be useful for the field secretary. However, if I were field secretary, I wouldn't want to travel by plane, not yet. If we could get a millionaire to finance such a plane, I most certainly would be willing to risk my neck to reach the Lacandones or the unexplored regions of Brazil with the gospel by plane.
>
> From what I have heard from Mr. Legters of the conditions in the interior of South America, it would be practically impossible to establish mission stations, or at best, very slow and dangerous to work

without the support of an airplane. Admiral Byrd is spending great sums of money on his South Pole expedition. Shouldn't we Christians be willing to spend as much money to reach people who are completely inaccessible to the gospel? I believe we could reach these people within ten years without any greater loss of life than already has occurred with the old methods of travel. Anyway, it's something to dream about.

By the end of March 1929, the translation team had completed the seventh chapter of Revelation. While Cam said they were beginning to see light at the end of the tunnel, there was still much that remained to be done. Acts needed to be revised. Additional editorial readings of the entire New Testament were necessary. And after that Elvira would type the final draft to be sent to the American Bible Society for printing.

Everything appeared to be progressing well, except that Trinidad Bac had grown homesick for Guatemala. His desire to return shattered the notion that life in the States would "spoil" him, making him unwilling to return to his people. While Trinidad had gained a great deal from his time in California—he had learned to speak English and to play the organ (thanks to Elvira)—still, this was no substitute for the Land of Eternal Spring. Cam booked passage for Bac on the SS *Venezuela* to sail on April 27.

On October 10, 1929, at a special service of praise, the translation of the Cakchiquel New Testament was dedicated to God at the First Presbyterian Church in Santa Ana, California. Cam's mother and father carefully wrote the final two words of the book of Revelation in the Cakchiquel New Testament—*Rix, Amén*. Dr. P. W. Philpott, then the vice president of the Central American Mission, officiated and gave his blessing to the project. One of the speakers was a former missionary to Guatemala, who said:

This is one of the most significant moments in the history of the Cakchiquel nation. They now have the Word of God in their own language for the first time. For centuries, the Indians of Guatemala have been held in serfdom; held down and neglected because they lacked the basic opportunity for education. This book, written in their language, will help restore this lost self-esteem.

Most people attending that special service were ignorant of the reality that the Cakchiquel New Testament completion came at a high price. When Cam began in 1920, most of his colleagues accused him of wasting money and time. The pressure to stop had been great. There had been opposition from *ladino* believers against a Cakchiquel New Testament—mostly from *ladinos* who preached to or taught the Cakchiquels using Spanish Bibles. Cam's concern with this had been that Spanish-speaking *ladino* preachers frequently gave misinformation and erroneous interpretation when preaching from the Spanish Scriptures, "passing on just what they want to and in a manner they see fit." Without a New Testament in their language, Cakchiquels were at the mercy of *ladino* teachings.

But Cam had been resolute and stubborn. Though he was tempted to give up on several occasions, men like Dr. Haven, Rev. R. R. Gregory of the American Bible Society, Rev. W. F. Jordan, and Dr. Paul Burgess encouraged and cheered him on. And now it was completed. On October 11, 1929, Cam and Elvira sent the manuscript to the American Bible Society in care of Dr. Eric M. North:

> Today Elvira and I have the pleasure of mailing to you the completed manuscript of the Cakchiquel New Testament. I am enclosing an account of the praise service held last night in the First Presbyterian Church in Santa Ana.
>
> Would it be possible to have some of the New Testaments bound in leather? The Indians take great pride in beautifully bound Bibles. We believe a leather-bound volume would greatly enhance the value of our translation in their eyes.
>
> Also, we are anxious to know how long it will take to publish this and how soon we will have to read proof. Between now and then we plan a short rest. We would like to know how to plan our lives around this since we are laying plans to return to the field.

Meanwhile, Cam was in correspondence with Legters, who was holding meetings across the U.S. In a report to Cam and others, he wrote:

After being called home to attend my sick wife for three months, I once again began my conference speaking. During the last twelve months I have spoken three hundred and forty-seven times. As well, I made one survey trip to Mexico. I have to tell you the enemy of our souls, the devil, is contesting every foot of ground where Mexico's Indians are located. The work that was opened in Oaxaca had to close down. The missionary has left the field. The work promised in Chiapas by another mission was never opened. One piece of good news is that Dr. Dale, of the Associated Reformed Presbyterian Mission, has begun work among the Huaxteco people.[4]

There is much need of prayer for all of us to know the will of God with regard to the work among Mexico's Indians. I am not sure whether the work should be done by the nationals themselves or by trained expatriate workers. I hope to leave for Mexico by October 28 to meet with a group of missionaries for prayer and counsel with the hope of arriving at a plan for how we might reach the unreached Indians of that land.

Legters had no idea how prophetic his words and action would be. Within three years, at the Keswick Bible Conference in New Jersey where Legters was the principal speaker, God used an all-night prayer meeting to confirm to Cameron Townsend that God would have him give his talent and energies to Mexico. In later years, Cam would speak of this juncture in his life as the most important in his career and the most crucial to WBT and SIL. But first there was the published Cakchiquel New Testament to be presented to the president of Guatemala, along with an extensive literacy campaign to prepare the people to read the New Testament. He would also have to face the fact that he had overworked his body.

Enjoying the winter weather in the northern U.S.

Chapter Nineteen

Faith and Imagination

No one was a more successful stump speaker and fundraiser for the cause of ethnic minorities in Mexico and South America, than L. L. Legters. Cam thought Legters's ability was nothing short of remarkable. The Central American Council, however, did not share Townsend's enthusiasm. Many council members considered Legters to be something of a "loose cannon." Legters thought nothing of writing a Central American missionary and asking for assistance with a survey trip, even if it meant taking him from his post for weeks or even months. He might also suddenly descend on a missionary to ask for interpretation help at a Victorious Life rally—without first contacting the missionary's supervisors.

There were also Legters's celebrated speaking eccentricities. He used his stentorian voice as a club. In the midst of an address, he would often descend the platform to interact with the congregation. Then he would pick a person, lock eyes with them, and boom at the top of his voice, shaking his bony index finger in the person's face, demanding to know why they hadn't made a commitment to missions. "Don't you know it *'tain't fair! It 'tain't fair* that we in the West have heard the gospel over and over and the Indians of South America haven't heard it once. *It 'tain't fair!*"

Unhappy over what they considered his dramatic presentation and penchant for overstatement—usually involving inflated population figures, in those days often undeterminable by the government—the Central American Mission council had previously turned down his proposal to do a survey of the ethnic people in Central America. Yet in spite of Legters's drama, dozens of men and women responded to his message, committing themselves to overseas mission service and raising their own financial support.

Cam knew about Legters's eccentricities but was untroubled by them. Cam, in fact, had a number of his own that people chuckled over—one being his constant complaint that he was cold. (Earl Mooney, his clothier when Cam was in Santa Ana, California, said, "Cam had a warm heart, but a cold body. He always wanted the heaviest weight suit in the store. He would frequently wear an overcoat and hat when everyone else was in shirt sleeves.") In an effort to persuade the Central American Mission Council to change their minds and allow Legters to do language survey work, Cam wrote:

> He is a remarkable conference speaker. His zeal for the Indians knows no bounds. We owe him a vote of confidence. I don't see why, in view of his great contribution, we can't run the risk of a little friction over his eccentricities. I would be happy to lend him half our national staff to accompany him on a survey trip to help ascertain the true needs of the Indian work. I understand he is interested in surveying Panama and Northern Colombia. He should be encouraged to go.

Karl Hummel's response to Cam's plea was, "Thanks, but no thanks." Hummel acknowledged that Legters's trips to El Salvador were helpful and appreciated. Nevertheless, the Central American Mission Council voted against Legters's participation in another survey. If this negative decision affected Cam's view of Legters, he never showed it. In fact, Cam firmly decided that if the Central American Mission council wanted to dissociate themselves from Legters, *he* most assuredly did not. To show appreciation to Legters for his unique ministry (raising interest and support for ethnic minorities) and for Legters's personal interest in them, Cam and Elvira invited Legters to be their special guest in California for Thanksgiving in 1929. He was guest number fifty-six!

After enjoying the Townsends' Thanksgiving celebration in Santa Ana, Legters accompanied Joe Chicol on the train, helping him reach Siloam Springs, Arkansas. Joe had been accepted as a student at John Brown Schools (now known as John Brown University). Unlike Trinidad Bac, who had returned to pastoral responsibilities in Guatemala, Joe had no commitments beyond helping Cam with translation work. Earlier, he had said that he wanted to prepare himself for future ministry. Now he could further his education.[1]

Following the October 10, 1929, celebration of the completed Cakchiquel New Testament, Cam and Elvira waited for the galley proofs from the American Bible Society (naively anticipating their return before the end of the year) and took a needed rest at Big Bear, a mountain retreat in Southern California. They also took several trips to see the sights in their own "back yard."

In early January 1930, Cam and Elvira moved to Chicago, stopping in Dallas to attend a Central American Mission conference. Since Elvira had family in Chicago, and since the printing of the New Testament was to be done by a Chicago printer, Cam and Elvira reasoned this would a good place to proofread the New Testament. They stayed with Elvira's younger brothers, then later rented an apartment. With the Depression, all the Central American Mission missionaries were receiving only about forty percent of their monthly stipend. The Townsends soon discovered how much more expensive it was to live in Chicago than California.

The first hint there might be a delay in receiving their galley proofs came early in January. Dr. Eric M. North, of the American Bible Society, wrote Cam to tell him he was sorry, but because they hadn't reached an agreement on how to format the Cakchiquel New Testament, the galleys were delayed. The problem was with the facing-page diglot of the Spanish text that Cam had requested. North explained this was a new procedure for them, since most of their diglots used parallel columns. There were other technical and orthography problems, including the use of inverted commas over certain words, the selection of font type, and the use of diacritical marks that Cam had used but which were now discouraged by the Bible Society.

On January 9, Cam responded:

> Dr. North, I hardly know what to say regarding the Cakchiquel or-
> thography. Readers of the Gospel of John have become accustomed
> to the inverted comma which has been in use for eight years. You
> suggested the inverted comma be placed just after the letter instead
> of directly over it. If the space occupied by the comma would not
> be so great as to give the appearance of separating the word, I believe
> it would be all right to use it after *k, h, z,* and *t,* and use the *g* with
> the dot over it since you have that character in the font you plan to
> use. This would be less expensive, and since you would have to
> wait for new characters to be made, less time-consuming. Further, it
> would not confuse the readers who have already become accustomed
> to the inverted comma.

A flurry of letters between North and Cam began. At issue was how
best to resolve the complex problem of standardizing the Cakchiquel
orthography and conform it to existing norms of the International Pho-
netic Society. North pointed out that the Institute of African Languages
and Cultures discouraged the use of diacritical marks.

Cam was anxious to return to Guatemala with the New Testament
by September. As in many instances when he was at variance with
popular opinion, he gently—but with resolute determination—tried to
persuade North to his point of view. One classic persuasion technique
he used was introducing an expert in the field who supported his own
ideas. In this case, Cam's support came from the eminent linguistic
scholar from the University of Chicago, Dr. Edward Sapir.

Sapir, a kind, gentle scholar, was one of America's foremost linguists.
Cam had been introduced to Sapir through Dr. Gates, the American
archeologist Cam met in Guatemala. Sapir offered Cam his invaluable
and practical linguistic suggestions. Some years later, Cam would send
a promising linguist, Kenneth L. Pike, to Sapir for training and advice.
Meanwhile, Cam wrote North to tell him of his lengthy conversation
with Sapir:

> I had to wait a few days before I could get an interview with Dr.
> Sapir regarding the letters you asked about. After a lengthy conver-
> sation, he advises we use *c* and *qu* in italics instead of *g.* He also

thinks the final *b* should be changed to an italic *p*. Otherwise he thinks the alphabet we have decided to use is, from a practical standpoint, satisfactory, though not from a scientific standpoint.

He thinks the Bible Society would be wise to adopt the orthography generally accepted by the linguistic community and to inform all missionaries [doing translation] to try and follow it. He has agreed to scientifically systematize the complete Cakchiquel alphabet with accurate descriptions of each sound. However, to do this correctly, he would need the assistance of Joe Chicol in order to get the correct Cakchiquel pronunciation.

Personally, I think that making the two changes mentioned above will be sufficient. We are anxious to return to the field. To go over the entire manuscript and revise the orthography would require a great deal of time. As far as the Indians are concerned, it would not make the translation any easier for them to read.

I have another matter that concerns me that is difficult for me to mention. Since arriving in Chicago, we have been living with relatives. But when we actually get down to proofreading, our efficiency will be greatly reduced without a place where we can be by ourselves.

We have checked into rents and find them high. A two-room furnished apartment costs $69.50 per month. It's so small we would have to clear our desk away before rolling the bed out of the closet. A roomier unfurnished flat costs $57.50. Our salary is supposed to be $115.00 per month, but our mission is seldom able to send one hundred percent. Last year we averaged $87.50 a month. As living was cheaper in California, with occasional gifts from friends and relatives, we were able to get along. However, it is different here in Chicago. While we are here and involved in proofreading, I was wondering if the Bible Society could assist us in securing a flat. Can you give us an idea when you can send us the proofs? We are anxious to formulate our plans.

Believing it would be at least a month before they would see any galley proofs, Cam and Elvira decided to visit Cam's uncle in Iowa where, said Cam, "the milk is good and cheap and has the properties to restore one's youth."

Almost every letter Cam and Elvira received during the first three months of 1930 brought news of some surprise. On January 18, they received word from a Dr. and Mrs. Roe of Colony, Oklahoma, expressing interest in Joe Chicol, whom they had heard about from Legters. The Roes had adopted a Winnebago Indian boy and saw him graduate from Yale with a master's degree. He then went on to earn a degree in theology from Auburn. So enthusiastic were the Roes over their adopted son's scholastic achievements, they were prepared to provide a full scholarship for Joe Chicol "providing he would use his education in the service of his people." Cam wrote Legters to assure him that it was precisely for this reason that Joe had gone to John Brown Academy. A note from Legters on January 28 informed Cam that Legters's wife was "losing ground daily." (She died in April.)

From Dr. North, Cam received happy news. The New Testament was scheduled to go to press by the end of February if all the orthography problems could be worked out. On March 11, 1930, North wrote Cam that the New Testament manuscript had been sent to the Chicago printer, R. R. Donnelley & Sons. He suggested Cam go there to proofread the manuscript soon, as the printer was anxious to begin setting type. Even though North indicated there were still some technical problems to be worked out, Cam was "overjoyed." To North, he wrote:

> We have secured two rooms in an old building located near the Lake on Winthrop Ave. The landlord has arranged for light housekeeping. The best news is that the rent is only forty dollars per month. When we compare it with other places we have looked at, we consider this to be a great bargain. It costs more to live in Chicago, but we are confident God will supply our needs, even when we stop speaking and give all our time to proofreading. Whatever your Bible Society committee decides to do about our request for financial help, will be fine.[2]
>
> I am extremely pleased with the proposed layout and binding. The page layout will be a practical help to the unskilled reader. I am also pleased with the attractiveness of the book. The Cakchiquels, who are inclined to be ashamed of their language, will be proud of *this* New Testament.

Though Cam intended to give up speaking engagements to devote himself to full-time proofreading, in reality he found invitations to speak difficult to refuse. In April, he spoke to a large African-American church of 1,400 people.[3] Then Dr. P. W. Philpott, who was now pastor of the

Church of the Open Door in Los Angeles, asked Cam to consider speaking at a special conference at his church. Though Cam declined that request, he did agree to speak at a large mission rally at the Moody Church on April 30. And his acceptance gave him a platform to speak about his new project—airplanes.

Ever since his encounter with Major Dargue, Cam's imagination had soared with new ways airplanes could be used in the service of missions. With this vision linked to his faith and imagination, all Cam needed to do was convince his colleagues, the public, and members of the Central American Mission Council that airplanes could enable evangelization of the isolated people groups of South America.

The Moody Bible Institute radio station gave Cam a half-hour of air time to talk about what was on his mind. Though he had difficulty talking into a "mike"—the public forum and letters being his strong suit—he nevertheless willingly spoke to the public about his vision for airplanes.

He also wrote Karl Hummel, asking him to consider heading up what he called an "aeronautical department":

> Karl, I am convinced God is leading toward an air project. I would love to see something develop in a month or so. It would be great if this could happen in connection with the Central American Mission. I plan to present the idea of an "air crusade" to a group of Christian leaders right after the Moody Missions Rally and wish that you or Mr. Rees could be here. The Catholics are using airplanes successfully for their mission work in several fields. Why can't we do the same?

To Legters, on April 24, he wrote:

> I am convinced that God is leading toward a big undertaking for the wild tribes of South America. I realize the need and opportunity in Mexico and Central America. Right now the attention of the Christian public is focused on the Indians of South America. But their attention would be drawn even more by a spectacular undertaking. What if we choose a name like "Air Crusade to the Wild Tribes," or something like this, and put it before the public? We could invite the public to contribute a dollar apiece to become a member of the Air Crusade. With their dollars will come their prayers, which will help

more. I trust, dear Mr. Legters, that you will pray about this. Perhaps you should be the general director. With such a membership program, the whole continent would be benefited. God likes to do marvelous things, and he likes to use small instruments to do them.

P.S. Major Dargue is willing to cooperate in an advisory capacity. I have sent him a copy of *Borden of Yale*. I am praying he might get a vision of service for God.

In mission strategy, Cam was twenty years ahead of his time. Most council members saw the advantage of using airplanes to save time, but not all were convinced the heavy investment in equipment would justify a departure from conventional mission strategy. Dr. North had become keenly interested in Cam's projects during the months they had worked together, and he wrote Cam a long, thoughtful letter on the use of airplanes for mission work:

I have given a great deal of thought to your project for hastening the evangelization of the "wild tribes" of South America with the use of airplanes. As you know, the Bible Society has an interest in pioneer work that will reach the unevangelized tribes with the translated Word. I also have a personal interest since I am chairman of the Commission on Indian work in Latin America that is endeavoring to serve all missions engaged in such work of common interest.

However, I have received the impression that some of the Indian work is marked with a good deal of unsteadiness. An eager missionary will open up a small territory, then ill health will reduce the staff, or the resources may not be adequate, or restless spirits will cause the missionary to leave. The perception is that the area is being covered, but, in fact, real accomplishments are slight.

While I favor reaching Amazonia and Central America with the gospel as soon as possible, my feeling is that it is more imperative at the present moment to strengthen and consolidate the work already going on among the great tribes where the foundation is already established. (This is one reason why I encourage you to return to work among the Cakchiquels. I know that Dr. Gregory also shares the same opinion.) Further, I have not heard from travelers or investigating missionaries who have explored the Amazon that there are any large homogeneous groups waiting to hear the Gospel.[4] There are any number of unevangelized Indians who are much more accessible and would not need the services of an airplane.

I agree the airplane saves time and overcomes many obstacles to travel. But when one is in an airplane, one loses all contact with the people. It is contact with the people where real missionary work is done and the missionary himself is trained.

North's letter continued with several more pages of sound argument as to why planes would be impractical for mission work. He ended his letter with an apology for having to give such a negative report to one whose heart was set on employing airplanes in this new way.

Dr. North's arguments notwithstanding, Cam continued speaking of his vision all during the spring and summer of 1930. And the famous biblical scholar, Dr. Henry Allan (H. A.) Ironside, was one of those who cheered him on: "I rejoice to know that your heart is set on reaching the millions of unevangelized Indians, and I pray the airplane will prove successful. Surely these people should be reached in the shortest possible time, not only for their own blessing, but to hasten our Lord's return."

On May 12, 1930, Cam wrote Legters an extraordinary letter telling him about the missionary rally at Moody and about a new awakening in his soul:

> We had a short meeting in Pastor Ironside's study to consider the airplane project. Unfortunately it was too short to be of any consequence. The general director of the Scandinavian Alliance Mission was present and told of great obstacles to working in places like Venezuela. This, of course, wasn't news to me. A few minutes after we separated, I began to wonder if this project was of God. Then a calm contentedness settled over me as I thought about our future.
>
> At first, it seemed as if we could stay on at Panajachel among the people we love and where the surroundings are so beautiful. But then I suddenly felt my ardor for Panajachel cooling off and a sense of deep concern for the lost [in South America] take possession of me. The feeling and the spiritual chill that followed was so strong that I immediately cried out to God. "No matter how great the obstacles, I will go in quest of those who are without the hope of the Gospel, if

this is Your will." After praying this, the warmth of the Spirit returned. As I write this I am satisfied that in his own time He will open the way. When you come to see me we can go into this more fully.

By the spring of 1930, the Central American Mission, like many other mission agencies in the country, found itself short of money. In urgent need, Karl Hummel asked Cam and Elvira if they would consider doing official deputation for the Mission: "We wonder if you and Elvira would spend the remainder of the Spring and Summer speaking around the country. I know you are not anxious to do deputation work, but our need is great. We wonder if you could walk by faith rather than by sight during the next few months?" Since they had sent in the last of the corrected proofs by mid-May of 1930, Cam and Elvira agreed to Karl's request. In April a woman from Denver (one of Legters's contacts) had given Cam and Elvira a Whippet automobile, stipulating that it always be used for "the Lord's work." With this blessing supplied, they felt they couldn't refuse.

And so, during the late spring and summer of 1930, Cam and Elvira spoke in Colorado Springs, Grand Rapids (at what he called "deHaan's Church"), Denver, at Keswick Grove Conference in New Jersey, and in Gull Lake. They also spoke to Cam's mother's relatives in Tennessee, to a Scandinavian young people's conference, and to groups in Kansas City. And through it all, Cam never failed to advocate his idea for an "Air Crusade to reach the forgotten people of South America."

With these speaking engagements Cam and Elvira purposed to raise both money and the public's awareness for cross-cultural missions. The American public in the thirties was creating a mood of cultural isolationism. But this did not deter Cam. He believed all believers had been entrusted with the message of reconciliation and therefore needed to be awakened to both the responsibilities and blessings that come from obedience to God's Word. As a result, Cam and Elvira wrote that they often were well-received and God blessed their efforts—even if the financial returns were, in Elvira's words, "a failure": "Dear Karl, Our trip to Kansas City and St. Joe [in June], if looked at by the receipts (six people gave a total of $50.70), would be considered a failure. However, we felt led of the Lord to speak to the folks there and are happy to leave the results with him."

After their whirlwind speaking trip, they returned to Santa Ana at the end of September in time for Elvira to undergo a series of operations. Leaving the "results with God," even with upside-down circumstances, continued to be fundamental for Cam and Elvira. On October 1 she had her appendix removed, as well as other corrective surgeries. This required a two-week hospital stay, after which she had her tonsils removed. The doctors also became concerned about Elvira's heart. Not exactly sure what the problem was, they knew only it wasn't as strong as it should be.

When Dr. Ironside heard about Elvira's extensive surgery and heart problem, he wrote Cam and Elvira telling them of his concern and informing Elvira that the church had a special prayer meeting on her behalf. Had they known, they would have had a special prayer meeting on behalf of Cam's health as well. Seven weeks after her operation, on November 24, Elvira wrote Karl Hummel about her concern for Cam's health:

> Since we are due to be back on the field by the end of December, I feel I should let you know a little about Cameron's physical condition. I am writing because I know he would never mention how he felt to you, or anyone else. The worst part about his physical condition is that he is as thin as a rail. He looks as if he had been pulled through a knothole.
>
> But that aside, I am worried most over his sleeplessness. He admits the only way he keeps halfway right is to be free from mental strain. Well, Karl, you know Cameron's makeup. The minute he gets back on the field, he's going to be head over heels with problems. And he is carrying many of them right now.
>
> My heart aches for him over this airplane project. Personally, I believe this air service will eventually be a splendid way to reach the hundreds of tribespeople who are at present inaccessible to any gospel witness. However, this project has gotten such a hold on him that night and day he thinks of nothing else. The correspondence on this project is piling up. His speaking engagements and the articles several Christian magazines have asked for are more than we are equal to. Unless the Lord does something supernatural for both of us, neither of us will have the needed strength for such an undertaking.

Presentation of the Câkchiquel New Testament to the president of Guatemala, May 19, 1931 (left to right: Reverend Gregory, President Ubico, Trinidad Bac, Cameron)

Chapter Twenty

A New Epoch

The May 19, 1931, issue of the newspaper *El Liberal Progresisto* ran it as the lead story, complete with a photo: the president of Guatemala, General Jorge Ubico, holding a copy of the Cakchiquel New Testament. On the president's left was the secretary of the American Bible Society for the Caribbean area, Rev. R. R. Gregory. On the president's right, dressed in a handsome new suit, was Trinidad Bac, who presented a special leather-bound copy of the New Testament to President Ubico. And standing beside Trinidad Bac was William Cameron Townsend.

At the ceremony President Ubico said, "This book marks a great forward movement for our civilization." The Minister of Public Education commented, "This book is a work of great cultural value for our people." And still another cabinet official noted, "The Indian is one of our nation's richest treasures. Our future greatness depends on his being lifted above a subsistence level. This book will help us in this great task." Upon receiving his copy, President Ubico turned to Cam and said, "Mr. Townsend, I hope some day you and the Bible Society will translate the Bible for the Quiché people."

The presentation, which was supposed to take only a few minutes, lasted a half hour. And the camera-shy president even allowed his picture to be taken with his three special visitors. This was a moment unforeseen when Cam began his translation project in 1919. Cam's obstacles then were great: a sick wife, his own poor health, a marriage that was under strain, little money, and poor working conditions. He struggled against his own limited knowledge in order to gain technical understanding of the nature of linguistics and Bible translation. In addition, he handled administrative difficulties and squarely faced colleagues who, in various ways, tried to block the Cakchiquel translation of God's Word.

Now, twelve years later, he was receiving accolades and affirmation from the highest office in the land. Not only was God's Word given significant recognition, but the Cakchiquels were honored as people of worth. This was a golden moment to be savored in Cam's memory, a moment for which to thank God for his faithfulness.

But, as Cam revealed in a hand-written letter to his parents on May 21, 1931, a variety of mishaps had preceded this moment:

Dear Home Folks,

This week should be called "New Testament Week." Let me explain. On May 7, I received word from the Bible Society that they had sent eighteen Cakchiquel New Testaments. They were to have arrived the following week. When they did not and we were getting closer and closer to the time for the presentation, I drove to Guatemala City and asked officials at the Post Office to search through their archives. Sure enough, there they were, waiting for some clerk who was taking his time forwarding them to Antigua. What a wonderful and glorious feeling to finally hold the completed New Testament in my hands!

Next I went to the hospital with Rev. Gregory. He was being treated for a bad case of malaria. From the hospital, he, along with Paul and myself, went to the president's home and tried to make an appointment for the following day, without success. I did, however, have an interview with the chief of staff on Saturday. He dictated a telegram for us to send to the president and assured us we would be received on Monday. After driving back to San Antonio in a terrific downpour, we returned to the capital on Sunday afternoon. Rev. Gregory had to go back to the hospital for another malaria treatment. I wanted Elvira to go with us, but she said she did not want to leave her correspondence and housework. It probably was just as well because we had a flat tire. The lock on the spare tire was frozen, which delayed us for almost two hours.

Monday morning we went to the new airport and saw Mr. Haymaker off. It was altogether fitting that this senior missionary to Central America should be the first to fly from Guatemala to the States.[1] Axel Anderson, acting dean of our Spanish Bible school, was there and told me a telegram had come for us from the president, giving us an appointment at 4:00 P.M. Tuesday. Our excitement knew no bounds. We were expected for a conference in Patzún on Monday evening and therefore had wired Carl [Malmstrom] of our delay and asked him to postpone the service with the believers until Wednesday.

On the day we were to meet the president, we met for prayer at 3 o'clock and then as instructed, arrived at the palace ahead of time and were shown into a waiting room. We had arranged for a photographer to go with us even though we were told the president was reticent about having his picture taken. However, without knowing it, the Lord led us to secure the services of the president's official photographer.

A little after 4:00 P.M., we were ushered into the inner waiting room where we waited for another half hour. Finally we were admitted. The president received us most cordially. In fact he made us feel so much at home I almost forgot my speech. I told him what the Bible had already done for Guatemala and what it would do in the future. I introduced Rev. Gregory who explained the work of the Bible Society. We then presented him with the specially bound copy with his name printed in gold letters on the cover.

Cam's letter also described their visit to the minister of education, who received them with similar warmth and cordiality. The minister said he thought the government could buy a New Testament for each government teacher. Shortly after 6:00 P.M., Cam and his party left the government offices and celebrated at a local restaurant. And since the church's dedication of the New Testament was the following day, they then left for Patzún.

The church in Patzún, despite continuing antiforeign sentiment, remained strong. The chapel that Wednesday was packed with over a hundred people. There were songs, testimonies, and speeches given, but the highlight of the day came when Trinidad Bac was presented with his own copy of the New Testament by Rev. Gregory, after Bac had given his dramatic testimony. Forgetting his Cakchiquel reserve, he waved his New Testament high in the air and said, "This is the greatest day in the history of the Cakchiquel people. We have finally received God's Word in our own language. This will ever be my most precious treasure, and when I die I will bequeath it to my oldest son. Thanks to God." At that point the congregation shouted as with one voice, "*Matiox chire Dios, Matiox chire Dios, Matiox chire Dios!*" (Thanks to God!).

Cam continued in his letter:

> I closed the service with a short résumé of how God had taken care of Elvira (she was there with us and took part in the service) and me through the long difficult years it took to complete the New Testament. I then urged an advance into new territories, especially mentioning the president's wish that the New Testament be translated into Quiché. Before the service ended, it began to rain heavily and came through the roof. Amidst the rain dripping down over us, we appropriately sang "There Shall be Showers of Blessing."
>
> It was hard to close the meeting. Everyone wanted to tell something of what the Lord and the New Testament in their language meant to them. Finally the last excited speaker was Gregorio Sirim who said, "This book marks a new epoch for each of us. Each year we should celebrate the 20th of May as the day upon which we received God's Word in our language." The roof leaked, we were wet, but each one left with feelings of praise, warmth and happiness.

Cam's happiness, however, soon gave way to sorrow. A letter from Cam's sister relayed the news that their saintly dear mother was in the hospital taking radium treatments for cancer. Cam wrote to tell his mother how she had affected his life, and how thankful he was to God for her encouragement, support, and godly example: "When I heard of your illness, I went immediately to the Word for his help. The first word I read was, 'Fear not, Abraham.' Then from 1 Peter 3:12, the Lord gave me this promise, 'The eyes of the Lord are over the righteous, and his ears are open unto their prayers.' I am asking the Lord to bless the treatments and to quickly restore you to health."

On June 10, Cam's and Paul's father wrote to tell them that, in spite of the doctors' best efforts, their mother was "going down fast":

> It would be nice if you folks had money to come home and see your mother again. If I could hear from you, maybe I would not feel so lonesome. Your mother says she is ready to go. She is trusting in Jesus, and it will not be long until I have to go as well. Let us all be ready to meet one another where death cannot enter and where there will be no more parting. Pray for me that I will be enabled to please him in all things and rejoice in God my Saviour; that will be my strength. May the Comforter dwell in us richly. With a lot of love from Father T.
>
> P.S. Yesterday was our 48th anniversary and my 76th birthday.

Though the completion of the New Testament was a major achievement, there was more work to be done. Cam and Elvira began implementing reading and literacy campaigns throughout the Cakchiquel area. Assisting Cam and Elvira were Cam's nephew, Ronald White (who was home from college), Anne Edson (who, in December 1930, had come with Cam and Elvira to Guatemala), and three national helpers. Cam prepared a primer that used what he called "[my] own psycho-phonetic method." With this simple method, each letter represented a single sound, and only a few new letters were introduced. This enabled students to begin reading simple words almost immediately.

To the group's delight and surprise, they discovered that, with motivation, students learned to read quickly, some within two weeks. When word spread that people could actually read and understand the words, the reading classes grew to almost four hundred men, women, and young people. In July, Cam and Elvira held a two-week reading campaign in the town of Comalapa. It was a cold, miserable time, raining every day. And they slept in dank and drafty huts. Cam caught a bad cold on that trip—a harbinger of things to come.

In July Cam sent a letter to Legters saying he wanted to do survey work, as President Ubico wished, for Quiché translation work:

> Should the Lord open the way, I would like to take Elvira and make a survey of the Quiché area to see if the Lord is calling us into such

a work. We are moving the Cakchiquels into becoming self-directing and self-supporting. With the introduction and good reception of the Cakchiquel New Testament, plus the San Antonio and Panajachel schools to train leaders, we are now in a position to leave this work.

I am most anxious to go to a new tribe. However, Elvira's health will not permit our going to the jungle tribes; thus, I fear I will have to look into the Quiché situation (using a chartered airplane). The other possibility is to look into working with the Indians who live around the San Cristóbal de Las Casas area in Mexico. Please remember us in your prayers (Romans 15:20).

In spite of the mission board's continued lack of enthusiasm for using airplanes, Cam's vision for aviation continued. His letters during this time referred to a chilling December 1930 incident that crystallized the reason his vision continued. Pioneering a mission station in Brazil, two thousand miles inland in impenetrable jungle and over five hundred miles from the nearest railway station, missionary Arthur Tylee, his two-and-a-half-year-old daughter, and a missionary nurse, Mildred Kratz, were tragically massacred by the Nambikuara Indians.[2] Cam wrote, "I still believe airplanes are the only possible method of reaching the jungle peoples. I believe men like [potential pilot] Van Sickle[3] and others will be able to carry out this adventure in Petén and southern Mexico."

On August 19, Cam and Elvira received official commendation from Karl Hummel for the important contribution they had made with the publication of the Cakchiquel New Testament, and he advised them that the board felt strongly that they should continue work with the Cakchiquels "in order to ensure adequate returns on this large investment." Hummel also advised Cam to curtail his concerns with the "hydro-airplane" project.

To the Pioneer Mission Agency on August 24, Cam reported his first use of an airplane to "scout out the land" in the Petén area of Guatemala:

Mr. Van Sickle and I have not yet reached Petén. We have been delayed for three weeks for a variety of reasons. The aviation company promised for sure to take us through. We had our packs and provisions for a month of hiking and got into the plane at seven in the morning. But after flying over the mountains for about forty minutes, one of the three motors developed trouble, and we had to land. The pilot fixed the trouble, but in the meantime, a dense black cloud bank came up. The pilot was afraid to continue, and we returned.

These delays have convinced me that God's time has not yet come for us to use air travel, and I have postponed the trip until after we hold a series of meetings at the Robinson Institute. I want to give intensive reading lessons to the men who have not yet learned to read. Elvira will teach music.

With the airplane project on hold, Cam returned to work on another plan: changing the leadership of congregations from expatriate to national leaders. As Cam prepared to begin this project, he received a letter from Axel Anderson, chairman of the newly formed field committee. This letter challenged Cam's plan for self-governing congregations. Also in this letter, Anderson asked Cam and Elvira to take over Carl and Genevieve Malmstrom's work during their furlough. Cam's response, on August 26, 1931, created a firestorm: "Dear Axel, I am writing to let you know that in view of the committee's changed position on turning over the direction and support of national churches to the nationals, I revoke our promise to take over Carl and Genevieve's work when they go on furlough."

Axel responded to the letter by writing field committee member Fern Houser (Houser had strongly opposed Cam over the issue of national and *ladino* church leadership):

> His letter sounds to me like he wrote it in the spirit of, "If you don't do as I want, I won't play." Besides falling down on his promises, he seems to forget the clause in the Mission's Principles and Practices that states missionaries should be willing to fill in for another missionary in an emergency.
>
> Some of us have had to move and suspend our programs for the good of the work. Why should he show such a spirit of independence? Why does he think he is such a favorite? As it is, no one hindered him from his Petén plan.

The battle of wits and wills had begun. The more the field committee insisted he abide by mission policy, the more Cam resisted. This fundamental principle, Cam felt, could not be compromised—developing indigenous churches was not a "fanciful dream."

Previously in 1927, Cam had proposed that the churches organize themselves under a semi-Presbyterian form of government. This proved too ambitious and in Cam's words, "too unnatural for a people untrained in representative government." Learning from this failed experiment, Cam now sent a letter to all the indigenous congregations saying the time had come. They should now govern and support themselves. Expatriate missionaries would now organize and hold Bible conferences, train teachers, pastors, and evangelists, and function as advisors for the congregations. Since most of the national workers were paid from Central American Mission monies, their support would continue for a limited period on a regularly diminishing scale until the churches themselves could assume, and/or decide what paid staff they needed and wanted.

In the fall of 1931, Cam faced two dilemmas. He was convinced that it was God's will to invest his energies into a new work; but how was he to do that and what would the work be? He also didn't know if he should obey the administration's wishes and take up the Malmstroms' work; would that mean compromising his vision for a self-supporting indigenous church?

On September 3, 1931, Cam drove to Guatemala City to explain his point of view to Axel Anderson, but Axel was not at home. The following day Cam wrote a lengthy letter explaining his position—a position, he said, that had been newly "strengthened":

> We regret more than we can say that it is against the wishes of Carl Malmstrom, the Field Committee, and the Home Council, but we dare not disobey what we are firmly convinced is the Lord's will for us. Humanly, we would like to obey the powers that be and take up Carl and Genevieve's work for this coming year, but we feel we can accomplish more by using our gifts in the way I have outlined.

With the letter, Cam sent a detailed plan of his proposed activities, including organizing a traveling evangelistic clinic with Dr. Ainslie in the Quiché or Mam area, working on the airplane project, and many more grand plans, none of which included the Field Committee's directive to help the Malmstroms. The committee saw this as an absolute refusal, full of rationalizations, which masked as the need to uphold a fundamental principle.

Though Cam couldn't talk to Axel, he succeeded in talking with Carl. As a result, Carl modified his position to be more in Cam's favor. Writing on September 11, this time with a softer stance, Cam said to Axel Anderson: "I do hope you understand that we made our plans not in the spirit of independence, but rather in the realization that [God] may change them entirely. The point we are sure about is that he is leading us into more or less a new work, and we cannot turn back."

The field committee did not fully understand or agree with Cam's position. Anderson did not want to tell anyone what the Lord's will for them might be. But he was swift to quote Proverbs 11:14 and 24:6: "In the multitude of counselors there is safety," and then asked why everyone else had to subscribe to the principles and practices of the mission, but Cam Townsend did not. Fern Houser wrote:

> It looks as though Cameron is disposed to obey no other authority but his own. Should we force him to our appointment [taking over Malmstroms' work while they were on furlough] and cause his dismissal from the mission? From the looks of things, this seems to be what would happen if we press our field committee authority. On the other hand, if we cannot work in harmony, are we better off without him? It would not, in my opinion, be good for the general discipline of the mission to let him do as he pleases.

In October 1931, Cam and Elvira learned that L. L. Legters had remarried. Cam invited Legters and his new bride, Edna, to honeymoon in Guatemala. "If you come," said Cam, "we could then discuss your idea of us working among the San Blas Indians of Panama." But before they made a decision, they could both go to Panama to see if this would be the right thing for them. He then added:

> A great deal of pressure is being brought to bear upon us to stay with the Cakchiquels. But the leading from the Lord is for us to keep free from "compromise" and to be ready to step forward when he

opens the way. Now that Carl and Genevieve are leaving on furlough, we'll have to give some time to their work. However, when the way opens, we are ready to move on toward Mexico.

Whether it was the board's and field committee's pressure that influenced Cam, or the two conferences he attended, or the prompting of the Holy Spirit to reconsider his decision to fill in for the Malmstroms, we will never know. No letters or diaries explain his change of mind. But it is this pivotal decision that stands at the apex of Cam's Guatemala career. This turning point was to give meaning to happenings in the future. If Cam had been unwilling to help in Panajachel, or unwilling to let God lead him "in the way," he, in all probability, would never have met the stranger by the lake.

The eruption of Volcano **Fuego**

Chapter Twenty-One

Goodbye to Guatemala

One October afternoon in 1931, Cam noticed a well-dressed tourist strolling beside the lakeshore, enjoying the quiet beauty and tranquillity of Lake Atitlán. Cam introduced himself with his usual warm smile and handshake. The stranger was the distinguished educator, Dr. Moisés Sáenz, then the undersecretary of Mexico's Department of Education. He explained that he had come to Guatemala as part of an intergovernment conference on rural education. Cam invited him home.

Even in the midst of his urgency to get work done and see things happen, Cam was seldom in a hurry. And this was never more true than when he showed hospitality. Even in the middle of a day brimming with high-level appointments and meetings, Cam knew how to drop everything and give himself fully to the person who had come to his door. Like Abraham's servant, Cam was guided by the truth in Genesis 24:27: "I being in the way, the Lord led me" (KJV). Cam had made this a fundamental and conscious prayer from his days as a colporteur. Thus he was open to the unexpected, to new possibilities and new worlds.

Cam spent the entire day with Sáenz, showing him around the various points of interest in Panajachel and the lake. Of course, Cam lost no opportunity explaining his own interest in public education. With pride he showed Sáenz the Robinson Bible School, his curriculum in

Cakchiquel, and his translation. Cam also told him about the school and clinic in San Antonio and how the government had once given him permission to open schools in Patzún, Palopó, and Balanya.

Cam told Dr. Sáenz that ever since he first came to work among the Cakchiquels, his dream had been to establish a large school system administered by national teachers and supported by local indigenous congregations. However, the depression had made it impossible for the local congregations to continue supporting several of the schools, even though they could have remained open for as little as twenty-five dollars per month. He told Dr. Sáenz about the reading and literacy campaign he had been conducting throughout the countryside and also related a story about the school in Patzún:

> I knew the day was coming when the government would no longer allow mission schools. I approached the minister of education and offered to turn over the school in Patzún with all its equipment, on the condition they would continue to run the school for Indian children with the same Indian teachers who were then employed. My offer was accepted, and the school was nationalized. But after a month, the *ladino* authorities in Patzún objected to Indian children being educated in a government-run school. The school was closed and the equipment turned over to a *ladino* boys' school.
>
> When this happened, the Cakchiquel chiefs strongly objected and asked me to help them get permission to reopen the school. I was able to raise enough money from the merchants in Antigua and Guatemala City to pay for the teachers' salaries since the government said they had no money to pay the teachers.
>
> I secured ten teachers, all of them Cakchiquels and all believers, and the school was reopened. The teachers used the Cakchiquel New Testament and the primer the government had printed for me as their textbooks.

Since Moisés Sáenz had been known as a champion of Protestantism during a time in Mexico when it was not politically correct to be associated with any church, he was impressed with Cam's work. At the end of the day, he said, "You, as a foreigner, have done more for rural education than anyone I know. Mexico is most anxious to see the Indians of our land progress and become part of the national culture. What you have done and are doing here in Guatemala is exactly what Mexico needs. If you were to come to Mexico and do there what you have done here, I am confident the Mexican government would help you."

On November 11, 1931, Cam wrote Legters about this fortuitous visit with Sáenz:

> When Dr. Moisés Sáenz came through here as a representative of the government of Mexico on a fact-finding mission to study the problems of the Indian people, he told me about the need among the Aztec people. He said there was a town, a four-hour drive from Mexico City, where the Aztec people speak less Spanish than do the people here in Panajachel. He said they should have the New Testament translated for them, just as I had done for the Cakchiquels.
>
> We continue to be in the dark as to where God would have us work next. But when the need is so great, and our desire to go to those who have had no opportunity to hear is so impelling, he surely must want us to undertake a new field. In the meantime, while he makes his will plain to us we will keep plugging away at the wonderful opportunities surrounding us here. The doors are wide open.

So it was that a providential meeting one afternoon opened the door to Mexico—where Cam would begin the second stage of his Bible translation career and where the Summer Institute of Linguistics would be born.

On January 18, 1932, Cam reported to Karl Hummel that the local congregations, who had assumed responsibility for their own leadership, were proving themselves equal to the challenge:

> Several of the local congregations have surprised us by the enthusiasm with which they are taking hold of the direction and support of their work. One congregation (the San Martín) took over the entire support of their pastor, and two others have done the same. One worker, who serves two congregations, has his support divided between two congregations. The result is that the mission has almost no financial responsibility for these works. It seems strange that we didn't get our eyes open long before now. With

this new independence, the workers themselves are becoming more industrious. There's a reason!

Cam concluded with a word of appreciation for the council's recently passed resolution in favor of turning over the local congregations to national and indigenous leadership. He then said he was continuing to pray for the privilege of going to a new field and that the new field was beginning to look more and more like Mexico.

On the heels of this letter to Hummel, Cam wrote Legters that he had received a letter from Moisés Sáenz, confirming what he had already said to Cam in October and asking him to think seriously of coming to Mexico to work in education. Legters reported to Cam on January 21 that, from the vantage point of his several trips to Mexico, his opinion was that the time was ripe to begin a work there. He wrote, "I do wish it were possible for you, now that Dr. Sáenz has given you an invitation to come to Mexico, to consider that a very definite door of opportunity has opened for you [to begin a new work among the Indians]."

On the afternoon of January 21, 1932, Cam, Elvira, and the entire population surrounding San Antonio, Escuintla, and Panajachel experienced the eruption of the volcano *Fuego*. To her family Elvira wrote her feelings and a description of that incredible moment. The letter was later printed in the *Central American Bulletin:*

> How can one describe a volcanic eruption? It's at once most beautiful and awe inspiring. It's also a most horrible and frightening sight. Early yesterday morning we began to feel the ground shaking under us. This kept getting stronger and stronger until 1:30 P.M. Then the volcano *Fuego* (fire) started to roar! In just a few minutes, thick smoke began belching into the sky. By 3:00 P.M. we were in almost total darkness, with ashes coming down like rain.
>
> The earthquakes became stronger and stronger until the earth began to lift itself, and all the while the volcano was roaring louder and louder while thick columns of smoke poured forth.
>
> That night we had an evening chapel service and wondered if anyone would come. To our amazement the chapel was filled. Cameron spoke even though he said he felt almost too weak to

preach. The air was heavy with the smell of sulphur and tended to make one nauseous.

We had a good meeting. But just as the last ones were leaving, it began to thunder and flash lightning. What a sight! The volcano was shooting great tongues of fire into the sky and roaring its awful roar while the earth continued to shake. As the volcano increased in power, flames would leap hundreds of feet into the air. Then great boulders, red hot, that looked like skyrockets, shot into the sky and rolled down the sides of the volcano.

This kept up until five o'clock in the morning. What a sight in San Antonio. Everything is covered with sand and ash. Houses, trees, everything. (I was told later that one town was covered with over a foot of sand and some of the houses were crushed by the weight.) As I write this letter, the ash continues to fall and only occasionally do we feel a jolt or earth-shaking. We suffered no real damage except for cracked walls, and no loss of life. Cameron read Psalm 46 last night, "God is our refuge and strength, a very present help in trouble." He said he thought this was an appropriate verse for earthquake days.

A month later, on February 23, 1932, Cam received another jolt. This time it was from pain and bewilderment as he learned of his mother's death. He received the news that she had been buried on February 15 in Santa Ana. On February 26, Cam wrote his father, displaying the introspective side few ever saw:

Dear Father,
Word of Mother's home-going came as a shock. The last letter I received from you told of a seeming improvement. This gave me confidence the Lord was going to restore her health. I didn't teach my reading classes that afternoon but spent the time in prayer. I know, of course, the rest and glory of life she is enjoying in heaven must be wonderful.

I was not a bit rebellious at the Lord taking her, after having spared her life all these years. At the same time, I couldn't understand why he had refused my petition when I had received such assurance that he was going to answer my request. My only answer is that I fear I had been presuming, on the Lord, and I must learn not to do that if he is going to use me to accomplish the things which need to be done among the Indians here. After a long time in prayer the Lord strengthened my soul, and I was able to teach my classes that evening.

Since then I have thought a great deal about what Mother meant to me and the rich heritage she left us all: her indomitable courage as she struggled against great obstacles, her resourcefulness, cheerfulness, and constant hope for improvement and progress of every kind. I thought of her desire to serve, her absolute integrity, her love of work, her humility and nobility of soul and last, but not least, her love and patience.

I hope all we, her children, may be able to more and more take possession of that inheritance. I look forward to the day with joyful expectation when we'll meet again, nevermore to part. How much we have to be thankful for! Praise his name.

I must close now and head back to Patzún. Elvira took sick up there, and I had to take her to the hospital. Your son, Cameron.

Cameron Townsend sometimes operated on the principle that what is not forbidden is permissible. If a colleague or the board or field committee happened not to be pointedly specific in relaying a proposal, project, or course of action, Cam, with his own agenda well in mind, might use such ambiguity to his own advantage. But Dr. Ainslie gave him no such loophole when he "ordered" Cam to come to Guatemala City at the end of March for a complete physical checkup.

When Dr. Ainslie examined Cam, he was concerned. Cam was clearly run-down, overworked, and had a severe bronchial inflammation that had not responded to conventional treatment. For months, Cam had been having severe bronchial problems. Ainslie suspected tuberculosis. Though Cam's sputum examination proved negative, Ainslie was not satisfied. He ordered Cam to leave the cold Patzún area for a complete two-month rest in the hot desert area of the country called El Rancho Guatemala.

Cam said he would take "every precaution until the inflammation disappeared." But immediately after he wrote this, he took part in a high-level field committee meeting and dug into heavy correspondence to family, friends, and the Central American Mission board. On June 10, Elvira, who herself was quite unwell with a degenerative heart condition, wrote a fuller account of Cam's examination and condition in a letter to her friend, Mildred Spain:

It is now over three months since we came to this hot, dry desert. Dr. Ainslie said Cam has a serious bronchial infection. At first he thought it was T.B., but they can't seem to find the bug to confirm this. Both Dr. Ainslie and Dr. Pinkerton have given strict instructions that Cam do absolutely no work. He is supposed to do nothing but rest, sleep, and eat.

The problem is that Cameron's health is not improving. Dr. Pinkerton has suggested we move back to Panajachel to see if this will help. If Cameron's condition does not improve, we will have to return to the States. We know the Lord can heal his lungs, and count on your prayers. I hate to complain about myself at such a time as this, but I am absolutely pepless. The days are long, and neither of us have been able to sleep very well here in El Rancho.

Then on August 26, 1932, Elvira wrote a letter to Karl Hummel that shocked the board and colleagues of the Central American Mission:

When x-rays were taken of Cam's lungs last week, the doctor found they were in worse condition than he had thought. He now insists we leave as soon as possible for the States. We have prayed a great deal about this. At first we thought I would remain on the field and just let Cameron go back. The doctor said he thought with a year's rest, Cameron's strength would return. However, we did not feel at peace about this and just yesterday morning made a decision that both of us believe is clear guidance from above.

As you know we have had our hearts and minds set on moving into a new territory for a long time. Since our return from the States, we have felt at a loss to find our place. That does not mean we haven't been working. Just the contrary is true. We have had a strenuous period of service and have felt happy and satisfied that some of the difficult problems have been solved. We are also pleased we have had a small part in getting the congregations among the Cakchiquels better organized and into the hands of the national workers.

But now that Cameron is broken in health, and the doctor is anxious for him to leave Guatemala as soon as possible, we feel this is the time for us to make a clean break with this field. You all can appreciate how hard this is for us. We love Guatemala and the people here. In some ways, we feel like we are Guatemalans ourselves. We have so many wonderful friends here that when we leave, it will truly be like leaving home.

At the same time, since having made the decision, the Lord has filled us both with a great peace, and we take this as his seal upon this move. We are selling all our furniture and other things and saying "goodbye to Guatemala." We expect to sail for Los Angeles next Sunday. It is hard to think of putting Cameron in a sanitarium, besides the expense would be out of reach for us. We are thinking about trying to find a little shack in the desert of California or Arizona.

We thank God for the privilege we have had for these years to work with the Mission, and for the happy fellowship with our colleagues. We especially count on your prayers on Cameron's behalf that he may regain his health and strength.

The age-old question of how to know God's will reappeared in Cam and Elvira's life. They were serious believers, people who wanted their lives, actions, and talents to be used in God's design for them. But how could they have the surety of knowing that a certain action was in line with God's plan? By believing that God guides his people through obedience to his Word. This is what Cam and Elvira believed, and they trusted that fulfillment of God's guidance would come as a result of that obedience.

The day after Cam and Elvira arrived in Santa Ana, California, in September 1932, Karl Hummel sent a letter telling them how shocked and saddened he and the board were over their decision to leave Guatemala. He assured Cam of their prayers for a complete recovery and understood perfectly the need to return home to regain his health. He said he was going to find it difficult, as were many other missionaries, not to have them be a vital part of the work in Guatemala. And then in response to the issue Cam seemed to interject (his sickness notwithstanding) in most of his correspondence—the question about the airplane project—Hummel said:

One of the things in my last letter (that you did not receive) was that if you do pursue the [airplane] project, I hope you will not have to organize another mission. There has been such multiplicity of independent missions in recent years that it is making it very difficult on the established missions. (The continuing depression has hit our missionary budget very hard indeed.) To lower our overhead, the Central American Mission is currently considering amalgamating with another Latin American faith mission.

Cam's response on October 14, 1932, in the light of the future formation of WBT, SIL, and JAARS, is nothing short of prophetic:

Our plans for the moment are a little indefinite. We know only that God is calling us to attempt something different, on a scale larger than anything we have yet tried in order to reach the "wild" tribes of South America. For safety and efficiency, Mr. Legters and I are convinced that hydro-plane transportation must be used to reach these out-of-the-way people.

Just when and how God will open the door for us to move ahead, we do not know. If funds were available next spring I would like to visit some of the countries where these unreached people live. It might be we could ask the government officials in some of these countries favorable to our project, if they could help us in some way.

In the meantime we need to be lining up young men (single, under twenty-five) who are qualified to go. These young men would be given a six-month training course in some swampy wooded region of the U.S. Dr. Pinkerton thinks he can secure such a spot in North Carolina. The young men who pass the training test and qualify would then be ready for field work.[1]

My idea is that actual contact would be done by young men with no homes to keep up until they make progress in the language and are given permission to live and work for a time right where the people live. (A working station should be established in the center of the tribal area.) At the moment, the Brazilian government does not permit single men to enter its protected areas. I am hoping that an exception can be made for our project.

Cam ended his letter by informing Karl that he was feeling much better and gaining weight. He had been diagnosed with tuberculosis, but the attending physician did not recommend confinement to a sanitarium.

One reason may have been that after he had examined Elvira's heart, the doctor ordered *her* to have complete bed rest with a minimum of emotional stress. Since Cam was feeling a bit better, he took over the household duties.

In November 1932, the same month Franklin D. Roosevelt was elected president of the United States, Cam began a fifteen-minute daily radio broadcast over station KREG in Santa Ana to acquaint people with the needs of minority peoples in Mexico, Central, and South America, as well as introduced opportunities for reaching these people groups. November also was the month Cam received official word from the Central American Mission board informing him that they did not in any way feel called to be involved in South America: "You can count on our prayer fellowship and interest from individual board members. But it does not appear to be the part of wisdom for the Mission to undertake such a responsibility as your project envisions."

Legters, on the other hand, continued to fire Townsend's vision and imagination with the needs and opportunities for work in South America, particularly in Brazil.

L. L. Legters, Edna Legters, Elvira and Cameron

New Directions

In 1933, most people in the United States and Canada knew that when they switched on the radio and heard, "Good evening Mr. and Mrs. America and all the ships at sea," they were listening to the voice of the popular news and gossip commentator, Walter Winchell. In the thirties, radio had become the single most powerful communication instrument in the world. President Franklin D. Roosevelt used the power of the airwaves to soothe, calm, and reassure those alarmed by the Depression with his "fireside chats." If one had something to sell or important information to give, radio was the way to reach the masses. And that's exactly what Cameron Townsend wanted to do—reach as many people as he could with his vision.

In January 1933, Cam's radio program, "The Foreign Missions Period" over Santa Ana station KREG, was a month old. Admittedly, it was only a fifteen-minute program, and his time slot of 10:00 to 10:15 A.M. wasn't exactly prime time, but it was a beginning. Cam shared the programming with visiting missionaries, local pastors, and speakers, with Saturdays dedicated to programs for children. On January 4, Cam wrote to Karl Hummel: "We know our time slot is not the best, but people tell us they try to listen every day. The financial support came in for a while, but there has been a bit of a lull, and we may have to give it up."

A day later, Cam scribbled a three-line note to Hummel with the news that the station manager had told him he could continue broadcasting indefinitely and not to worry about paying for air time. For the moment it seemed it was God's will for Cam's radio ministry to continue.

Cam was happy over this unexpected good fortune and also for the progress in his general health. The doctor had prescribed good food and rest. He and Elvira were living in a small wooden house next to his sister Lula and her husband, Eugene Griset. The Grisets' small farm provided the good food; southern California provided the sunshine. Both were doing wonders for Cam. The prognosis for Elvira, however, was not good. Her congestive heart ailment was becoming increasingly painful, giving everyone cause for concern. In addition, Elvira was unhappy with her living conditions, adding to her stress. Cam knew he needed to make a change, but wasn't sure exactly what to do. This, after all, was at the height of the Depression, and they were living rent-free. In the meantime, he looked forward to a visit from his greatest encourager, L. L. Legters, with his new wife, Edna.

Legters came to Southern California in February to hold four conferences in the area. He also came to talk with Cam about his future. From the time of the Chichicastenango Conference in 1921, Legters and Cam had shared the vision for taking the gospel to indigenous peoples in Mexico and South America. This vision, in the early days of 1933, was still coming into focus.

There is a curious footnote to this moment in time: Wycliffe history properly accords L. L. Legters as the co-founder with Cameron Townsend of Wycliffe Bible Translators and the Summer Institute of Linguistics. There is, however, no recorded formal agreement to mark the union of purpose between these two men. The only record of this reality is from Cam who once said: "When Legters came to visit me in February of 1933, we talked at length about our future service and particularly about a school. Finally, I said, 'I will cooperate with you if you will cooperate with me in starting a linguistic training course for missionaries.' Mr. Legters said simply, 'All right.'"

In 1929, Cam had written a letter in response to a mission policy that discouraged fellow missionaries from learning Indian languages. He

said, "It is my opinion that all new recruits for Indian work should spend their language study at a place where specialized Indian work is being done in order that they not become sidetracked from learning the Indian language." Now, Legters and Townsend incorporated plans to both encourage that language work and provide learning help. Of this Cam later related that, "Inasmuch as one of the greatest barriers in reaching [ethnic minorities] was the difficulty of learning their languages, I suggested we found a summer institute where pioneer missionaries could be taught how to reduce a language to writing and to translate the Scriptures."[1] Cam and Legters agreed that when the school started it should be called "Camp Wycliffe."

Perhaps more than any other single person in Townsend's life, L. L. Legters refused to let Cam's vision evaporate or be compromised. He gave practical shape to Cam's vision. Now, in view of the depressed economy and Elvira's health, Legters once again urged Cam to consider Mexico as the next field of service. Cam was open to the idea but not entirely convinced God was calling him there. Elvira's health precluded his earlier desire to work with the Lacandones in southern Mexico. She simply wasn't strong enough for any more primitive living conditions.

At this stage, Cam said, his plans were indefinite. Karl Hummel asked him to take part in Moody Church's large mission conference in May. But then on March 16, 1933, Cam wrote Hummel a distressing letter:

> Last week, when I took Elvira for treatment, her heartbeat was 140 per minute. The doctor immediately put her in the hospital. It took a long time to get her heart under control. Even now she has to take digitalis and other heart medicine every day. She is home now, but the doctor has ordered strict bed rest. I have to do everything for her including all the cooking. On top of that, we had an earthquake here last Friday. We thought when we left Guatemala we would not have to experience any more shakes.
>
> Elvira's condition since leaving the hospital, continues to be weak. I am afraid her recovery is going to be slow. We are much perplexed at what the Lord's will might be in this matter. We both want to be active in his vineyard. But for the moment, his plan is different than ours. I am sure someday we will see his was the best. In the meantime, pray we will have patience. The doctors say it will take a long time for her heart muscles to strengthen.

Don't count on us for the missionary rally. The doctors advise against Elvira taking a trip to Chicago. Did I tell you that Charles Fuller has left his church in Placentia and plans to go into home mission radio work? I wish we could get him for foreign missions. He told me his heart had always been with foreign missions, but his radio program is a big success. He gets $850.00 each month in contributions.

Our own program, "The Foreign Missions Period," continues (our contributions are nowhere close to Fuller's). A committee of local pastors and Bible teachers is now sponsoring it. I have been talking to my friend William G. Nyman, who formerly owned a lumber business in Chicago and is on the board of several missions, including the Orinoco River Mission. He believes we can start a similar radio ministry on a larger station in Los Angeles. I would have done this already if I didn't have to stay at home to be cook and nurse for Elvira.

On April 11, Cam sent Hummel an update on Elvira's condition, also indicating his desire to return to "active" service on the mission field. He simply felt out of place in the States:

For the moment, returning to the field is out of the question. Elvira's doctor told me it will be several months before she should try a move to Chicago. He said it would be a year or two before we should consider going back to the field. And if Elvira should return, her activity would be severely limited. Elvira and I feel we will get back to the mission field sometime, but the days of waiting are hard. Doubtless the Lord has a purpose in all this.

Cam concluded his letter by telling Hummel that he was to have a part in the Church of the Open Door's mission rally. Cam didn't have any slides to show, but he did have Elena Trejo, a young Cakchiquel woman whom Elvira and Cam had taken into their home. "Just think, ten years ago this young girl ran away from a forced marriage to a drunken Indian. Since then she has learned two languages, gotten her bachelor's degree, and is to graduate in June from her pre-medical course."

A month later Elvira was showing small signs of improvement and wrote a letter of condolence to a friend mourning the death of a family member. She revealed that Cam, with William Nyman's help, had begun another missionary broadcast over station KMPC in Los Angeles. It was being aired every Monday morning between 11:00 and 11:30.

By early July, Elvira had weathered the worst of her heart problem. Her physician was encouraged with her progress and said she might be strong enough in the fall to travel to Chicago. Elvira was also encouraged, realizing this meant leaving the old wooden farmhouse in Santa Ana. To Mildred Spain she wrote:

> I must tell you how the Lord has supplied our need. It came out of a clear sky, or should I say a clouded sky. I say this because it came to us on a morning when I told the Lord I couldn't stand it any longer [living in this house].
>
> Mr. and Mrs. Nyman live in Glendale, California, and have fixed up a darling three-room apartment over their garage. It has a large bathroom, a hallway, and back porch. It's furnished beautifully, even has floor and table lamps. The Nymans will make this available for their many missionary friends. We are the first ones to occupy this apartment. The Nymans have invited us to spend the next two months in this lovely place. The grounds of their home are like a beautiful park. I can't tell you how much better I am feeling since we arrived. We often take our meals outdoors. Mrs. Nyman is a wonderful sister in the Lord.

During the spring and summer of 1933, support for most Central American Mission missionaries in Guatemala was almost nonexistent. Elvira's friend Mildred Spain, who worked in the Central American Mission office in Dallas, said she could hardly live through the experience of having to write missionaries on the field with the news that no money had come in for them. Besides struggling with the severe economic crisis of a world depression, the Central American Mission missionaries and board were caught in the upheaval of Guatemala's liberal reforms.

Military and administrative reforms in the thirties were designed to strengthen the central government's authority in Guatemala City. These reforms moved away from a feudal agrarian tradition, seeking to modernize, to expand trade, and to expand government revenues. And along with its new liberal powers, in both Guatemala and Mexico, the government instituted an official policy of anticlericalism. Both of these countries closed their borders to foreign missionaries, clergy, and self-described do-gooders who wanted to work with ethnic peoples.

Where did this leave Cam and Legters and their dream? It left Cam with the care of Elvira (who was nearly an invalid), with little money, and with poor health himself ("a half-man," as Ken Pike would one day describe him). Cam wrote that perhaps the purpose for the obstacles he was encountering was to eliminate the "dross" that remained in his life. In light of the remarkable events that occurred from August to December of 1933, the "dross" that God wanted Cam to eliminate seemed to be Cam's complete absorption with *his* own vision. Later God showed Cam, and those who held to Cam's vision, that the dream would be realized on *God's* terms and in *God's* timing. To hear those terms, Cam had to listen to the still, inner voice of God. In years to come, WBT and SIL leadership would require training in how to discern and listen actively to God's quiet voice that said, "This is the way, walk ye in it (Isa. 30:21, KJV)."

The August Victorious Life Conference in Keswick Grove, New Jersey, was coming soon. Legters invited Cam to attend. Cam would have enjoyed going but declined. His nephew and nieces attending John Brown University in Siloam Springs, Arkansas, had driven Cam's small car to school. Cam planned to retrieve his car in the early fall after he and Elvira took the train to Dallas. They would stop in Eagle Pass, Texas, where Cam wanted to investigate a new radio station that beamed into Mexico and Central America. Using Dallas as a base in September and October, they planned to travel to various mideast areas.

In the meantime, Legters went to speak at the Keswick Conference with two visions burning in his heart. With his usual flamboyance, he spoke first about the (what he then believed were) fifty-one distinct tribal groups in Mexico who had never heard the gospel in their own language. He challenged the people to pray for an open door to this land that had sealed its borders against all outside missionaries.

Legters's second vision and burden for prayer was for the linguistic training school where prospective pioneer missionaries, or missionaries from the field who were having difficulty learning and translating an unwritten language, could come for professional help.

While Legters's critics sometimes accused him of manipulating an audience, they could not fault a man who lived his beliefs. When he challenged people to pray, he also accepted the challenge of his own words, becoming part of the worshiping community praying for an open door to Mexico. And Addison Raws, director of the Keswick Conference, told how the Spirit of God touched those conferees that August morning in 1933:

> On Thursday morning, August 10, I began as usual to play the early morning hymns on the cornet to waken the people. While I was doing this, I noticed two people coming from the direction of the auditorium. The man carried a flashlight and wore no necktie. The woman carried a small blanket. Both had Bibles. As they came closer, I recognized them as Mr. and Mrs. Legters. At first I thought they had been out for an early morning walk. But then it suddenly dawned on me that they had spent the entire night praying in the auditorium prayer room.
>
> After breakfast, just as the Bible hour was to begin at 9:00, we all began to sense a new consciousness and presence of the Lord. It was a consciousness that the Lord wanted to do a new thing for his people. During the ten-minute break between the Bible and missionary hour, some of the conference leaders began to talk about the urgency the Lord seemed to be laying on us to pray for an open door to Mexico. We soon became of one mind that God wanted us to set aside our regular scheduled meeting and turn the remainder of the morning into a time of prayer and intercession for God to open the doors of Mexico to the gospel.
>
> In an amazing way, all of us forgot about time. The hours just seemed to slip by. When the lunch bell sounded, a few left the auditorium, but most continued to pray through the lunch hour into the afternoon. There was still a large number praying at five o'clock. When the day was over, all of us had a deep sense of assurance that God had heard our prayers and that he would show us great and mighty things as he promised in Jeremiah 33:3. Later, the evening service was filled with praise and thanksgiving for what God had done that day through the power of His Spirit.

What God had done that day was just the beginning of the fulfillment of his promise to show his people "great and mighty things" when they call upon his name.

Unknown to those at the U.S. Keswick Conference was the startling fact that God had placed a similar burden upon those who met at the

Keswick Conference in England. Dr. George Cowan, president emeritus of WBT, learned about this fact in 1956 from John Savage, a missionary who had attended the British Keswick Conference. Said Cowan:

> In 1933, Savage had returned on his first furlough from Peru and attended the Keswick Conference in England. When he was invited to give his report, Savage shared the burden he had for the tribal peoples he had seen in the Amazon. And just as he did in Keswick, New Jersey, God laid on his people a burden of prayer for the tribe-speople of the Amazon. To this day, we've never been able to establish any human connection between those two meetings. It was God's time for a fresh missionary initiative to get his Word to the peoples of Latin America. And his first move was to call his people to prayer.

Legters lost no time in writing Cam, urging him to go with him to Mexico. Legters told Cam he had been given a car and $160 toward their expenses. He said he and his wife wanted to cross the Mexican border on November 10 or 11. Legters concluded his letter by saying he believed Cam's presence with him in Mexico was absolutely necessary for their future plans. Wrote Legters:

> At Keswick, God made it plain to us all that he has power to do the impossible. I believe He will work in the hearts of the authorities in Mexico and the doors will be open to us. Please let us know whether you can go with us.
>
> Just a word about the linguistic school. I don't think the time is ripe just yet. It seems to me that before we begin, we should have a definite opening into Mexico, then we will have something to work toward. It would, in my opinion, be valueless to have men trained and nowhere to send them. I do agree that your idea of a course of study of Indian languages, as you outlined, would be a valuable thing. If you go with me to Mexico, you could study Aztec, and my wife and I could go to Oaxaca and Yucatán. Please answer soon.

When Cam received Legters's letter is unclear, for most of September and October he was speaking to a variety of civic and student groups in the Midwest and the Ozarks. At a civic group in Wichita Falls, Texas,

Cam, "by chance," met an Episcopalian rector. He gave Cam a letter of introduction to the Episcopalian dean of Mexico City, who "can put you in touch with some influential people," he told him. Cam had no idea how important that letter was to become. And in just a few weeks, he was to receive another letter of great importance.

After returning to Dallas from Siloam Springs, Elvira went with her parents to Chicago to wait for Cam. Cam had responded to Legters's letter, and on November 9, 1933, joined Legters and his wife, Edna, in Temple, Texas. They planned to drive to the Mexican border through Laredo, Texas.

Two days before, on November 7, 1933, Cam had written the executive council of the Central American Mission in Dallas the following brief letter:

> Dear Brethren,
> Since I feel that the need of the unreached tribes of Central America is exceedingly great, I would like to be free to undertake work on behalf of some of them. After waiting long for guidance, I have decided to present my resignation from membership in the Central American Mission. I do this partly because of my desire to work in Mexico, and there I would not be permitted to represent any religious organization.[2]
>
> Words cannot express my appreciation of the precious fellowship which I have enjoyed with you. Your prosperity and blessing shall ever be my petition at the throne of grace.

With just two short paragraphs, Cam closed the door on fifteen years of remarkable service in Guatemala, thirteen of which were with the Central American Mission. With this chapter of his life closed, he now waited expectantly for God to open another door. However, at times on that trip to the Mexican border, Cam wondered if he would live long enough to see that new door. On the morning he and the Legterses left for Laredo, Cam wrote to Karl Hummel:

> I have just heard the Legterses are up, and will be going down to breakfast soon. I want to get started by 7:30. We have 309 miles to

drive to Laredo. Mr. Legters is not the driver you are, Karl. He makes me nervous. Maybe he was too tired yesterday afternoon! Our plan is to be in Monterrey, Mexico, by Friday night, in Victoria Saturday night and all day Sunday, and in Valles on Monday night.

But when Cam and the Legterses arrived in Laredo on November 11 and tried to cross the border, they were met by an unsmiling immigration official who said, "Religious missionaries are not permitted to enter Mexico."

From 1924 to 1934, Mexico's liberal federalist government, under President Calles, strongly opposed pro-church, aristocratic, centralist groups. His government enforced the Reform Laws of 1856–57 that brought about the separation of church and state. Other laws, codified in the 1917 revolutionary constitution, brought a variety of anti-church provisions that applied to all religious groups, but the Catholic church was especially targeted.[3]

If Cam and Legters held any assumptions that crossing Mexico's border would be like the Israelites crossing the Red Sea, they were mistaken. Before them was a patriotic official upholding his government's directives. Under the reform laws, only native-born Mexicans could be priests. And while Legters and Townsend were not clergy (Cam had resigned from the Central American Mission precisely because he had anticipated this problem), the officer at the border had information that Legters was a religious conference speaker. In the official's mind that put him in the same league as a priest. He could, with perfect justification, deny Legters's entrance into the country. As far as Townsend was concerned, the official denied him entrance on the grounds that Cam was a religious person who wanted to investigate Mexico's indigenous languages. This also went against government policy. Besides, he was traveling with Legters, and this tarred him with the same brush.

Thus the two men sat at the border, praying, waiting, and pondering their next move. While Cameron Townsend believed in prayer, he also believed that little was accomplished for the kingdom of God by simply giving in to the status quo. He believed such a posture usually blocked God's purposes. Then, in the middle of silent prayer as he asked God for wisdom, Cam remembered the letter—the letter he had received from the distinguished Mexican educator, Dr. Moisés Sáenz.

They returned to the immigration office, and with diplomatic decorum Cam presented the Sáenz letter to the immigration officer. The official took a long time to read the two-page letter, then with a softer look of suspicion he said, "Well, if you are a friend of Professor Sáenz, and he has invited you to Mexico, we can allow you to come into the country. But just to make sure this is indeed a true letter from Professor Sáenz, we will phone Mexico City for verification."

Later that night in their hotel room in the city of Monterrey, Cam wrote a postcard, dated November 11, 1933, to Mr. and Mrs. Lewis Gall in Santa Ana, California: "The Legterses and I left Dallas on Wednesday after lunch and entered Mexico yesterday. It was hard to get across the border. Much prayer is needed that our journey will be successful. I know you will be faithful. The officials won't permit Mr. Legters to hold any conferences even though he has resigned as a clergyman."

In his diary, Cam gave a fuller account of that border crossing, adding that they waited seven hours before being allowed in, and that both he and Legters had come into the country under bond. If Legters were caught holding a conference, he would be fined seven hundred pesos. Cam, likewise, would be fined if he were to investigate an Indian language. And to make certain he would comply, this stricture was written across Cam's entry permit.

Since L. L. Legters was forbidden to hold the planned conference in the city of Valles, he thought he and his wife should return to the States. Cam, however, persuaded them to accompany him to Mexico City, making stops in Monterrey and Valles. After they had made the decision to stay, Cam wrote:

> After settling into our hotel, we decided to refresh ourselves in the Lord and read *Daily Light*. The Scripture reading for November 11 came from Exodus 23:20. The words we read immediately dispelled all the disappointment, perplexity, and sorrow that came out of our border crossing: "See, I am sending an angel ahead of you to guard you along the way and to bring you to the place I have prepared." After reading this, the Lord gave us all a deep sense of peace that in spite of the strictures laid upon us at the border, the rest of the trip would be successful.

He was right. This trip that led him to Mexico City and beyond proved to be one of the most successful Cam had ever taken. It laid the groundwork for a future SIL work in Mexico. This, in turn, led to SIL's involvement in more than fifty countries of the world. The promise of the words from *Daily Light* suddenly filled the day with vibrancy and expectation.[4] In letters to Elvira and excerpts from his diary during late December 1933, Cam wrote the following: "God is leading me here in strange but wonderful ways. I hardly know from one day to the next what [God] expects me to do. I have no definite plan, but the events of these past weeks are remarkable and often contrary to all logic. No one can tell me God isn't guiding my steps."

One of the "contrary to all logic" chain of events was Cam's visit to meet the Episcopalian dean that he had been given a letter of introduction to by the Episcopal rector he met in Wichita Falls, Texas. And though Legters thought it was a waste of time, the meeting proved worthwhile. There, Cam was introduced to Bernard Bevans, an English writer and traveler, who decided to honor Cam with a special luncheon in a Mexico City hotel on December 7. That was the day the Legterses had already decided to leave Mexico, and Cam had agreed to drive them back to Nuevo Laredo. But once again Cam prevailed, and they stayed over an extra day.

During the course of the luncheon, Cam's host, the English writer, introduced Cam to noted sociologist, political science professor, and author from Columbia University, Dr. Frank Tannenbaum, who just "happened" to be in the same hotel dining room. When Tannenbaum learned why Cam had come to Mexico, he gave Cam a letter of introduction to Mexico's Director of Rural Education, Professor Rafael Ramírez. When Cam learned Ramírez and his staff would arrive in Monterrey on the exact day he and the Legterses would also be there, he took the introduction from Tannenbaum and made an appointment to see Ramírez. Cam noted:

> Professor Ramírez said he knew of a petition asking for permission for expatriates to translate the Bible for the Indians. He said he thought the Indians had too much religion and they certainly didn't need any more. When the Lord gave me the wisdom to tell him the problem was that the Indians had never had an opportunity to have the Bible in their own language, his attitude toward me completely

changed. He was impressed with Dr. Tannenbaum's letter of introduction, and expressed amazement that I would come all the way to Monterrey to see him. He promised to aid me in every way possible.

Professor Ramírez was as good as his word. When Cam told him about the limitations that had been placed on his passport, Ramírez introduced him to an educator staying in the same hotel. He gave the educator instructions to take Cam to Nuevo Laredo and tell the immigration officials to issue Cam a new passport without restrictions. Cam was given a new passport as well as a special pass that allowed him to travel on the railroads and to access the aid of the authorities wherever he went.

Professor Ramírez had suggested that Cam study Mexico's unique rural school system, rather than Indian languages, and then write articles that could be published in the States. And that's exactly what Cam did. He spent the remainder of December, January, and most of February 1934 studying, making contacts, and traveling back and forth across three Mexican states. He wrote the articles Professor Ramírez asked him to write. Three were published in a Dallas newspaper and one in an educational magazine. When Cam sent him copies, Ramírez said, "I was well pleased with your articles. Maybe the young folks you want to bring down here can be of service to Mexico. I'll see what I can do to get the permissions you will need."

Back in the fall of 1931, just after Cam had met Moisés Sáenz walking along the shore of Guatemala's Lake Atitlán, Cam, in a pensive mood, had written a letter. Somewhat unsure when or how it would happen, he was quite certain God had a new adventure planned for him. His confidence was high:

> Professor Sáenz told me about a large group of Aztec Indians just four hours from Mexico City. He said they should have the New Testament in their own language, that surely there was someone who could do this. At the moment we are in the dark as to where God would have us work, but the need is so great and our desire to go to those who have no opportunity to hear is so compelling, He must want us to undertake a new field. The doors are wide open.[5]

Afterword
Continuing by Faith

Faith, mighty faith, the promise sees,
And looks to God alone;
Laughs at impossibilities,
And shouts, "It shall be done!"

In September 1959, to commemorate the twenty-fifth anniversary of SIL, Cameron Townsend wrote the following:

> Twenty-five years ago [at our first Summer Institute of Linguistics school] we sang the chorus, "Faith, Mighty Faith," seated on nail kegs for chairs beside an abandoned farmhouse in Sulphur Springs, Arkansas. Everything seemed to be against us. The door was closed to the land we wanted to enter. Only two students came to our first linguistic school. Our methods were untried, I was in poor health, had a very sick wife, and had no money.
>
> But when L. L. Legters led us in singing that chorus, he led us with such confidence that he was completely oblivious to the "impossible" barriers that lay between us and our goal of taking the Bible to all the world. By the enthusiasm with which he led the singing, one could tell he was greatly burdened for the hundreds of ethnic peoples who were without the Scriptures in their own language. But when he sang the chorus, one could tell by the emphasis he put on the words, "It shall be done," that Mr. Legters was unusually conscious of God's power.
>
> Today, twenty-five years later, hundreds of SIL members sing that same chorus all over the world. Doors have opened faster than we could enter. A thousand pioneer workers for Bible translation are almost in sight. In a miraculous way, money has kept pace with the increase

in personnel. The success of the spiritual, linguistic, and service methods into which God has led us is self-evident. Our physical health and strength have been replenished as our tasks have grown.

L. L. Legters is no longer here to lead us in the chorus. But Ken Pike has taken over with almost the same vim and vigor. Ken seems to be as oblivious to the present cost of success as Legters was to the magnitude of the problems we faced in the early thirties. Indeed, we all are. We now know the task we face today is much larger than it was twenty-five years ago. How are we going to accomplish the task before us? By faith. By faith alone. It was by faith we crossed the border into Mexico, and it was by faith we began our first linguistic school.

Our hope and expectation continue to be in God alone. Of course, we must be true to the proven methods he gave us. But along with them, and far beyond them, we are utterly dependent upon his miracle-working power, his love, and his Holy Spirit. As we sing "Faith, Mighty Faith" in this anniversary year, we realize that in the next twenty-five years the Word of God must be taken to ten times as many ethnic groups as we have reached during the past twenty-five years. We realize, too, that there are still many, many barriers to overcome. However, we have tasted of God's faithfulness and power and are not frightened by the obstacles that face us. We dare to sing again with utmost confidence of the mighty faith that laughs at impossibilities and shouts, "It shall be done!"

Now, sixty-one years after its inception, Wycliffe Bible Translators will celebrate the completion of its four hundredth New Testament. In 1934, the linguistic school Cameron Townsend and L. L. Legters envisioned began with two students. As of this writing, there are over five thousand workers in some fifty countries, with several hundred young men and women in various stages of preparation for service.

And it all began with a plain man who had the faith and imagination to move beyond the constraints of the status quo, with Spirit-enlightened eyes, to see a deeper reality. Beyond frustration and obstacles, he saw the hand of God guiding, directing, moving, and a still small voice saying, "This is the way I want you to walk." And William Cameron Townsend obeyed.

Notes

Chapter 1. Home Sweet Home

1. Over five thousand feet and set in a beautiful fertile valley surrounded by three volcanos, Antigua once rivaled Mexico City and Lima, Peru as one of the great centers of Spanish culture in the Western hemisphere. Between 1541 and 1773, Antigua (then called Santiago de Los Caballeros) had fallen victim to successive earthquakes, monstrous floods, plus the manmade turmoil of political and economic instability that included the terror of the Inquisition. When Cam and Elvira arrived in Antigua, it had risen, phoenix-like, to once again display much of its Old World charm.

2. William Cameron Townsend, *Tolo, the Volcano's Son* (Huntington Beach: Wycliffe, 1981), p. 29.

3. "The working population of Guatemala today divides about equally into two culturally distinct groups. One group termed *Indians*, in both popular and scholarly discourse, is [comprised of] those who retain a considerable amount of Mayan tradition, including the use of Mayan languages. The other group, known as *ladinos*, is popularly assumed to be descendants of Spanish/Indian liaisons (i.e. *mestizos*), but in fact are mostly Mayans in biological heritage who have assimilated the national language [Spanish] and culture" (Carol A. Smith, *Guatemalan Indians and the State, 1540 to 1988* [Austin: University of Texas Press, 1990], p. 72).

Chapter 2. Implicit Trust

1. Eunice Victoria Pike, *William Cameron Townsend: Pioneer in Modern Linguistic Research and Founder of the Summer Institute of Linguistics* (n.p.: n.d.), pp. 14–16.

2. In an effort to get away from a drunken father, Antonio Bac left his own Quiché people and settled among the Cakchiquels in Patzún.

Chapter 3. A Companion in Lice Cracking

1. *Guillermo* is Spanish for "William." Cam was called by his first name since "Cam" or "Cameron" sounded too much like the Spanish word *camarón* meaning "shrimp."

2. Robert Crawford McQuilkin (1886–1952), not to be confused with J. Robertson McQuilkin, now chancellor of Columbia International University.

Chapter 4. The Chichicastenango Twelve

1. Most of the research material on this conference and the Chichicastenango Twelve is taken from "Trailblazers for Translators: The Chichicastenango Twelve," © 1995 by Anna Marie Dahlquist (to be published by William Carey Library, Pasadena, Calif.). Used by permission.

2. Lawrence Dame, *Maya Mission* (New York: Doubleday, 1968), p. 13.

3. Anna Marie Dahlquist, *Burgess of Guatemala* (Langley, British Columbia: Cedar Books, 1985), pp. 96–97.

4. Dahlquist, "Trailblazers for Translators."

5. Ibid.

Chapter 5. Testings

1. Louise Treichler, "Serving-and-Waiting Missionaries: Latest News from the Front Where Our Friends Are Fighting the Good Fight," *Serving-and-Waiting* (a Philadelphia College of the Bible publication), vol. 11 (May 1921): p. 15.

2. Taken from "Trailblazers for Translators: The Chichicastenango Twelve," © 1995 by Anna Marie Dahlquist (to be published by William Carey Library, Pasadena, Calif.).

Chapter 6. The Dark Night of the Soul

1. For the story of the earthquake, see Hugh Steven, *A Thousand Trails* (Langley, B.C.: CREDO Publishing Corporation, 1984), pp. 127–39.

Chapter 10. A Great Loss

1. One of the emerging realities over Elvira's and Cam's relationship was that Cam's vision and drive seemed to aggravate her "nervous" condition.

2. At the Central American Mission council meetings held September 15–19, 1922, the home council voted to move the Mission's office from Paris, Texas, to Dallas, Texas.

Chapter 12. Fellow Dreamers

1. Peggy Noonan, *What I Saw at the Revolution: A Political Life in the Reagan Era* (New York: Ballantine Books, 1990), p. 90.

Chapter 17. A Formidable Challenge

1. Harald Schultz, "The Waurá Brazilian Indians of the Hidden Xingu," *National Geographic*, vol. 129, no. 1 (January 1966): pp. 131–32.

2. General Rondón was Theodore Roosevelt's companion in the 1913 expedition to the River of Doubt, now called Roosevelt River. See Petru Popescu, *Amazon Beaming* (New York: Viking Penguin Group, 1991), p. 108.

3. Though Legters's survey in 1926 was not as sophisticated as language surveys of the 1990s, the effect and importance of his survey paved the way for SIL's future work in Peru, Brazil, Bolivia, and beyond.

Current survey work rests on many of the basic principles Legters used: Before translators commit to translating the Scriptures and literacy materials into a given language, they must first determine the need for the translation. The translator must discover whether it is a unique language or a dialect of another language. And before a translator settles to a specific area, he or she must determine that the variant spoken there is the central dialect.

They determine this by answering the questions: How many people speak the language? Do only older people speak the language? What are the linguistic boundaries of a given language? If a trade language like French, Portuguese, or Spanish is the vernacular language spoken in the home, how fluent are the people in the trade language? Many more questions must also be answered before a translation team is

assigned to do Scripture translation. To determine this need, a "Language and Linguistic Survey" is used (see July/August 1994 issue of *In Other Words*).

Chapter 18. A Most Significant Moment

1. Two women, Grace Barrows and her sister Lavanchie, came to run the elementary school at San Antonio. Lavanchie and Grace set up a fine curriculum and taught grades one through six. Later, Archer married Grace.

Impressed with the Barrow sisters' skill as teachers, Cam recommended that even expatriate missionaries send their children to Grace and Lavanchie. Cam once said these two women left the indelible imprint of their Christian character on the lives of their students. The effect was such that many were inspired to become evangelists, teachers, church leaders, and, in one case, a physician. Elena Trejo, a young Quiché girl who lived with Cam and Elvira, became a doctor, and Joe Chicol became Cam's co-translator.

Today, the school continues to operate with over six hundred students.

2. Sulphur Springs later played an important role in Cam and Elvira's lives as Wycliffe purchased property there from John Brown Academy. For over twenty years, WBT and SIL held their biennial conference there.

3. In 1930, Cam wrote a warm account of Antonio's life, including the remarkable details of his journey into faith. Ethel Wallis, translator and friend of Cameron Townsend, compiled an anthology of stories, including Cam's account of Antonio Bac, in *The Cakchiquel Album*, published by Wycliffe in 1981.

4. Dr. James Dale would later form his own group called the "Mexican Indian Mission."

Chapter 19. Faith and Imagination

1. Later, Joe Chicol graduated from John Brown University and then attended Columbia Bible College.

2. The Bible Society agreed to contribute forty dollars per month toward the Townsends' living expenses.

3. Many years later in North Carolina, during the height of the Civil Rights Movement, Cam showed his solidarity for their cause by joining an African-American church.

4. Working among large groups of people versus smaller, obscure ethnic minorities would become a fundamental debate between the American Bible Society and Wycliffe Bible Translators in later years. Townsend, of course, was passionately dedicated to reaching *all* ethnic minorities who had no Scriptures, but his special vision was for the small people groups. He believed no ethnic minority was too small to have a translation of the Scriptures in its own language.

Chapter 20. A New Epoch

1. A new air service had just begun between the U.S. and Guatemala.

2. During the massacre, Arthur Tylee's wife, Ethel, was painfully injured, but later recovered.

3. Van Sickle accompanied Cam and Elvira on their return to Guatemala in December 1930 in order to gain firsthand exposure to aviation needs of the field before taking pilot training.

Chapter 21. Goodbye to Guatemala

1. In 1961, JAARS was given 256 acres of land in the very state Cam had talked about, an area near Waxhaw, North Carolina. The wooded area is ideally suited to train and approve new JAARS pilots.

Chapter 22. New Directions

1. Ethel E. Wallis and Mary A. Bennett, *Two Thousand Tongues to Go* (New York: Harper and Row, 1959), p. 37.

2. While it was true that Cam was no longer part of a religious organization, he did later work under the supervision of the Pioneer Missionary Agency and received some support from that agency.

3. The Mexican reform laws were daunting. For example, the government did not recognize marriages performed by the Catholic church. All citizens had to be married first by a civil authority before any church ceremony. Under the reform laws, all cemeteries were secularized, ecclesiastical property was expropriated, and convents and religious orders abolished. Priests and ministers were denied the right to vote and were not permitted to wear clerical robes in public. Under the harsh reforms of the 1920s, priests were rounded up and forced to marry, thereby breaking their vows of celibacy. Those who refused were executed, like the "whiskey priest" in Graham Greene's novel, *The Power and the Glory.*

In 1926, the Catholic church's opposition to the 1917 Constitution led to the Cristero Rebellion, a state-versus-church civil war that lasted until 1929. Many people died, including the President-elect Alvaro Obregón, who was assassinated by a religious fanatic. Things remained tense but generally nonviolent throughout the 1930s. It wasn't until President Manuel Avila Camacho (1940–46) proclaimed that he was a Roman Catholic believer that religious peace was truly restored. For further information see Patrick Oster, *The Mexicans, A Personal Portrait of a People* (New York: Harper & Row, 1989), pp. 203–204.

4. To commemorate the significance of that day in the history of WBT and SIL, each year, November 11 is set aside for members on all fields of service with SIL and WBT to celebrate with thanksgiving, prayer, and praise to God.

5. It was Cam and Elvira who, in 1934, went to that group of Aztec people in the town of Tetelcingo. And years later, Cam's own daughter (by his second wife, Elaine), Joy, and her husband, David Tuggy, completed the New Testament for the Aztec people of Tetelcingo, Mexico.

Index